Praise for

The **Politically Incorrect Guide**™ to

# THE FOUNDING
# FATHERS

"Brion McClanahan does far more than merely rehabilitate the Founders. In his devastating and relentless presentation, he reminds us, on one issue after another, how utterly opposed they were to what has since become fashionable opinion. Here's the stuff our competent historians know but would rather you didn't."

> —**Dr. Thomas Woods,** author of *New York Times* bestsellers *Meltdown* and *The Politically Incorrect Guide*™ *to American History*

"Brion McClanahan's bang-up new book gives us the Founding Fathers as they really were, providing what intelligent readers of history want: the plain truth. In short, the men who made the USA deserve our admiration, and McClanahan's fascinating account shows just why."

> —**Dr. Kevin Gutzman,** author of *The Politically Incorrect Guide*™ *to the Constitution*

"Our American Founding Fathers were the leaders in the creation of a unique and noble experiment in liberty and self-government. The passage of time, the misunderstandings of superficial commentators, and misrepresentations by those pushing agendas incompatible with the Founders' wisdom, have hidden and distorted our real history. Dr. Brion McClanahan, one of the ablest of younger historians, has gone a long way toward uncovering who the Founders were and what they really intended."

> —**Dr. Clyde Wilson,** Professor Emeritus, University of South Carolina and Editor of the *John C. Calhoun Papers*

"Brion McClanahan affords us an excellent look at the major issues addressed by the Founders and the real nature of the Constitution. He debunks many liberal myths and makes it clear that the Founders were not idealistic revolutionaries, but conservatives looking to maintain the 'ancient constitutions' of their forefathers."

> —**Dr. Bart Talbert,** history professor at Salisbury University and author of *Maryland: The South's First Casualty*

Praise for

The **Politically Incorrect Guide**™ to

# THE FOUNDING
# FATHERS

"Brion McClanahan presents us with a delightfully contrarian and refreshing perspective on the Founders, one that can help us rediscover their wisdom for our time."

> —**Dr. Jeff Rogers,** history professor at Gordon College in Barnesville, GA

"The American history profession ignores or denigrates our founding fathers because they were champions of liberty and feared Big Government. Brion McClanahan's *Politically Incorrect Guide*™ *to the Founding Fathers* sets the record straight and revives the true history of these great men. Every student—and teacher—in America needs to read this book."

> —**Dr. Tom DiLorenzo,** author of *Hamilton's Curse*

The **Politically Incorrect Guide**™ to

# THE FOUNDING FATHERS

The **Politically Incorrect Guide**™ to

# THE FOUNDING FATHERS

★ ★ ★ ★ ★

Brion T. McClanahan, Ph.D.

*Since 1947*
**REGNERY**
**PUBLISHING, INC.**
*An Eagle Publishing Company • Washington, DC*

Cataloging-in-Publication data on file with the Library of Congress

ISBN 978-1-59698-092-1

Published in the United States by
Regnery Publishing, Inc.
One Massachusetts Avenue, NW
Washington, DC 20001
www.regnery.com

Manufactured in the United States of America

10 9 8 7 6 5 4 3 2

Books are available in quantity for promotional or premium use. Write to Director of Special Sales, Regnery Publishing, Inc., One Massachusetts Avenue NW, Washington, DC 20001, for information on discounts and terms or call (202) 216-0600.

Distributed to the trade by:
Perseus Distribution
387 Park Avenue South
New York, NY 10016

*To Samantha*

# CONTENTS

Contents

Contents

# INTRODUCTION

O n a cold, damp, blustery, gray day in March 1775, prominent Virginians gathered at Saint John's Church in Richmond to consider action against the British Crown and Parliament. Foremost among this group stood resolute patriot Patrick Henry, a man Thomas Jefferson called the "leader in the measures of revolution in Virginia." The mood was solemn and the atmosphere thick. Despite the bitter weather, windows were opened to alleviate the stifling air of the packed building. A faint hope of peace still prevailed in the Old Dominion, and many members of the Second Virginia Convention appeared ready to accept any conciliatory proposal from the British. Not Henry. After offering a series of resolutions that moved Virginia closer to war with Britain, Henry delivered a speech on the "illusions of hope" that became a battle cry for a new republic. He said, "I know not what course others may take; but as for me, give me liberty or give me death!"

It used to be that students not only knew this line, they knew the speech and its context; they knew that Henry was a devout Christian, that the Second Virginia Convention met in the oldest established church in Richmond, and that Henry's belief in liberty stemmed from the assumed birth right of a free born Englishman. Today, students are far less likely to know any of these things—and they won't learn them from most high school and college textbooks. Rather than learning that the convention

1

took place in a church, and that Henry made frequent references to God, they will be taught to focus on the contradictions between Henry's claim of liberty and his status as a slaveholder. You can even find college textbooks that ignore the speech altogether.[1] If you look at these textbooks, you might well wonder what has happened to the teaching of American history, especially about the Founding Fathers.

Tom Brokaw labeled the World War II generation the "Greatest Generation," but he was wrong. That honor belongs to the Founders, the men who pledged their lives, fortunes, and sacred honor for the cause of liberty and independence. This is the generation that produced Washington, Adams, Jefferson, Madison, Henry, and a host of other patriots; this is the generation that established the United States, framed two successful governing documents and a host of state constitutions, and provided the foundations of American civil liberty; this is the generation that gave us the greatest political thinkers and constitutional scholars in American history, from Jefferson and Madison to John Taylor and St. George Tucker. The Founding generation has no equal, and it deserves to be rescued from politically correct textbooks, teachers, and professors, who want to dismiss the Founders as a cadre of dead, white, sexist, slave-holding males.

In 1971, Richard Nixon proclaimed that the national celebration of George Washington's birthday would be re-named Presidents Day. The presidential directive had no legal effect, and Congress has never officially changed the name, but Americans no longer have a federal or state holiday marking the birth of our first president. In effect, Nixon attached his corrupt, insecure, and power-driven presidency to that of Washington's, and Washington's stature has been reduced by lumping him with every other man to have held the office—from William Henry Harrison to Millard

---

[1]See, for instance, David Goldfield, et al., *The American Journey* TLC 4th Edition Combined (New York: Prentice Hall, 2006).

Fillmore, from Chester Alan Arthur to Warren Harding, from Jimmy Carter to Bill Clinton. Today, the only American to have a federal holiday named in his honor is Martin Luther King Jr. Washington is relegated to being one president among many, rather than the "Father of our Country."

Current "national history standards" consider Washington important—but only reluctantly. The original "standards" established in 1995 eliminated Washington and many other Founding Fathers from public school curricula and replaced them with more politically correct individuals and issues. Even with reluctant backtracking of the national history standards guidelines, American history textbooks are light on the men who established the United States and heavy on issues concerning feminism, civil rights, immigration, and American Indians. High school students spend weeks studying how various social and minority groups "felt" about the Revolution, and how the Declaration of Independence contradicted "the realities of chattel slavery," yet detailed biographies of Washington and the other Founding Fathers, the "gallant gentlemen" in Douglas Southall Freeman's phrase, have been removed. Students, instead, know about the limited participation of blacks and women in the Revolution, but little about Washington's deep faith, his commitment to the cause of independence, or his impeccable character.

For example, David Goldfield's *The American Journey*, published in 2006, dedicates more space to discussing Washington's fashion preferences—two pages—than to his contributions to the Revolutionary War—one paragraph.[2] In contrast, Thomas Bailey's 1966 edition of *The American Pageant* discusses Washington on thirty-seven pages and describes him as a "giant among men," who was "gifted with outstanding powers of leadership and immense strength of character."[3] In forty

---

[2]Ibid., 54, 55, 152.

[3]Thomas A. Bailey, *The American Pageant: A History of the Republic,* Third Edition (Boston: D.C. Heath and Company, 1966), 100, 104.

years, Washington has moved from a pillar of masculine strength, courage, and integrity to an effete dandy.

Why does this matter? The Left likes to argue that students are better served by a "complex" history that incorporates race, class, and what they call "gender studies" into the curriculum. The net result of this approach is that students learn little of the sagacity of the Founders and their heroic deeds and instead are indoctrinated into a politically correct worldview, where the Founding Fathers and the nation they created are seen as nothing special. Instead, America is almost irredeemably scarred by oppression: racial, sexual, financial, you name it. "America is a downright mean country," as Michelle Obama recently proclaimed.[4] This message is buttressed by historians like Howard Zinn, whose popular leftist textbook *A People's History of the United States* describes the Founding Fathers as geniuses only because they figured out a way to plunder "land, profits, and political power" and in the process "hold back a number of potential rebellions and create a consensus of popular support for the rule of a new, privileged leadership."[5] James Loewen echoes this sentiment in *Lies My Teacher Told Me*. Washington is not a hero, but a "heavily pockmarked" slaveholder. And Thomas Jefferson fares worse. Loewen claims that "Jefferson's slaveholding affected almost everything he did, from his opposition to internal improvements to his foreign policy."[6] The Revolutionary generation, in short, was mean, racist, and downright ugly.

---

[5]Howard Zinn, *A People's History of the United States: 1492-Present (P.S.)* (New York: Harper Perennial Modern Classics, 2005), 59.

[6]James Loewen *Lies My Teacher Told Me: Everything Your American History Textbook Got Wrong* (New York: Touchstone, 2007), 76, 146–47.

[4]Lauren Collins, "The Other Obama," *The New Yorker*, March 20, 2008; article available online at http://www.newyorker.com/reporting/2008/03/10/080310fa_fact_collins?currentPage=all

De-emphasizing, or disparaging, men like Washington, Jefferson, and Henry serves a purpose. It is meant to sever our attachment to, and our respect for, the Founders and their principles and to replace them with the Left's own ideal of a "living" Constitution that better reflects our increasingly diverse nation and the interests of those (such as ethnic minorities, women, and others) who have had to struggle for their due rights.

The irony is that the Founders had a better understanding of the problems we face today than do our own members of Congress. If you want real and relevant insights into the issues, for example, of banking, war powers, executive authority, freedom of the press, freedom of speech, freedom of religion, states' rights, gun control, judicial activism, trade, and taxes, you'd be better served reading the Founders than you would watching congressional debates on C-SPAN or reading the *New York Times*. This book intends to restore a bit of our patrimony, to reconnect us with the greatest political thinkers in our history. The Founding Fathers didn't always agree, but it is from their debates, and, as we'll see, their underlying conservative principles, that we secured our liberty. It is only by understanding their principles that we'll be able to keep the freedom that Americans have cherished for generations.

# Part I

★ ★ ★ ★ ★

# MYTHS, REALITIES, AND THE ISSUES OF THE FOUNDING GENERATION

## Chapter One

**THE MYTHS**

Just as Parson Weems wrote about Washington chopping down the cherry tree, liberal historians today have taken their axes to the Founding Fathers themselves, highlighting what they think will discredit them in modern eyes, exposing some of them as slaveholders or as philanderers or as spawning illegitimate children. Some of what these historians write is true, but much of it is not—it is gossip, often ill-founded gossip at that, instead of history. If Parson Weems's famous story was a myth, liberal historians have been propagating many more myths of their own—and they're much more harmful than Parson Weems's illustrative tale of Washington's moral probity. Here are some of the more common myths liberal historians propound about the Founding era.

## Myth: The Founding generation created a democracy

Please repeat: the United States is not a democracy and was never intended to be a democracy. The United States is a republic, and a great number in the Founding generation, if not the majority, classified themselves as republicans (not to be confused with the modern Republican Party). Most of the Founding Fathers considered democracy a dangerous extreme to be avoided.

9

Elbridge Gerry of Massachusetts said at the Constitutional Convention that "the evils we experience flow from the excess of democracy. The people do not want virtue, but are the dupes of pretended patriots." George Mason guarded against being both "too democratic" and running "incautiously" to the "other extreme" (monarchy). Mason equated the United States House of Representatives with the British House of Commons, and suggested, as did James Madison, that the other branches of government should have some check on rampant democracy. In the words of Madison, "Where a majority are united by a common sentiment, and have an opportunity, the rights of the minor party become insecure"—in other words, the Founders wanted checks against the tyranny of the majority. That was why the Founders wanted a republic of separated powers. While the government was to "be derived from the great body of society, not from an inconsiderable portion or a favored class of it," the Constitution included a system of indirect appointments, including the Supreme Court, the Electoral College System, and, originally, the United States Senate, whose members were appointed by their respective state legislatures.

The only level of government that was to be directly responsive to the people was the House of Representatives. It was granted the most constitutional power, but was to be checked by the executive branch, the upper house of the Senate, and the judicial branch.

Madison warned against a "pure democracy" in *Federalist Essay No. 10*. Pure democracies, he surmised, could not protect the people from the evils of faction, which he defined as a group whose interests were alien and counteractive to the good of society. Madison believed that in a pure democracy, factions could easily

## Wisdom of the Founders

"A democracy [is] the only pure republic, but impracticable beyond the limits of a town."

**—Thomas Jefferson, 1816.**

take control of the government through alliances (or dishonesty) and subject the minority to perpetual legislative abuse. A representative or federal republic, such as the United States, offered a check against destructive factionalism. Madison thought the states would help control factionalism by rendering a small group from one geographic or political region ineffective against the aggregate remaining states.

## Wisdom of the Founders

"Give all the power to the many, they will oppress the few. Give all the power to the few, they will oppress the many. Both, therefore, ought to have the power, that each may defend itself against the other."

—**Alexander Hamilton, 1787.**

During the New York ratification debates, Alexander Hamilton also disputed the observation that "pure democracy, would be the most perfect government." He said, "Experience has proved that no position in politics is more false than this. The ancient democracies...never possessed one feature of good government. Their very character was tyranny; their figure, deformity." The Constitution created a system far superior, in his estimation, to a pure democracy. John Adams echoed this sentiment and once wrote that "there was never a democracy yet that did not commit suicide."

Edmund Randolph of Virginia saw the Senate, with its members elected by their respective state legislatures, as a "cure for the evils under which the United States labored...the turbulence and follies of democracy." United States senators were not elected directly until the Seventeenth Amendment to the Constitution (1913)—a change that destroyed the Framers' original intentions for the upper house. No longer would it be the bastion of state's rights and an aristocratic check on both the House of Representatives and the executive branch; no longer would it be what it was meant to be: a guardian against demagoguery, an evil the Framers associated with unbridled democracy. As Samuel Huntingdon, who was not only a signer of the Declaration of Independence but president of the

Continental Congress (and governor of Connecticut), said in 1788: "It is difficult for the people at large to know when the supreme power is verging towards abuse, and to apply the proper remedy. But if the government be properly balanced, it will possess a renovating principle, by which it will be able to right itself." That balance was to be provided by the indirectly elected Senate; if the federal government has become more demagogic since World War I, the Seventeenth Amendment might be to blame.

## Myth: The Founding Fathers really believed everyone was equal

The most famous line in the Declaration of Independence is "We hold these truths to be self evident, that all men are created equal...." But the Founders meant something very different by that phrase than most of us have been taught to believe.

It was written, of course, by a slaveholder—by Thomas Jefferson—and politically correct historians mock him, for that very reason, as a hypocrite. But they do so by ignoring what he meant.

When the Founders talked about liberty and equality, they used definitions that came to them from their heritage within an English culture. Liberty was one of the most commonly used terms in the Founding generation. When Patrick Henry thundered, "Give me liberty, or give me death!" in 1775, no one asked Henry to define liberty following his speech. Similarly, when the Founders talked about equality, they thought in terms of all men being equal under God and of *freemen* being equal under the law. But the distinction of freemen was important. The founders believed in a natural hierarchy of talents, and they believed that citizenship and suffrage required civic and moral virtue. Jefferson wrote, "If a nation expects to be ignorant and free in a state of civilization, it expects what never was and what never will be." To that end, *restricting* the status of freemen was essential, in the Founders' view, to the liberty of the republic, which is why some states initially had property qualifications for voting, and why equality did not extend to slaves (or for that matter to women or children). Most of the Founding generation favored a "natural aristocracy" consisting of men of talent and virtue. They believed that these men would be, and should be, the leaders of a free society.

The Founders were not at all egalitarian in their sentiments, as might be clearer if we quote Jefferson at greater length:

"We hold these truths to be self-evident, that all men are created equal, that they are endowed by their Creator with certain unalienable rights,

## Why the Framers Created the Electoral College

At the Constitutional Convention, most of the Framers initially favored Congress appointing the president. It was only after much deliberation that the Electoral College was established (only a few argued for the direct election of the president). The Framers wanted an executive who was independent, and they wanted the states to have a direct role in his election. The Framers assumed that the state legislatures would choose the electors and the people would vote for an elector who would then vote for president. The whole system was designed to *prevent* direct democracy and its attendant evil of demagoguery, including the corruptions of money and patronage, and to preserve the power of the states. It is telling that no one even bothered to count the popular votes for president until 1824, the first election without a member of the Founding generation as a candidate. Modern "reformers" who think the Electoral College is dispensable want to jettison what the Founders considered a necessary check against the possible tyranny of the majority.

that among these are life, liberty, and the pursuit of happiness—that to secure these rights, governments are instituted among men, deriving their just powers from the consent of the governed...."

Jefferson declares the equality of men under God, but then is quite clearly referring to freemen—they are the men who consent to granting power to the government, because they are the men who elect representatives. Jefferson was not, in this instance at least, being hypocritical; he was thinking in terms that his fellow Founders, raised in the same English tradition, completely understood. He begins with every man being equal under God, but does not end in the idea that all men are equal in their talents, rights, and duties.

## Myth: Slavery was a sin of the Southern founders

The importance of this myth is that it is used to divide the country into progressive and enlightened (the North) and reactionary and racist (the South), and allows historians to portray all of American history through that divide, dismissing the Southern founders and Southern arguments about limited government and states' rights while praising ever-expanding powers for the Federal government in its long war to ensure racial and social equality.

But slavery was not a purely regional sin, largely because it was northern ships that conducted the slave trade.

It is true that most New England states had abolished slavery by 1789, and the importation of slaves was abolished in 1808 by an act of Congress, but most Northern states retained anti-black laws, northern shipping interests continued to participate in the slave trade, and small numbers of slaves remained in the North. For example, slaves were still found in Connecticut as late as 1848 and in New Jersey until 1865. In 1790, there were more than 21,000 slaves in New York, more than 11,000 in New Jersey, more than 3,700 in Pennsylvania, more than 2,700 in Connecticut, nearly 1,000 in Rhode Island, and a handful in New Hampshire (158) and Vermont (17). (Of course, these numbers were miniscule compared to more than 293,000 in Virginia, more than 107,000 in South Carolina, more than 103,000 in Maryland, and more than 100,000 in North Carolina. In addition, Georgia had more than 29,000 slaves, Delaware had nearly 9,000, and in the territories, there were also nearly 12,000 slaves in what would become the state of Kentucky and more than 3,400 in what would become the state of Tennessee.) Included in the group of Northern slaveholders were prominent names in American history. William Penn and John Winthrop, the most important individuals in the early history of Pennsylvania and Massachusetts respectively, both owned slaves. John Hancock (of Massachusetts) and Benjamin Franklin (of Pennsylvania) owned slaves during the course of their lives, and many of the Northern signatories to the Declaration of Independence and delegates to the Constitutional Convention were slaveholders.

All New England states had a connection to the international slave trade. The small New England towns of Newport and Bristol, Rhode Island, were the slave trading hubs of the North American colonies. Rhode Island had a virtual monopoly on the North American slave trade in the eighteenth century, and as many as 100,000 slaves passed through its slave markets. Faneuil Hall in Boston, Massachusetts, commonly known as the "Cradle of Liberty," was financed by slave merchant Peter Faneuil. The Easton family of Connecticut and the Whipple family of New Hampshire amassed considerable fortunes on the importation of slaves. Slave merchant James De Wolf of Bristol was one of the wealthiest men in America, a fortune obtained almost entirely from the slave trade. Brown University derived its name in part from John Brown, a prosperous slave trader who once wrote that "there was not more crime in bringing in a cargo of slaves than in bringing off a cargo of jackasses." Once the international trade was closed in 1808, many of the slave traders simply transitioned to the interstate slave trade or illegally continued the practice. Interestingly, John Adams, who was himself something of an abolitionist, professed to see no great difference in condition between laborers in the North and slaves in the South: "In some countries the labouring poor were called freemen, in others they were called slaves; but that the difference as to the state was imaginary only.... That the condition of the labouring poor in most countries, that of the fishermen particularly in the Northern States, is as abject as that of slaves."

In the South, of course, slavery was a fact of life. The overwhelming majority of black people (about 95 percent) lived in the South. But Southerners, particularly Virginians, were vexed by the institution. Washington, Jefferson, and Madison cursed slavery, and George Mason called the slave trade the "nefarious traffic" and thought that "every master of slaves is born a petty tyrant." Washington, Jefferson, Madison, and Mason (among others) are deemed hypocritical, because they denounced slavery but did not free their own slaves. But they were no more hypocritical than Benjamin Franklin, who at one time owned slaves and then argued for abolition.

The real dividing line is that the South had to wrestle with the reality that slaves were not only central to the Southern agricultural economy, but were an actual numerical majority in some states (at least in some periods), and certainly a large minority in others. In 1790, for instance, slaves made up at least 40 percent of the population of both Virginia and South Carolina. To leaders in the South, the granting of freeman status to hundreds of thousands of slaves who were by no means grounded in the English tradition of inherited rights and moral duties would have imperiled the very liberty they were trying to guarantee; it would have, in their

## Books They Don't Want You to Read

*Complicity: How the North Promoted, Prolonged, and Profited from Slavery,* by Anne Farrow, Joel Lang, Jennifer Frank (New York: Ballantine Books, 2006).

*North of Slavery: The Negro in the Free States, 1790-1860,* by Leon F. Litwack (Chicago: University of Chicago Press, 1961).

view, overturned the Republic into a mobocracy. For Southerners, it was, as Jefferson would later say, a case of justice being on the one side and self-preservation on the other.

The North and South had a shared responsibility in the institution of slavery. But a better way to think of slavery is not as a uniquely American sin—because it wasn't—but to put it in the context of what the Founders North and South, regardless of their views on race and slavery, had in common, which was the vital importance of defending the inherited rights of Englishmen and resisting tyrannical government. *That* was the cornerstone principle of the newly constituted American government, *that* was the Founders' most lasting contribution to American politics, and *that* is the contribution that the "politically correct" and "progressive" centralizers would like you to forget when they disparage the Southern Founders and their devotion to liberty, limited government, the English common law tradition, and states' rights.

## Myth: Paul Revere single-handedly warned the Boston countryside of the impending British invasion

This myth falls under the historical embellishment category. If you attended school in the United States after the early nineteenth century—and if you are reading this, I am certain you did—then you probably heard the story of the midnight ride of Paul Revere, about how he singlehandedly alerted the Minutemen of Lexington and Concord that "The British are coming!" and helped spark the Revolution. This makes for a good story (or poem), but like Washington chopping down the cherry tree, it is almost entirely false.

The fabrication of the Revere story can be traced to 1860. On the eve of the American Civil War, New England poet Henry Wadsworth Longfellow penned a poem entitled "Paul Revere's Ride." His purpose was to stir patriotic sentiment in New England by reminding his countrymen of their past. The last stanza of the poem was a direct call for action against the South. "A voice in the darkness, a knock at the door, / And a word that shall echo for evermore! / For, borne on the night-wind of the Past, / Through all our history, to the last, / In the hour of darkness and peril and need, / The people will waken and listen to hear / The hurrying hoof-beats of that steed, / And the midnight message of Paul Revere." The Union was in peril, and Paul Revere became the symbolic figure of action, the "night-wind of the Past."

Thus, a politically aimed work of fiction became the accepted story for the events of 18–19 April 1775. But what really happened? On the night of 18 April, British troops, "regulars," were ordered to arrest John Hancock and Samuel Adams in Lexington, Massachusetts, and then to seize arms and provisions at the Concord arsenal. After he discovered the plot, Revere and another rider, William Dawes, took opposite routes to Lexington to warn Hancock and Adams. (The idea was that if one were captured, the other would arrive safely with the warning.) Along the way, Revere and Dawes tried to warn people that the "regulars are coming out." Other riders joined them, spreading the message, and by the early hours of 19 April, probably forty men rode through the countryside warning their neighbors of the impending invasion.

Revere arrived in Lexington first and met with Hancock and Adams. Dawes arrived thirty minutes later. Joined by Samuel Prescott, they rode on to warn the people of Concord of the impending attack. But before they reached the town, British sentries stopped them at a roadblock. Revere was arrested, but Dawes and Prescott escaped. Dawes, however, fell off his horse and was injured, leaving Prescott to alert the Minutemen of Concord on his own. Meanwhile, a group of Patriots freed Revere from the three

## Books They Don't Want You to Read

*Don't Tread on Me: A 400-Year History of America at War, from Indian Fighting to Terrorist Hunting,* by H. W. Crocker III (New York: Crown Forum, 2006).

British guards who were escorting him to Lexington. Revere, reunited with Prescott, managed to help Hancock and his family escape Lexington before the British arrived.

Revere's actions were heroic, but Longfellow took a little poetic license with the facts.

## Myth: Benjamin Franklin had thirteen to eighty illegitimate children!

This myth has been around for a long while, and is even, apparently, perpetuated by tour guides in Philadelphia. In my experience as a professor lecturing students, the image of the balding, portly Franklin as the consummate ladies man incites giggles from women and shocked astonishment from men. Those reactions are justified because the image is based on a myth, or at least an enormous exaggeration.

Franklin never married in a religious ceremony, and this fact might have contributed to the myth that he fathered numerous illegitimate children. Franklin courted young Deborah Reed of Philadelphia when he was only seventeen. Because Franklin was being sent to London by the Pennsylvania governor's request and would not be back for some time, Reed's mother refused to allow her daughter to marry. Reed married John Rogers, a notorious debtor who soon fled to Barbados to avoid possible incarceration. Franklin, meanwhile, had returned to Philadelphia and fathered an illegitimate son named William, but was also eager to rekindle the relationship with his lost love, Deborah. Reed never obtained a legal divorce from her husband, and John Rogers was never heard from again. Therefore, without a divorce or a death certificate, Franklin and Reed were forced to marry through a common-law union in 1730.

Shortly thereafter, Deborah Reed took the infant William Franklin (who had been born earlier that year) into her home. It has been speculated that William Franklin's mother was a servant in the Franklin household. This might help explain the apparent strained relationship between Deborah and William. Some historians have claimed that Franklin fathered another illegitimate child, a girl, who later married John Foxcroft of Philadelphia. Details of this child are difficult to find, and it might be nothing more than speculation or hearsay, but it also could have fueled the wild imaginations of Franklin detractors. Benjamin and Deborah Franklin did have two children together, a son named Francis Folger who died of smallpox at the age of four, and a daughter, Sarah, who married Franklin's successor to the office of postmaster general, Richard Bache.

Deborah Franklin died in 1774 when Benjamin Franklin was approaching seventy. This is when the story becomes more interesting and possibly salacious. Franklin was a man of fine taste who loved European court life, particularly in France. Franklin drew considerable attention from French women, and he, in turn, enjoyed their company. He was sent to France in 1776 to act as a special envoy on behalf of the American cause of independence. While in Paris, he became close with Anne-Catherine de Ligniville, the widow of the French *philosophe* Helvetius. Franklin apparently proposed marriage, but she declined in deference to her deceased husband. Franklin and Madame Helvetius were both in advanced age, and it would be highly unlikely that she could have produced children even if they sustained an intimate relationship. She did organize one of the more popular salons in France and enjoyed the company of many notable men and, of course, many ladies of society, women Franklin frequently charmed.

In 1777, Franklin was introduced to thirty-three-year-old Madame Anne-Louise d'Hardancourt Brillon de Jouy. She was enamored with the American philosopher and is reported to have called him "Papa." Their relationship, while flirtatious, appears to have been nothing more than innocent. Franklin often complained that she too often withheld her kisses and rejected his affection. For her part, Brillon often corrected

Franklin's French and tried to convert him to Catholicism. From the written evidence, it would be difficult to deduce anything more than the image of Franklin as a persistent suitor and Brillon as a coy object of affection.[1]

Interestingly, both Franklin's son and grandson fathered illegitimate children, making the practice a "family tradition." But, while Franklin's moral reputation suffers from his past indiscretions (William Franklin), his common-law marriage to Deborah, and the sheer volume of letters and references to French female interests, nothing connects him to more than two possible illegitimate children. Franklin loved the company of women, but the evidence that he was a prodigal fornicator is anecdotal at best and fabricated at worst.

## Myth: Thomas Jefferson kept a concubine slave and fathered children with her!

In 1802, James T. Callender published an editorial in the Richmond *Recorder* that claimed President Thomas Jefferson had fathered a child with Sally Hemings, one of his own slaves. The story gained traction in the Federalist press (Jefferson was a Republican), but Jefferson ignored the allegation and never commented on it. His non-response has created two hundred years of speculation, a process that culminated in the 1998 DNA tests of several families that claimed connection to Jefferson. To those who wanted to believe the story, the DNA results "proved" that Jefferson did indeed father at least one of Hemings' children. This conclusion has now been stated as "fact" in many newer books on the subject, and one History Channel documentary on United States presidents spent almost as much

---

[1]See Claude-Ann Lopez, *Mon Cher Papa: Franklin and the Ladies of Paris* (New Haven: Yale University Press, 1964) for a detailed look at his female acquaintances in France.

time on Sally Hemings as it did on Jefferson's accomplishments as a statesman. The Sally Hemings story is a fine example of irresponsible scholarship based largely on contestable circumstantial evidence.

Even before he wrote the story linking Jefferson to Hemings, Callender had earned a notorious reputation. He had written a stinging pamphlet in 1796 that accused Alexander Hamilton of corruption and adultery. Hamilton admitted to the latter but denied the former. He was ultimately exonerated of having done anything illegal. Jefferson, ironically, had encouraged Callender when his targets were Federalists, like Hamilton, and even financed some of his projects.

Callender was arrested under the Sedition Act in 1800, was fined $250, and spent almost a year in jail. After Jefferson assumed the presidency in 1801, he pardoned Callender. Shortly thereafter, Callender, in need of money, pressed Jefferson for the job of postmaster in Richmond, Virginia. True to form, Callender's request included an insinuation of blackmail if Jefferson refused. Jefferson had come to see Callender for the scamp that he really was and refused to appoint someone with such a seedy past to any federal position.

Callender took a job with the anti-Jefferson newspaper the *Recorder*. He revealed that Jefferson had bankrolled some of his earlier scandalous writings—a charge that Jefferson was forced to admit. Callender then hit him with the Hemings story. Callender had never visited Monticello and based his information on the fact that several of Jefferson's slaves were light skinned. Callender later implicated Jefferson in the seduction of a married woman. Jefferson eventually confessed to that charge, but deflected the Hemings accusation by pretending it did not exist (at least in public; privately he denied it). In 1802, one of Callender's public targets clubbed him over the head. A year later, Callender was found drowned...in two feet of water. By the time Jefferson died in 1826, few remembered the accusations, save for the occasional snide attack in the Northern abolitionist press. That changed in 1873.

Madison Hemings, the youngest son of Sally Hemings, granted aboli-tionist newspaperman Samuel Wetmore an interview in 1873. Madison had intimated to close family and friends that he was Jefferson's son and disclosed this alleged relationship to Wetmore, who published it in his newspaper in Ohio. The story quickly spread across the country. Critics argued that Wetmore's article was a mere rewrite of Callender's original (the same word was even misspelled), and Jefferson's grandchildren denied its accusations. For most people that again put an end to it.

Fast forward one hundred years. Fawn Brodie's 1974 book *Thomas Jefferson: An Intimate History* revived interest in the "affair." Brodie sided with Madison Hem-ings and argued that Jefferson fathered all of Sally Hemings' children. Historians, includ-ing Jefferson's most important biographer, Dumas Malone, doubted the Hemings story, but the general public seemed eager to accept it. Twenty years later, lawyer Annette Gordon-Reed published *Thomas Jefferson and Sally Hemings: An American Contro-versy* in an attempt to vindicate Madison Hemings. The book and mod-ern advancements in DNA technology led to several members of the Jefferson and Hemings line having their DNA analyzed. The results showed that a "male" in Thomas Jefferson's family was indeed a direct ancestor of the Hemings children, principally Madison Hemings, but did not conclusively prove that Thomas Jefferson was the link. A 2000 study conducted by the Thomas Jefferson Foundation, however, determined that Jefferson was, unequivocally, the father of Madison Hemings and possibly Sally Hemings' other children. Omitted from the report was the one dissenting voice on the committee, the medical doctor charged with

## Books They Don't Want You to Read

*Anatomy of a Scandal; Thomas Jefferson and the Sally Story*, by Rebecca L. McMurry and James F. McMurry Jr. (Shippensburg, PA: White Mane Books, 2002). This book conclu-sively takes apart the Jefferson-Hemings myth.

verifying the DNA tests. Though noting that Jefferson *could* have been the father of Hemings' children, he preferred to leave the question open due to the circumstantial nature of the evidence, and argued that the majority of the committee had arrived at their conclusion before examining all available information. In essence, most of the committee believed the burden was to prove Jefferson innocent, not guilty.

In 2001, the Thomas Jefferson Heritage Society, a group that possessed more academic clout than the Foundation, released a report that directly contradicted the Foundation's conclusions. In the summary to their findings, the scholars stated, "With the exception of one member... our individual conclusions range from serious skepticism about the charge to a conviction that it is almost certainly false."[2] The scholars' report identified various inconsistencies in both the oral and written records that the Foundation used to indict Jefferson, and argued that Madison Hemings was upset because he felt Jefferson and his family had not treated the Hemings family well. The scholars also noted that Jefferson's overseer, Edmund Bacon, had not only flatly denied that Jefferson had fathered any of Sally Hemings' children, but reported that he had seen a white man—not Thomas Jefferson—leave Hemings' bedchamber many mornings before work. The scholars pointed to Jefferson's brother, often called "Uncle Randolph," as the probable father of Heming's children. Randolph Jefferson was reported to have a social relationship with the Monticello slaves and had possibly fathered other children through his own servants.

Because of the circumstantial nature of the evidence in the case, it cannot be proven conclusively that Jefferson fathered *any* of Sally Hemings' children. It is *possible* but not *probable.* If Jefferson were to stand trial for paternity with the current evidence in hand, an honest jury would find him "not guilty." So should historians and so should the public.

---

[2]Jefferson-Hemings Scholars Commission, Final Report of the Jefferson-Hemings Scholars Commission, 2001, 3.

## Myth: Washington had an affair with his neighbor's wife!

This myth has been a rumor since the publication of a suspect letter in the *New York Herald* in 1877. The contents of the letter seemed to indicate that Washington and Sally Fairfax, the beautiful, intelligent, graceful, and potentially flirtatious wife of his good friend and neighbor George William Fairfax, had a passionate, romantic interest in one another.

Washington attended the union of Sally and George William Fairfax at Mount Vernon shortly before the outbreak of the French and Indian War in 1753. Sally Fairfax and Washington also spent time together at balls and while Washington was recovering from a bout of dysentery in 1757 (George William Fairfax was in London). One year later, Washington proposed marriage to Martha Dandridge Custis, a wealthy and socially popular widow, but not the same reported picture of beauty and grace as his neighbor's wife.

According to the "discovered" letters, Washington professed his love for Sally Fairfax shortly after proposing to Martha Custis, but he realized the impossibility of a romance under the circumstances. In a second letter to Fairfax, Washington compared the two "romantics" to fictional characters Cato and Juba in the famous Joseph Addison play *Cato*. Combined, the letters seem to indicate that Washington considered his impending marriage to Custis as nothing more than a matter of social convenience, more of a consolation prize, and that he would have preferred the forbidden fruits of a married woman.

There are several problems with this line of reasoning. First, no evidence of an affair exists. Washington's primary biographer, Douglas Southall Freeman, wrote that such an affair would surely been the subject of considerable gossip in Virginia's elite circles. Freeman believed Washington loved Sally Fairfax, but she did not return the admiration and never spoke a word to anyone about it. Fairfax was described as a "prudish" woman, and Washington wished to remain in the good graces of the Virginia gentry. An affair would have tarnished his reputation and violated his ethics as a gentleman. Washington may have wished to know that Fairfax loved him, but he never pursued her either before or after his engagement to Custis.

After their marriage, George and Martha Washington frequently invited the Fairfax family to Mount Vernon, and Loyalist George Fairfax was the first to correspond with Washington from England at the conclusion of the Revolution. Washington even invited them to stay at Mount Vernon while their home was rebuilt after the war. Such cordial conversation would probably have been impossible between two men who loved the same woman, unless Washington had always hidden his feelings and maintained a proper state of decorum. [3]

Second, while these letters have been cited on numerous occasions since John C. Fitzpatrick, who worked at the Library of Congress and had an enormous interest in Washington, included the letters in his thirty-seven volume series of Washington's writings and correspondence (published between 1931 and 1944), their authenticity has always been in question. The letters were sold at auction the day after they were originally published in 1877, were never subjected to proper scrutiny, were doubted at the time, and have since disappeared. Fitzpatrick considered omitting the letters but reluctantly included them in the collection. Freeman believes this was justified since the style of the letters points to their authenticity and "forgery would not be easy,"[4] but he also concluded that they offered no evidence of anything more than the memory of an infatuation. The only honest conclusion, based on the existing evidence, is that Washington and Fairfax never consummated an affair and indeed behaved

---

[3]Douglas Southall Freeman, *George Washington: A Biography* (New York: Charles Scribner's Sons, 1951), II: 337-339; V: 449.

entirely honorably. It is true that women considered Washington to be dashing and gallant, but it is equally true that his marriage to Martha Custis appeared to be a happy union without any known improprieties.

## Myth: Alexander Hamilton had a gay lover!

One often gets the impression that myths like this are perpetrated to justify modern moral impropriety. Hamilton certainly had a colorful career and death, but this accusation is based on amateur psychoanalysis and extremely circumstantial evidence. If Hamilton was gay, he certainly did a fine job of hiding it throughout his adult life.

The myth of Hamilton's homosexual past centers on his relationship with John Laurens of South Carolina. Both men served under George Washington during the American Revolution. Washington referred to his staff officers as his "family" during the war, and Laurens and Hamilton developed a close relationship. When the two were apart, they corresponded frequently. Their letters were written in the flowery language of the eighteenth century, and while they would raise suspicion in modern American society, they were typical in style and tone for their time. Hamilton told Laurens that he loved him, and Laurens referred to Hamilton as "My Dear." They were both young, involved in a dire situation, and had idealistic notions about life and society. They were kindred spirits, but no hint of a sexual relationship exists.

Hamilton in fact requested that Laurens find him a wife. He described her desired attributes in detail, particularly her looks. Within a year, Hamilton married Elizabeth Schuyler, the daughter of a wealthy American general Philip Schuyler. The two had eight children together and from all appearances had a healthy relationship, though with some indiscretion on Hamilton's part. There were rumors that Hamilton and Elizabeth's sister, Angelica, had an affair, but the family edited Hamilton's letters after his death, so no conclusive evidence exists.

Hamilton did have an affair with a married woman in 1791. Maria and James Reynolds concocted a scheme to milk Hamilton for money. Maria Reynolds planned to seduce Hamilton, and James Reynolds, her husband, would then extort "hush" money from him. The scheme worked perfectly, only Hamilton continued to pay James Reynolds for the "use" of his wife long after the initial blackmail. James Reynolds was eventually arrested for counterfeiting, and in the process implicated Hamilton. James Monroe and Aaron Burr interviewed Hamilton, but found Hamilton innocent of the charges of corruption and counterfeiting, though Hamilton was forthcoming about the affair. Monroe and Burr decided to keep the affair secret, but James T. Callender caught wind of the illicit story and exposed Hamilton. Surprisingly, Hamilton publicly admitted to the affair. Thus, while Hamilton was an adulterer, his known and suspected affairs were all with women, not men.

The Hamilton rumor, unfortunately, has been seized upon by activist groups who want to make him a champion of gay rights, for which there is not a shred of evidence. Hamilton deserves to be remembered for many things, but homosexual activism isn't one of them.

## Chapter Two

# A CONSERVATIVE REVOLUTION

Whe Patrick Henry presented a series of resolves against the Stamp Act—the first direct tax on the American colonies— in the Virginia House of Burgesses in May 1765, he aimed to defend and preserve the traditional rights of Englishmen. Henry's verbal assault on the Stamp Act was not a radical cry for equality or democracy; it was not influenced by the wave of "liberal" thought sweeping Europe in the eighteenth century. Virginians, according to the resolves, retained "all the liberties, privileges, franchises, and immunities, that have at any time been held, enjoyed, and possessed by the people of Great Britain . . . as if they had been abiding and born within the realm of England." Henry insisted that by imposing a direct tax, the Parliament violated the "ancient constitution" of British common law, because the colonists were not and could not be represented in London. This led to the battle cry, "No Taxation without Representation!"

Henry's charge against the Stamp Act set other activities in motion. In the fall of 1765, representatives from nine colonies (Virginia, Georgia, North Carolina, and New Hampshire did not send a delegation) met at Federal Hall in New York City and adopted a series of resolutions that closely resembled Henry's Stamp Act Resolves. These were known as the Declaration of Rights and Grievances. They asserted that the colonists had all the rights and privileges of Englishmen, and because they could not be represented in Parliament, taxing power was the sole responsibility of the colonial legislatures.

The Parliament shortly thereafter rescinded the Stamp Act. Colonial leaders seemed satisfied with their success. They did not want a political showdown, merely the ability to keep the power of taxation within the realm of local sovereignty. Few colonists called for violent action against the crown, especially after the repeal of the Stamp Act. Even the famous Sons of Liberty, the most strident defenders of American rights, professed their loyalty to the crown.

But Parliament needed money to cover the enormous costs of the Seven Years' War (1756–63), the American component of which had been the French and Indian War. Parliament believed the colonists needed to absorb "their share" of the financial burden. Newly appointed Chancellor of the Exchequer Charles Townshend authored a new list of taxes that included duties on lead, glass, paper, and tea. The Townshend Acts (1767) were even more unpopular than the Stamp Act and faced considerable opposition. When the Virginia Royal Governor heard rumors that the Virginia House of Burgesses intended to resist the measures, he dissolved the legislature. No matter. The legislature simply moved to a private residence and adopted a boycott of British goods. As Thomas Jefferson later stated in the Declaration of Independence, legislative powers, meaning the rights of Englishmen, were "incapable of annihilation"; Englishmen always retained their legal rights, including their right to representation.

Violence eventually erupted in New York and Boston between British Regulars—the "Red Coats" or "lobsterbacks" as they were called in New England—and colonists. The Boston Massacre was the most famous incident, and it was used by patriot leaders to whip support for actions against the Parliament. The Townshend Acts were repealed, but even before they were repealed, smuggling rings in the North and a boycott of British goods in the South dampened the Acts' effects. It appeared the colonists had won their stand-off with Parliament, and at this juncture there was little talk of independence. As long as collective action through petition and remonstrance—with the threat of boycott and smuggling—maintained the rights established by the "ancient constitutions" of British tradition, most colonists appeared willing to keep the peace.

But men like the "Forgotten Founder," Samuel Adams, warned that the British would persist with their unconstitutional measures. In 1773, Parliament enacted the Tea Act. The Tea Act brought with it no new taxes, and in fact lowered the price of East India Company Tea in the colonies, but that was the problem to patriots like Samuel Adams, who saw the Act as an attempt to bribe compliance with the Townshend Acts and undercut American merchants (including smugglers). "Tea parties" in Boston, Annapolis, and Charleston highlighted the protest.

Maryland was already boycotting British goods in retaliation for the Townshend Acts when patriots apprehended a ship trying to bring British tea into Annapolis. Under threats of violence, they convinced the three joint-owners of the ship to personally set their own ship ablaze (though they were allowed to offload their tea and fifty-three indentured servants from England). Further south, Charleston patriots seized boycotted tea and sold it, using the money to support their efforts against the crown. The Boston Tea Party, of course, was the most famous event. Led by Samuel Adams, Bostonian patriots, masquerading as Mohawk Indians, threw chests of tea into Boston Harbor in December 1773.

The "tea parties" forced the British into a response. Parliament passed a series of laws, labeled the Coercive Acts, in an attempt to stem the growing tide of resistance to Parliamentary authority. These acts ordered that Boston Harbor be closed—in retaliation for the Tea Party, and until the East India Company was repaid for its damages and order was restored—that the Massachusetts government be brought under the direct authority of the crown (through the power of appointing all colonial officials), that court cases involving British officials be tried outside

Massachusetts (even in Great Britain) according to the discretion of the British government, and that crown-appointed governors quarter British troops where they saw fit in the colonies (which in practice tended to be in unoccupied buildings). Colonial leaders viewed these laws as a violation of English common law. Parliament intended these laws to crush dissent in Massachusetts and was surprised when patriot leaders throughout the colonies rose in opposition. The laws, in the view of many colonists, fundamentally altered and abridged long established rights of Englishmen, especially in removing the power of local legislatures and courts. If the British could enforce these new rules in Massachusetts, what would stop them from doing the same in Virginia or South Carolina? To patriot leaders, the Coercive Acts (or Intolerable Acts, as they came to be known) represented another assault on English civil liberties.

It is a politically correct myth that the colonists sought to create a radically new conception of political and civil rights. The popular historian Joseph Ellis has fueled this misinterpretation in his *American Creation* by concluding that the Declaration of Independence was a "radical document that locates sovereignty in the individual and depicts government as an alien force, making rebellion against it a natural act."[1] On the contrary, colonial protests and America's founding documents always relied on a common understanding, and a reassertion, of the rights of Englishmen, which is why the British statesman Edmund Burke supported the colonists in Parliament. Hardly a radical, Burke is considered the founding father of Anglo-American conservatism.

American leaders justified their protests against Parliament in terms of the Magna Charta of 1215 and the 1688 English Bill of Rights. The Revolution intended to preserve these "ancient constitutions" of their forefathers. In the eyes of the Americans, it was the British Parliament that was making

---

[1] Joseph Ellis, *American Creation: Triumphs and Tragedies at the Founding of the Republic* (New York: Vintage Books, 2007), 9.

a radical departure from tradition, usurping powers to itself (principally the power of taxation) that rightly resided in the colonial legislatures.

It was this sense of traditionalism, of conservatism, that separated the American Revolution from the later and more ideological French Revolution that sought to create an entirely new politics and even a new religion. The Americans were looking to keep what they had: liberties that had been developed over centuries of English history and law.

## The Declaration of Independence

As the gun smoke cleared around Lexington and Concord on 19 April 1775, colonial leaders realized the conflict between the colonies and the British Empire had reached a tipping point. The Continental Congress assembled and asked Thomas Jefferson to draft a petition to the king in the hopes of reconciliation. John Dickinson, a conservative from Pennsylvania, thought Jefferson's language was too harsh, so he toned it down. In essence, he told the king the colonists would accept one of two options: tight restrictions on their trade if there were no direct taxes from Britain; or taxes from Britain if in return the colonists were granted unrestricted free trade. The "Olive Branch Petition" was sent to the king in July 1775, but before the document reached London, British officials intercepted a letter from John Adams that questioned the sincerity of the petition. King George thus viewed the petition as disingenuous and refused to consider it.

The Continental Congress now believed it had no choice. Thomas Jefferson, author of the well-regarded pamphlet *A Summary*

★ ★ ★ ★ ★ ★ ★ ★

## Poll, July 1775

Do you believe the colonies should break with the crown and declare their independence? Yes: 25%; No 25%; Undecided: 50%. Granted, there were no Gallup Polls in 1775, but most historians believe that if such a poll had been taken, this, or something close to it, would have been the result.

## ★★★★★★★★
# Put Your John Hancock Right Here

It is a myth that John Hancock signed the Declaration of Independence in a big, bold hand so the king could read it without his glasses. That is a later fabrication. He signed it first and largest because he was the president of the Congress.

*View of the Rights of British America* (1774), was chosen to lead a committee in drafting a declaration of independence. Work began in June 1776. Congress approved independence from Great Britain on 2 July 1776, and the final wording of the Declaration was hammered out over the next two days. The final draft was sent to the printer on 4 July 1776. John Hancock might have signed the document that day—no one is certain—but all the signatures were affixed by 2 August 1776.

Many years later, Jefferson told Henry Lee that he wrote the Declaration "not to find out new principles, or new arguments, never before thought of . . . it was intended to be an expression of the American mind, and to give to that expression the proper tone and spirit called for by the occasion."

Many historians, including Jefferson's most important biographer, Dumas Malone, believe Benjamin Franklin changed Jefferson's draft of "we hold these truths to be sacred and undeniable" to "we hold these truths to be self-evident," a much more powerful expression. Jefferson himself probably borrowed language from George Mason's *Virginia Declaration of Resolves*, written a month before Jefferson authored the Declaration. Mason had argued, similarly to Jefferson, that "all men are by nature equally free and independent, and have certain inherent rights . . . namely the enjoyment of life and liberty, with the means of acquiring and possessing property, and pursuing and maintaining happiness and safety." It seems likely that Jefferson simply shortened Mason's wording. But even that wording was not new. The idea that Englishmen had a right to "life, liberty, and property" went back at least to John Locke and his *Two Treatises on Civil Government* in 1689, which itself was meant to couch England's "Glorious Revolution" of 1688 in the rights of English-men, established in 1215 when King John was forced to sign the Magna Charta at Runnymede. These rights were thus common parlance not only in Britain but in America. They were, for instance, part of the Carolina Charter, which Locke may have helped author. Most colonists did not consider themselves to be solely "Americans." They were British subjects pleading with the king for relief from taxes and laws that violated their "natural" rights as Englishmen. Indeed, Americans were proud to be British. And, why not? Englishmen were the freest and most prosperous people in the world.

Jefferson insisted that the colonists had suffered patiently while the king and Parliament assumed tyrannical rule over the colonies, but only the "present King of Great Britain" deserved the condemnation of the patriot leaders. Jefferson never declared that *all* kings were unjust, just George III. It is true that Jefferson was not a monarchist, but it is equally true that he thought there were worse things than monarchy. When the French Revolution, of which he was an early proponent, had proven itself to be unmistakably extremist, with the revolutionary government lopping off heads at a rapid pace, Jefferson called for a restoration of the royal family in France. Moreover, contrary to what the historian Joseph Ellis says, Jefferson never suggested that government was an "alien force." Government, in Jefferson's words, should pro-tect the "safety and happiness" of the people. Only after a "long train of abuses and usurpations" reduced the people "under absolute Despotism" did the people have the "right" and "duty, to throw off such Government and to provide new Guards for their future security." They could "alter or

## ✯ ✯ ✯ ✯ ✯ ✯ ✯ ✯

## Sic Semper Tyrannis

Virginia declared its independence a month before the Declaration of Inde-pendence was ratified in the Continental Congress. The Old Dominion did not need "approval" from other states to assert its right to resist tyranny and determine its own destiny.

abolish" a tyrannical government, but Jefferson did not consider the British system of government *per se* to be unjust, only the government of King George III. Even conservatives like John Dickinson knew their grievances would not be addressed by a Parliament determined to maintain its sovereignty over the king's subjects, no matter what the cost. Independence was justified because it was the only way left for the colonists to preserve their inherited rights.

## Who's sovereign now?

After the states declared their independence in 1776, work began on a new governing document. If Jay Leno conducted a "man on the street" interview and asked, "What was the first governing document of the United States?", most respondents would probably not mention the Articles of Confederation. It's unfortunate, but most Americans forget about the original "united States." That is not a typo. In the closing paragraph of the Declaration, Jefferson wrote that the document was ratified by the "Representatives of the united States of America…" and that the "United Colonies are, and of Right ought to be Free and Independent States; that they are Absolved from all Allegiance to the British Crown…and that as Free and Independent States, they have full Power to levy War, conclude Peace, contract Alliances, establish Commerce, and to do all other Acts and Things which Independent States may of right do."

Notice that Jefferson did not claim that the colonies were a "United State" or a "United States." They were a "united States" with each individual State having full power as an independent country. A state under an eighteenth-century definition is a sovereign political entity, not a mere subdivision of a larger unit. That would have been a county or shire. If Jefferson and other American leaders wished the States to be subservient to a higher political power, the Declaration would have labeled the colonies "united counties, shires, or parishes." It was no mistake that Jefferson and other American leaders classified each former colony as a state.

Creating another layer of government seemed unnecessary to American leaders during the Revolution. They were seceding from a powerful central authority, and by the close of the Revolution each State had developed a republican form of government modeled after the tested British system, excluding a king. Americans also had a prejudice in favor of reserving power to local communities. They believed this offered the greatest protection against tyranny.

A "union" was deemed beneficial for mutual protection against foreign threats, but no one was willing to grant a new central authority taxing and war-making power without restrictions; nor were Americans eager to see a central government that would regulate commerce. Thus, the Second Continental Congress commissioned John Dickinson to write a new charter for "union" keeping in mind that State sovereignty was to be jealously protected.

Though it took a year of debate to smooth out contentious issues, Dickinson produced a document that was agreeable to most (with the exception of "nationalists" like Benjamin Franklin and John Adams). Maryland first refused to ratify the document until every State, most importantly Virginia, had ceded their claims to western land. But more pressing matters took center stage. Small state delegations, such as those from Delaware and New Jersey, insisted on equal representation in Congress. Without it, they surmised that the larger states would overwhelm them on every issue. They were, after all, equal parties to this new confederation of independent states. Why shouldn't they have an equal role in the government? The new union was not to be "national" in character, but federal with a central authority limited by the sovereign constituents.

Another issue that arose during the debates was the apportionment of taxes among the states. John Adams spoke for many Northern delegates in pressing for each slave to be counted as one person in a state's population. Because taxes were apportioned according to population, this was in the interest of the Northern states, which had by far the fewest slaves. The Georgia and South Carolina delegations resisted, and in the end it was decided that taxes would be apportioned not according to population, but according to the value of land in each state. Moreover, Congress could not "require" states to pay taxes; it was only authorized to formally request money from the states. Incidentally, many of the states did not have an income tax and restricted the franchise to those who owned land or paid taxes. Article II of the newly created "Confederacy" of "The United States of America" explicitly affirmed that "Each state retains its sovereignty, freedom, and independence, and every power, jurisdiction, and right, which is not by the Confederation expressly delegated to the United States, in Congress assembled." If anyone had any doubts about sovereignty in the new Confederation, Article II silenced them. The states pledged their mutual support in maintaining the common defense, "the security of their liberties, and their mutual and general welfare." The rest of the document placed restrictions on the ability of the states to maintain an army, though the maintenance of a militia was deemed necessary, and on the ability of Congress to enter into war or treaties without a two-thirds majority of the states. Simple majorities were not enough. This provision kept the Congress from overreaching its authority on the mere "passion of the moment."

The standard interpretation of the Articles lambasts the document for its "weak" structure. At the time, most of the men who called for a new constitution were from states that either had trouble with raiding Indians, domestic insurrections over taxes, or wanted a more active central authority to promote commerce. Alexander Hamilton was one of the very few who believed in creating an American "empire" based on a strong central government.

The Articles were "weak" only to those who wanted more from government—whether that more was better protection from Indians, or troops to put down tax protesters, or a closer economic union; but these voices hardly spoke for all states, or even for most of them. It is a common misperception that the Constitution "saved" the United States from some sort of disaster. It did not, because no disaster was pending under the Articles of Confederation. It would be more appropriate to think of the Constitution as a delicate operation to adjust the balance between the interests of union and states' rights. The Founders were practical and traditional men who well understood the danger of giving too much power to a central authority. This fear would be manifested both in the drafting of the Constitution and in the ratification debates in the states.

## "Experience must be our only guide"

In 1786, delegates from five states met to discuss potential solutions for commercial problems under the Articles of Confederation. Noteworthy members of the Annapolis Convention included Alexander Hamilton of New York, James Madison and Edmund Randolph of Virginia, and John Dickinson of Delaware (formerly of Pennsylvania). After the delegates determined that the convention lacked a quorum, they drafted a letter urging the other States in the Confederation to attend a future meeting in Philadelphia. The contents of this letter did not suggest that fundamental changes would be made to the Articles, only that there were pressing issues that needed attention. In the interim, Madison penned the framework of a new governing document and prepared to present it at the Philadelphia Convention.

Of the fifty-five delegates who met in Philadelphia in May 1787, a majority had served in the Continental or Confederation Congress; close to half had been governors. Almost all of the Convention delegates would serve in the new federal government, many as United States senators or as members of the House of Representatives. Two delegates, George Washington and James Madison, would become presidents of the United

★★★★★★★★

## The Tar Heel Nation

Did you know North Carolina and Rhode Island refused to ratify the Constitution until 1789 and 1790 respectively? That made these two states independent countries while the other eleven states met in a government under the United States Constitution on March 4, 1789. Other states, such as New York and Virginia, reserved the right to revoke their ratification of the document should the new Congress not ratify a bill of rights.

States, and Elbridge Gerry of Massachusetts would serve as vice-president. Other members would hold cabinet positions or diplomatic posts. Most had considerable land holdings. Thirty-five were slaveholders. All but five were members of denominational Christian churches. They were men well educated in history and law. They ranged in age from the 26-year-old Jonathon Dayton of New Jersey to the 81-year-old "American sage," Benjamin Franklin.[2] Though the document they produced would be debated passionately and accepted only after the inclusion of a bill of rights, their experience in legal and political matters generally ensured the trust of the people from the several states. The Union was an "experiment" as Washington suggested, and one that all hoped would last, but it was based on experience, not lofty political philosophy. As John Dickinson emphasized at the Convention, "Experience must be our only guide. Reason may mislead us."

When the Convention opened on 14 May 1787, Edmund Randolph of Virginia presented the framework for a new constitution to the assembled delegates. This framework, known as the Virginia Plan or "large state plan," called for a bicameral legislature, a separate executive selected by the legislature, a judiciary, and representation in both houses based on population. In response, William Paterson of New Jersey submitted a counter-proposal that simply amended the Articles of Confederation.

---

[2]M. E. Bradford, *Founding Fathers: Brief Lives of the Framers of the United States Constitution* (Lawrence, KS: University Press of Kansas, 1994), xvi-xvii.

Paterson's plan, also known as the New Jersey Plan, envisioned a supreme court, a unicameral legislature with a one-state, one-vote provision, and divided executive power between two presidents, appointed by the legislature and serving separate terms, who had no veto power. The New Jersey Plan granted the Congress the ability to tax and regulate trade. Historians have characterized this plan as the "small state" response to the Virginia Plan.

Yet, the "large state" and "small state" designations suffer from conceptual misinterpretations. Madison's motive in basing representation in each house of Congress on population was not, as is often suggested, to increase the power of Virginia. He intended to decrease the power of the states *vis-à-vis* the new federal government. Madison was, at this point, a nationalist. He was troubled by the factionalism in his home state, in which men like Patrick Henry were power-brokers. Removing that power, as he mentioned in *Federalist No. 10*, would lead to a greater good. In contrast, Paterson and the rest of the New Jersey delegation believed they had no authority to scrap the existing Articles. Paterson was not an Anti-Federalist, he was not opposed to increasing the power of the central government, but he also firmly held that the states must remain equal partners in the Union, and he believed that most people agreed with him.

Hot weather, and the hot tempers the two proposals produced, led to a recess in July. When the delegates returned, the more moderate men in the Convention started to carry

## Books They Don't Want You to Read

*Original Intentions: On the Making and Ratification of the United States Constitution,* by M .E. Bradford (Athens, GA: University of Georgia Press, 1993).

the proceedings, and the compromises began. Madison's plan would be implemented with alterations. The new government would have a bicameral legislature with a lower house based on population and an upper house that maintained the equality of the states. The executive and judiciary would be separate branches and each would be checked by another branch. These "checks and balances" were supposed to provide safeguards against tyranny. The president would not be popularly elected as some wished, nor would he be chosen by the federal Congress or by the state legislatures, but by a new entity called the Electoral College, which both emphasized the role of the states and granted a moderated democratic element to the election of the president.

The Framers derived much of the language for the Constitution from British examples, and the bicameral system was in some respects similar to the British Parliament. John Dickinson, for example, likened the Senate to the House of Lords. Hamilton spoke at length of the liberty of the British system of government, and other delegates, such as Charles Pinckney of South Carolina and Edmund Randolph, echoed this sentiment. The eminent scholar Forrest McDonald wrote, "Whatever their political philosophies, most (though by no means all) of the delegates sought to pattern the United States Constitution, as closely as circumstances would permit, after the English constitution."[1] This is not to suggest that the United States Constitution in its final form was purely a copy of the British constitution; it had to be adapted to American circumstances and conditions, but there was nothing in it that an Englishman would find alien to his own political traditions, save for the absence of a monarch.

The final draft received the approval of the Convention on 17 September 1787. The Constitution was not "official" on that date. Not one state had ratified it, and there was strong opposition to it. Even Edmund Randolph, who presented the Virginia Plan, refused to sign the document because it lacked a bill of rights. The states, as sovereign, independent political entities, still had to say yes or no. This is the most important and forgotten component of American constitutional history. The Framers were not as important as the ratifiers. We can celebrate the genius of the Framers, but they still had to persuade the state ratification conventions that the new document maintained the "spirit of '76."

## "The public mind...is extremely uneasy at the proposed change of government"

Delaware ratified the Constitution on 7 December 1787 by unanimous vote of the state's constitutional convention. But the second state to ratify the Constitution, Pennsylvania, showed early signs that the process would not proceed smoothly. Federalist James Wilson, a Scot by birth, a slaveholder, and one of the wealthier men in Pennsylvania, dominated the ratification debate in his state. He argued against a bill of rights, because he deemed it unnecessary. The Constitution, he said, expressly delegated limited powers to the general government; all other powers were reserved to the states. He consistently used the term "sovereign states" to placate the Anti-Federalists who believed the Constitution arrogated too much power to a central authority. Wilson almost single-handedly carried ratification in his state, where the Constitution was approved by a 46 to 23 majority. But not everyone trusted assurances from a man who possessed a heavy debt and who rarely showed consistency on any issue. Shortly thereafter, Wilson was burned in effigy during an anti-Constitution riot, and the "backcountry" areas of the state continued to show disgust with the new government for years to come.

The margin of victory for those in favor of the new Constitution was closer in Massachusetts. Nathaniel Barrell of York, Massachusetts, summarized the sentiment of many in the convention when he stated, "I fear it [the Constitution] is pregnant with baneful effects.... Because, sir, as it now stands, Congress will be vested with more extensive powers than ever Great Britain exercised over us; too great, in my opinion, to intrust with any class of men...even though composed of such exalted, amiable characters as the great Washington.... " Anti-Federalists in this state continued to press for a bill of rights, and ratification only passed with assurances that one would be added. Still, the vote was 187 to 168, hardly a ringing endorsement.

Anti-Federalists in New Hampshire almost prevented ratification. Shrewd political maneuvering by Federalist John Langdon thwarted their attempts, but the vote was a close 57 to 47. In South Carolina, Patrick Dollard warned that the people of his district believed that the Constitution would bring "a great variety of impending woes to the good people of the Southern States . . . than all the plagues supposed to issue from the poisonous box of Pandora." He was more prophetic than he knew, but the Constitution passed 149 to 73. By the time Virginia and New York met in convention to discuss the Constitution, the new document had been approved by a two-to-one total majority in eight ratification conventions, including three unanimous votes (Delaware, Georgia, and New Jersey). But without the approval of Virginia and New York, arguably the two most powerful states in the Union, the Constitution would lack legitimacy.

## Books They Don't Want You to Read

*Novus Ordo Seclorum: The Intellectual Origins of the Constitution,* by Forrest McDonald (Lawrence, KS: University of Kansas Press, 1985).

*E Pluribus Unum,* by Forrest McDonald (Indianapolis, IN: Liberty Fund, Inc., 1979).

The Virginia Convention met first, in June 1788. Washington, Madison, and Edmund Randolph led the faction in support of ratification. Randolph was a young, attractive, and powerfully built figure, and an excellent orator. He commanded respect and was serving out his term as governor. Though Randolph refused to sign the Constitution at the conclusion of the Constitutional Convention, he believed that because eight other states had already ratified the document Virginia needed to follow suit and stay part of the Union. George Mason, Patrick Henry, James Monroe, and Richard Henry Lee (not present at the convention but a commanding force nevertheless), led the fight against ratification. Henry could match any man in oration, and Mason possessed a better pen than most Virginians. This was a clash of the titans, and the vote would be close. Henry opened for the opposition, saying, "The public mind . . . is extremely uneasy at the proposed change of government." He questioned the need for a new constitution and feared that the new federal government would be too powerful. "We are wandering on the great ocean of human affairs. I see no landmark to guide us. We are running we know not whither." Henry knifed the preamble to the Constitution by questioning the phrase "We the People." Shouldn't the phrase instead read "We the States," he asked? That would expressly maintain the sovereignty of the states.

Mason, for his part, pressed for a bill of rights and agreed to ratify the document "when such amendments as shall, from the best information, secure the great essential rights of the people. . . . " Without a bill of rights, the proposed Constitution had a similar form but lacked the substance of the British constitution of assumed rights. The Constitution, as it stood, seemed to put liberty at risk.

Madison and Randolph worked diligently to persuade the Anti-Federalists that their fears were unfounded. They assured their opponents that only the powers "expressly delegated" to the Constitution would be exercised; the states would remain sovereign within their sphere of influence.

In response to Henry's attack on the preamble, Randolph found no problem with the phrase and suggested that a substitution such as "We the States" could not be used because of Rhode Island's refusal to send delegates to the Constitutional Convention. Besides, he said, the document is "for the people." Madison, meanwhile, agreed to consider amendments to the Constitution and present them in the early sessions of the new Congress. With this assurance, Virginia ratified the Constitution on 25 June 1788 by a vote of 89 to 79.

The New York Convention met in the middle of June. Before ratification was put to a vote in New York, ten states, including Virginia, had ratified the Constitution, making the document technically legal. But Anti-Federalists in New York were undaunted in threatening to reject the Constitution. In fact, Hamilton believed the Anti-Federalists could win.

To counter their arguments, Hamilton, Madison, and John Jay anonymously authored a series of letters that appeared in New York newspapers after the conclusion of the Constitutional Convention. Later called the *Federalist Papers,* it is questionable how persuasive these letters were to the general public.

At the convention, Hamilton had taken a hard pro-Constitution line, going so far as to issue a veiled threat that New York City would secede from the state if the Constitution was rejected. The Anti-Federalists lost the vote, but did so while insisting on the inclusion of a bill of rights, as other states had insisted. It was close, with 30 delegates voting in favor of ratification and 27 against. In a circular letter sent to the governors of the other states, New York governor (and Anti-Federalist) George Clinton encouraged the states to consider a bill of rights, writing, "Our attachment to our sister states, and the confidence we repose in them, cannot be more forcibly demonstrated than by acceding to a government which many of us think imperfect."

What brought Federalists and Anti-Federalists together was their shared respect for George Washington. As long as Washington occupied the executive office, many felt safe in the belief that their liberties would not be abridged; they felt safer still when the Bill of Rights was finally added to the Constitution in 1791, though the battles between the Federalists and Anti-Federalists would reemerge after Washington's presidency.

Stripped to its purest form, the Constitution and Bill of Rights together constitute a natural expansion and transition of the British system of government. The rights of Englishmen were maintained by the first ten Amendments to the Constitution, and the traditional order of the British Parliament was manifested in a bicameral legislature that contained both democratic (the House) and aristocratic elements (the Senate). The principle of a constitutionally restricted executive is evident in the few expressed Constitutional duties of a president of the United States restrained by congressional oversight. The American legal system retained the traditional elements of the British system, most importantly, the adherence to a common law system that originated in the Magna Charta. The Founders were neither radical liberals nor idealistic revolutionaries. They believed in the "ancient constitutions" of their forefathers, with some modification, and the traditional order of society.

Successive generations, especially in the twentieth century, have greatly strengthened the executive at the expense of the states, the Congress, and the people at large. This raises an interesting question: What would the Founders say about that and other issues in our own American society?

## Chapter Three

# THE ISSUES

I f you want to know what the Founding Fathers would do, you only have to read what they wrote.

## Give me back my gun!

"A well regulated Militia, being necessary to the security of a free State, the right of the people to keep and bear Arms, shall not be infringed." (Second Amendment to the United States Constitution)

The Founders understood that gun rights exist to protect us (the people) from them (the government).

The right to "keep and bear arms" had British antecedents. King Henry II in the twelfth century ordered that all Englishmen keep weapons to protect and defend his realm. This became part of English common law, and though the ability for Englishmen to own weapons fluctuated, by 1689 this right had become entrenched throughout the empire, including the American colonies. Virginian St. George Tucker, the foremost early American constitutional scholar, noted in his work, *Blackstone Commemtaries,* "In America we may reasonably hope that the people will never cease to regard the right of keeping and bearing arms as the surest pledge of their liberty." All of the early state constitutions organized citizen militias based on this principle. During the ratification debates the Anti-Federalists insisted on an explicit recognition of the right to keep and bear arms, as did those states that ratified the Constitution conditionally (like Virginia, New York, and Massachusetts).

When Congress began debate over a constitutional amendment protecting the right to keep and bear arms, the issue was not "who was the militia;" that was understood; it was, in the words of the New York Constitutional Convention, "the body of the people capable of bearing arms." Most of the disagreement over the future Second Amendment centered on the original "conscientious objector" clause. The Amendment would have exempted religious objectors, such as Quakers, from rendering "military service in person." The Senate ultimately struck this clause and the final wording became the current Second Amendment to the Constitution.

## Wisdom of the Founders

"A militia, when properly formed, are in fact the people themselves, and render regular troops in a great measure unnecessary."

**—Richard Henry Lee, 1788.**

The Founding generation would find it inconceivable that the right to own guns—whether to hunt or to protect private property or to defend the nation's liberty—would not be respected.

## A godless society?

"Congress shall make no law respecting an establishment of religion, or prohibiting the free exercise thereof...." (First Amendment to the United States Constitution)

When Henry VIII broke with the Catholic Church in 1532, England descended into a century of religious civil warfare. Catholics hurried into hiding, while English Protestants worked zealously to destroy any remnants of the old religion. When Henry's daughter, Queen "Bloody" Mary (a Catholic) came to the throne, she struck back persecuting Protestants. Her half-sister and successor, the Protestant Queen Elizabeth I, persecuted Catholics with equal ardor. By the outbreak of the English Civil War in 1642, England was split between Catholics and orthodox Anglicans who supported the king, and dissenting Protestants (Puritans) who upheld the authority of Parliament. This terrible conflict resulted in the beheading of King Charles I and the establishment of a military dictatorship under "Lord Protector" Oliver Cromwell. Similar religious strife, or worse, took place in France, Spain, and the German states. Europe was a powder-keg of religious partisanship.

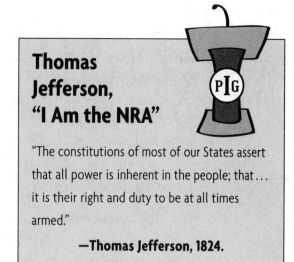

## Thomas Jefferson, "I Am the NRA"

"The constitutions of most of our States assert that all power is inherent in the people; that . . . it is their right and duty to be at all times armed."

**—Thomas Jefferson, 1824.**

Religious conflict, while far less frequent than in Europe, was not alien to the colonies. For example, efforts to establish the Anglican Church in Maryland and Massachusetts sparked violence, while James Oglethorpe prohibited Catholics from settling in Georgia. Rhode Island was founded by Roger Williams after he was banished by Puritan leaders in Massachusetts, and Quakers in Massachusetts faced the death penalty.

Still, however much they differed in the details, most American colonists were Protestant Christians. Northern settlers tended to be "more Protestant"—Puritans, Pilgrims, Quakers, Congregationalists. Southern colonists generally favored the established churches of the nobility and were either Anglicans or Scots Presbyterians. Maryland's colonial charter was granted to the Calverts, a royalist Catholic family. Maryland also enjoyed a Religious Toleration Act (foreshadowing the First Amendment) that guaranteed toleration of all Christians. Designed to protect Catholic

**Books They Don't Want You to Read**

*The Theme Is Freedom: Religion, Politics, and the American Tradition*, by M. Stanton Evans (Washington, D.C.: Regnery, 1994).

colonists from the emerging Protestant majority, the Toleration Act was suspended by Oliver Cromwell and later again by Protestant rebels so that, ironically, Catholics were occasionally persecuted in "their own" colony.

The Founding Fathers wanted to cap religious conflict and believed the best way to do that was to avoid an "established religion"—that is, a state-supported denomination, like the Church of England. The First Amendment prohibits the United States government from establishing a "Church of the United States" that would require all American citizens to attend and tithe.

The Founders believed in religious liberty, but this does not mean they were complete opponents of state-sponsored churches. For example, both Massachusetts and Connecticut maintained established churches well into the nineteenth century, and the constituents of each state would not have ratified the Constitution had they believed the document would destroy state authority over the issue. Patrick Henry argued that Virginians could belong to any church, but they *must* belong to *some* church and pay taxes to support it. Certainly, men such as Jefferson and Madison argued for the "separation of church and state," but Jefferson issued proclamations of thanksgiving while governor of Virginia. The "wall of separation" applied principally to the federal government. State government had greater flexibility and autonomy. Jefferson, in authoring the Virginia Statute for Religious Freedom, maintained that all men had freedom of conscience, but he also recognized that most if not all Virginians were religious people. The Virginia statute simply aimed to prevent the "hypocrisy and meanness" that he thought naturally followed from government-established churches. History, he believed, had already proved his point.

To say the Founding Fathers were Godless men—and this is usually said of Jefferson and Benjamin Franklin—is to distort their views. Allusions to God saturate early American documents. Jefferson opens the Virginia Statute for Religious Freedom with "Whereas Almighty God hath created the mind free," and believed it was God, being "the Holy author of our religion...Lord of both body and mind," who resisted religious coercion. Franklin did not attend church much of his life, but he spoke of the necessity of religion in letters to his devout Puritan sister. He also recommended prayer breaks during the Constitutional Convention in Philadelphia.

George Washington believed God saved the Revolution and became a decidedly devout Christian following his years on the battlefield. As president, Washington issued the first proclamation of a national thanksgiving on 3 October 1789, in order to "acknowledge the providence of Almighty God, to obey His will, to be grateful for His benefits, and humbly to implore His protection and favor...." Shortly before his famous duel with Aaron Burr in 1803, Alexander Hamilton formed a religious society in New York, and while writhing in agonizing pain on his death-bed, asked for last rites from an Episcopalian priest.

There seems no doubt that today the Founders would support religious toleration of Jews, Muslims, and Christians of all denominations, but they were, themselves, mostly devout, church-going Christians who did not object to religion (namely

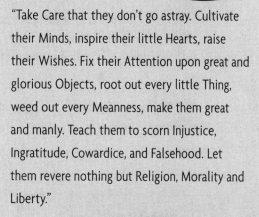

## A Founding Father to His Children

"Take Care that they don't go astray. Cultivate their Minds, inspire their little Hearts, raise their Wishes. Fix their Attention upon great and glorious Objects, root out every little Thing, weed out every Meanness, make them great and manly. Teach them to scorn Injustice, Ingratitude, Cowardice, and Falsehood. Let them revere nothing but Religion, Morality and Liberty."

**—John Adams, 1776.**

Christianity) in the public discourse. Only a few of the principal leaders in the Founding generation could be classified as non-Christian. The most likely candidates are Jefferson, Franklin, Madison, maybe even John Adams at times, but even here the evidence is somewhat tenuous, at least from what people knew during their lifetime. What is beyond doubt is that the Founders lived in a self-consciously Christian society. Congress frequently called for national days of prayer, and not one Founding Father would have considered public professions of faith "controversial," because faith was an accepted part of life. Twisting the words of the First Amendment—as the modern Supreme Court has done—to eliminate *all* public displays of religion would have been regarded as preposterous two hundred years ago.

## The states (and the people) are sovereign

"The powers not delegated to the United States by the Constitution, nor prohibited by it to the States, are reserved to the States respectively, or to the people." (Tenth Amendment to the United States Constitution)

James Madison, in *Federalist Essays No. 40–44*, introduced dual sovereignty to the American public. His concept rested on the idea that the new central government under the United States Constitution would be sovereign within its *delegated* sphere of power, and the states would retain all powers not expressly denied by the Constitution. In other words, both the central government and the state governments would be sovereign. Many delegates in the state ratification conventions feared this idea of dual sovereignty as dangerous to the states, and the Federalists had to offer constant reassurances that the

### Books They Don't Want You to Read

*The Founders' Second Amendment: Origins of the Right to Bear Arms*, by Stephen Halbrook (Chicago, IL: Ivan R. Dee, 2008).

new government would violate neither individual nor state rights. The states, jealously guarding their status as sovereign political entities, were not willing to relinquish too much power to a new central authority.

With the addition of the Tenth Amendment to the Constitution, Anti-Federalists believed they obtained a legal safeguard against central encroachment. How wrong they were. In 1798, the Federalist-dominated Congress authored a bill labeled the Sedition Act which provided for fines and possible imprisonment for any type of speech that brought the president or Congress into disrepute. This clearly violated the First Amendment to the Constitution, and members of the opposition party (namely newspaper editors) were the only individuals to be prosecuted under the law.

★ ★ ★ ★ ★ ★ ★ ★ ★

## States' Rights: Not Just for Southerners

Virginia, New York, and Massachusetts made state sovereignty number one on their proposed amendments to the Constitution.

In response, Jefferson and Madison secretly authored a series of resolutions that appeared before the state legislatures in Virginia and Kentucky. Both declared the Sedition Act to be a violation of the First Amendment and an infringement upon civil liberties. Jefferson, as the author of the Kentucky Resolves, declared that "whensoever the general government assumes undelegated powers, its acts are unauthoritative, void, and of no force...." In essence, a state could nullify—or interpose its sovereignty against—a federal law if it deemed that law unconstitutional. In Jefferson's view, the Supreme Court did not matter, the president did not matter, the Congress did not matter; it was the states that had the ultimate sovereign authority to protect the rights of the people.

Just five years later, a group of New England Federalists, led by former secretary of war and secretary of state Timothy Pickering, organized a plan to secede from the Union. They were appalled by Thomas Jefferson's election as president in 1801 and by his acquisition of the Louisiana

Territory in 1803. They did not want to be part of a union that would be dominated by Southern and Western farmers. The idea fell apart when their candidate for governor of New York, Aaron Burr, was defeated. But secession had been put forward as a more dramatic alternative to nullification.

Federalists again threatened secession in 1815 after the War of 1812. New Englanders thought President James Madison was fighting the war only for the benefit of the South and West and was oblivious to the cost of the war to New England shipping and dismissive of the strong anti-war sentiment in the New England states. The New England press condemned "Mr. Madison's War," particularly when Madison refused to pay the expenses of the Massachusetts and Connecticut militia after these states rejected directives from the War Department. In 1814, twenty-six delegates from five New England states met in secret to discuss potential action. The Hartford Resolves, issued in 1815, mirrored Jefferson and Madison's Virginia and Kentucky Resolves of 1798. These carefully worded attacks claimed New England had a "duty" to question unconstitutional infringements upon state authority. The Hartford Convention did not produce a clear pronouncement of the right of secession, but from evidence contained in private correspondence from the actors involved, secession was, at least initially, the primary goal of the Convention.

Legal scholars of the Founding generation provided additional justification for states' rights through secession. William

## Wisdom of the Founders

"I expressly say that Congress is not a representative body but a diplomatic body, a collection of ambassadors from thirteen sovereign States. . . . nor indeed, in any moment of my life, did I ever approve of a consolidated government, or would I have given my vote for it. A consolidated government under a monarchy, an aristocracy, or democracy, or a mixture of either, would have flown to pieces like a glass bubble under the first blow of a hammer on an anvil."

**—John Adams, 1824.**

Rawle, the United States attorney for Philadelphia from 1791 to 1799 and good friend of Benjamin Franklin and George Washington, wrote a treatise on the United States Constitution in 1825 that included a chapter on the right of secession. His work was used as a textbook on government at the United States Military Academy at West Point and no doubt influenced many Americans, especially many of America's top military officers. Rawle unequivocally stated that "The states, then, may wholly withdraw from the Union..." if the people of the states decided they no longer deemed attachment to a union necessary for their future security.

## Books They Don't Want You to Read

*View of the Constitution of the United States With Selected Writings*, by St. George Tucker, Clyde Wilson, ed. (Indianapolis, IN: Liberty Fund, 1999).

St. George Tucker, a member of the Founding generation who taught law at the College of William and Mary, reasoned in *Blackstone Commentaris* that since the states in essence seceded from the Articles of Confederation, they could legally secede from the United States Constitution. "Their obligation...to preserve the present constitution, is not greater than their former obligations were, to adhere to the articles of confederation; each state possessing the same right of withdrawing itself from the confederacy without the consent of the rest, as any number of them do, or ever did, possess." Tucker cautioned that secession should not be pursued for "light and transient causes," but the people had a duty pursuant with their natural rights to throw off governments that infringed upon their civil liberties.

Talk of secession might seem odd to the modern reader, but it was not odd to the Founding generation and to several generations that followed. For example, Northern states nullified a more stringent fugitive slave law during the 1850s, and abolitionists consistently spoke of secession during the 1830s and 1840s. John Quincy Adams, the son of Founding Father John Adams and sixth president of the United States, advocated the secession of New England during the Mexican War. And of course secession came to its final, bloody test during the War Between the States.

The Tenth Amendment, of course, has not been repealed, but states' rights have been curtailed nevertheless. It seems unlikely that the Founders would accept this state of affairs. More likely, they would remind us that, as the Declaration of Independence states, legislative powers are "incapable of annihilation." If we believe the Federal government is exceeding its constitutional authority, the remedy is for the people to defend themselves through their respective state legislatures and governors, where sovereignty rightly resides.

## A limited executive

The Founding generation would be taken aback by the power wielded by presidents today. The first five presidents—Washington, Adams, Jefferson, Madison, and James Monroe—had ties to the American Revolution and the founding of the United States. Four were from Virginia and the other, Adams, from Massachusetts. Washington and Adams were Federalists; Jefferson, Madison, and Monroe were Democratic-Republicans. Sectional and political differences aside, each man generally viewed the office in limited terms.

In contrast to the detailed outline of congressional powers in Article I of the United States Constitution, the executive powers contained in Article II are both vague and brief. The President of the United States has few defined, constitutional roles. He is commander-in-chief of the armed forces and the militia when

**War Powers Are Congressional Powers**

Charles Pinckney, patriot, governor of South Carolina, and United States Senator, thought giving the president the powers of war and peace "would render the executive a monarchy of the worst kind, to wit, an elective one."

called into service, he is head-of-state, and he is charged with executing the laws of the United States. No more. The president can make treaties with foreign nations, but the Senate must approve them by a two-thirds majority. All executive appointments, with the exception of lower level executive positions, require senatorial confirmation. He can from "time to time" give the Congress "information of the state of the Union and recommend to their consideration such

## No Emergency Powers for the Prez

P[I]G

"The President is bound to stop at the limits prescribed by our Constitution and law to the authorities in his hands, [and this] would apply in an occasion of peace as well as war."

**—Thomas Jefferson, 1806.**

measures as he shall judge necessary and expedient," and he can ask for advice from his cabinet members on particular issues. Those are the only duties the president can constitutionally perform. He is not the chief legislator, and contrary to popular belief, he cannot constitutionally make laws or issue treaties by decree. In essence, the president can't do much of anything without congressional approval. That is the dirty little secret in Washington, and one that the American public forgets. By removing congressional responsibility, the president has become (regrettably) the focal point in American politics.

For the first thirty-six years of American history under the Constitution, the primary job of the president was foreign policy. (It still is, but Americans now want much more from the office.) Jefferson, as first Secretary of State and third president, noted that the president was to be considered the "channel of communication" between foreign powers and the United States. Washington determined early in his first administration that treaties should be worked through by the president first (the channel of communication), and then submitted to Congress. This initially vexed the Senate, particularly Vice President John Adams, but it helped speed the process. A channel of communication, however, is not the final arbiter. The Senate still had a clearly defined role in the process.

According to Article I, Section 7 of the Constitution, the president also has veto power ("veto" comes from the Latin for "I forbid"). The first five presidents used the power sparingly by issuing a total of twenty vetoes. Since 1825, there have been more than 2,500 vetoes. Washington considered using the veto power only when legislation conflicted with the Constitution. He used the power twice. Adams and Jefferson did not veto any legislation. Madison and Monroe issued eighteen vetoes for legislation they considered unconstitutional (including bills for federally funded "internal improvements" like roads, canals, and harbors). Simply put, Congress passed laws, but the president could veto them if he deemed them unconstitutional. No president in this period used the veto for partisan political purposes or as a legislative hammer. This has become commonplace in the post-Civil War period (Franklin Roosevelt, for example, issued more than 600 vetoes as president). For the Founding Fathers, this would be an abuse of executive power.

During the state ratification debates, several opponents of the new Constitution surmised that when Washington retired from public life, the executive office as written (vaguely) offered potential for abuse. Hamilton, Madison, and other proponents of the Constitution assured these Anti-Federalists that the executive would always be checked by the legislative power. But it appears that the Anti-Federalists were right. George Mason stated during the Constitutional Convention that he feared the new document paved the way for "a...dangerous monarchy—an elected one." Ben-

## Put Not Your Faith in Princes

"It had been observed, that in all countries the executive power is in a constant course of increase. This was certainly the case in Great Britain. Gentlemen seemed to think that we had nothing to apprehend from an abuse of the executive power. But why might not a Catiline or a Cromwell arise in this country as well as in others?"

**—Pierce Butler, patriot, and United States senator from South Carolina, 1787.**

jamin Franklin agreed, and said that "the first man put at the helm [Washington] will be a good one. Nobody knows what sort may come afterwards. The executive will be always increasing here, as elsewhere, till it ends in monarchy."

Franklin approved of the new Constitution; Mason did not. Both understood the natural progression of power, even in a government designed to protect against abuse. The first five presidents accepted limits on their own power. The last thirty-eight, with a few exceptions in the antebellum period and one in the late nineteenth century, have not.

## Abolish the Fed!

No, not the federal government, though that could be helpful, but the Federal Reserve System. Many in the Founding generation, including Jefferson and initially Madison, warned against a central banking system. Jefferson called the First Bank of the United States "one of the most deadly hostilities existing, against the principles and form of our Constitution."

Central banking was a defining issue in the early Federal period. In 1790, Secretary of the Treasury Alexander Hamilton proposed a Bank of the United States. The historian Forrest McDonald writes that "Hamilton set out to plant the British system in America, corruption and all, and to do so within the framework of the Constitution and American institutions."[1] Corruption was the key. Adams, Jefferson, and other Founding Fathers were afraid of it, but not Hamilton, who believed that such corruption—with government favoring certain financial interests and industries—was necessary to build America's commercial might. Hamilton hoped to salvage America's postwar finances, and did so successfully in

---

[1]Forrest McDonald, *The Presidency of George Washington* (Lawrence, KS: University Press of Kansas, 1974), 48.

## ★★★★★★★★

## Monopoly Money

The idea of a national bank was raised during the Constitutional Convention. Many of the Framers considered a national bank to be a form of monopoly and opposed the power to charter one. George Mason of Virginia said he "was afraid of monopolies of every sort" and that the Constitution provided for no such institution.

part by establishing a line of credit, but the central banking system he helped create was constantly under attack. The most common charge centered on the constitutionality of the institution. The Constitution does not specifically give Congress the authority to establish a central bank.

Jefferson wrote in 1791 that Hamilton's proposed Bank of the United States was unconstitutional because "the powers assumed by this bill, have not, in my opinion, been delegated to the United States, by the Constitution." Moreover, a national or central banking system, Jefferson argued, violated the "ancient and fundamental laws of the several States" and created a dangerous standard that allowed Congress to pass laws for "convenience." Hamilton, surprisingly, agreed with Jefferson. The Constitution did not specifically authorize the creation of a central bank, he acknowledged, but it did not prevent it either. Furthermore, Hamilton believed a bank was "necessary and proper" for executing his powers as Secretary of Treasury. President Washington thought Hamilton provided a sound justification for the Bank and sided with him. The Bank Bill passed and received a twenty-year charter.

This did not mean that the opposition vanished. The constitutional argument had fallen on deaf ears in 1791, but twenty years later, with the Federalists out of power, the Bank's opponents won a victory against Hamiltonianism. Congress failed to re-charter the Bank in 1811. George Clinton, in casting the deciding vote against re-charter, stated, "If, however, on fair experience, the powers vested in the government shall be found incompetent to the attainment of the objects for which it was instituted, the constitution happily furnishes the means for remedying the evil by amendment." Even some of those who thought the bank was justified considered a constitutional amendment necessary to legally charter the institution.

Following the War of 1812, nationalist members of Congress pressed for a second Bank of the United States. The war created an air of nationalism (and a tremendous debt) that swayed most to support a bank, though a few conservative members voted against it on constitutional grounds. Nathaniel Macon of North Carolina wrote, "I seem to be the only person of those who were formerly in Congress, that still cannot find the authority for a bank in the Constitution of the U.S." Even President Madison departed from a strict constructionist stance and supported the Second Bank Bill in 1816. His reasoning stemmed from precedent. He argued that the bank was not unconstitutional, because the "general will of the people" supported a bank and it had been recognized as a "valid" necessity. John Clopton of Virginia argued that neither "time" nor "usage made an act of Congress constitutional." The Constitution could not be changed by Congress alone. Jefferson, out of the political spotlight but still acutely aware of the major issues in the government, sided with the conservatives.

At this juncture, John Taylor of Caroline became quite possibly the most vocal critic of a central banking system, though he described the magnitude of opinion against his position as "a contest between a dwarf and a half a dozen giants." His greatest fear was the consolidation of government and finance capital, or more appropriately, state-sponsored capitalism. Central banking facilitated this type of political economy and led to the corruption that Hamilton believed was an essential element of the British economy. Taylor thought that the Hamiltonian economic system, comprised of central banking, protective tariffs, and federal support for commerce and industry, not only violated the Constitution, it created a climate of centralization that logically ended in monarchy and the ruin of civil liberty. To Taylor, the Hamiltonian system could only be supported through "artificial phraseology," or "the vocation of stripping evils of unseemly attire in order to dress them more handsomely, or of subjecting the federal constitution to the needles of verbal embroiderers, in obedience to the saying, 'the tailor makes the man.'" This, to him, was the end of "sound revolutionary good sense."

Andrew Jackson ultimately killed the Second Bank of the United States in 1836, and Congress did not re-establish a central banking system until the Civil War. Of course, many in the Founding generation supported a central banking system, though the question of constitutionality was never conclusively solved. Chief Justice John Marshall defended the Bank in the *McCulloch v. Maryland* decision in 1819 through the "necessary and proper clause" of the Constitution, the same clause that Taylor suggested created "artificial phraseology." "Mystical interpreters," Taylor said, "extract from texts whatever doctrine is necessary for their purpose, but sound logick is not like money; an hundred light arguments cannot make a heavy one, as an hundred cents makes a dollar."

## Books They Don't Want You to Read

*Pillars of Prosperity*, by Ron Paul (Auburn, AL: Mises Institute, 2008).

*Meltdown: A Free Market Look at Why the Stock Market Collapsed, the Economy Tanked, and Government Bailouts will Make Things Worse*, by Thomas E. Woods Jr. (Washington, D.C.: Regnery Publishing, Inc., 2009).

*National Review* editor Richard Brookhiser argues that Hamilton's system was perfect and only distorted by later partisans who did not have Hamilton's fiscal or political aptitude. This may be true in part, but the Republicans who railed the first and second Bank of the United States believed that central banking would ultimately undermine the stability of the country. Corruption would not be easy to contain, and they feared that it would lead to "monarchy" and the destruction of "civil liberty." Opponents of the Bank of the United States, and central banking in general, have been criticized by historians as being provincial or influenced by their status as agrarian slaveholders. Yet, with the current economic mess in the United States, for which many blame the Federal Reserve and government involvement in the mortgage industry, perhaps this aversion to corruption and central banking is a needed antidote. The central bank arguably led to one depression in 1929, and the potential exists for another, due in large part to a fusion of finance capital and government. Have the Founding Fathers who opposed state-capitalism and central banking been vindicated?

## A "president's" war?

"The Congress shall have the power: To declare war, grant letters of marque and reprisal, and make rules concerning captures on land and water." (Article I, Section 8 of the United States Constitution.)

Since 1789, the United States has been involved in five declared wars. Quick, name them. If you thought of any past 1945, you are wrong. The last constitutional war in American history was World War II. In an increasingly bellicose world, much can be learned from the Founding generation. They established limits on the war-making powers of the government, warned against a perpetual standing army, and declared that foreign alliances were detrimental to American liberty. All of these precedents and limits are currently ignored. The United States spends more money on a "standing army" than any other power, has allowed the president almost single-handedly to involve the country in four major foreign wars, and has developed an extensive alliance system that could potentially drag the country into international conflicts that otherwise need not involve the United States.

During the ratification debates, Anti-Federalists consistently worried over the

**Books They Don't Want You to Read**

*The Politically Incorrect Guide to American History*, by Thomas E. Woods Jr. (Washington, D.C.: Regnery, 2004).

prospect of a standing army. The militia was fine, but an army organized by a central government and controlled by a president smacked of a European-style military establishment. English, French, and Spanish kings had been quite successful in silencing public opposition through a powerful military. After all, the British attempted to quell dissent in New England before the Revolution through the Quartering Act.

The Anti-Federalist Brutus (possibly Robert Yates of New York) wrote in 1788, "The liberties of the people are in danger from a large standing army...." History was his guide. The Third Amendment to the Constitution prohibited the quartering of troops in peacetime. This restriction on the military power of the central government alleviated some of the fear of the Anti-Federalists, but Congress could still maintain a standing army.

Even the most ardent advocates of the Constitution reasoned that a standing army was practically unnecessary. Washington wrote in 1778 that standing armies are "dangerous to a state." If the Founders were to look at America today, and at the problem of preventing potential terrorist attacks on American soil, they would no doubt argue that this task should be handled by the militia of the several states. Yet, on 3 December 2008, the Defense Department reported that 20,000 uniformed troops (a division) would be deployed domestically by 2011 to help prevent terrorist attacks or "other domestic catastrophe." Founders like Patrick Henry would regard that news with grave

## Let's Stick to the Militia

Patrick Henry, at the Virginia Ratifying Convention in 1788, warned against a standing army: "There is no control on Congress in raising or stationing them....This unlimited authority is a most dangerous power: its principles are despotic. If it be unbounded, it must lead to despotism.... We are told we are afraid to trust ourselves... that we shall not enslave ourselves....Who has enslaved France, Spain, Germany, Turkey, and any other countries which groan under tyranny? They have been enslaved by the hands of their own people. If it will be so in America, it will be only as it has been every where else."

disquiet. For the sake of civil liberty, he would argue for the role of the citizen-soldier in his state militia and against the idea of the domestic deployment of professional soldiers.

But the Founders were much more concerned with restricting Federal power than we seem to be today. Another example of this is the reservation to Congress of the power of declaring war, a power that has been essentially ignored since 1945. Yet to the Founders, rendering the military subservient to the civil power (the legislature) was seen as a safeguard against a potentially tyrannical executive. Only one delegate to the Constitutional Convention, Pierce Butler of South Carolina, advocated giving the president the power to declare war. George Mason responded that "he was for clogging, rather than facilitating, war; but for facilitating peace." An executive with full control over the ability of a government to go to war was dangerous to the liberty of the people. All agreed that a president could repel "sudden attacks," but a prolonged struggle required legislative approval.

**Books They Don't Want You to Read**

*A Foreign Policy of Peace, Commerce, and Honest Friendship*, by Ron Paul (Lake Jackson, TX: Foundation for Rational Economics and Education, 2007).

Constitutional limitations on war worked fairly well for the United States under the Founding generation. Both the French and the British presented problems for American sovereignty and neutrality in this period. The British constantly harassed American shipping and impressed American sailors, and the French often confiscated American cargo and captured American vessels. When French ministers demanded the United States bribe them for diplomatic correspondence in 1798, American calls for war reached a fever pitch. President Adams followed a cautious course, as did his predecessor Washington, and prepared to defend the United States against French hostility. Congress, however, authorized the navy to attack French shipping. While not a declared war, the purely naval Quasi-War of 1798 to 1800 showcased presidential restraint and congressional aggression.

A few years later, pirates off the northern coast of Africa captured the USS *Philadelphia* after it ran aground patrolling the Tripoli coast. The Barbary States had already declared war on the United States after President Jefferson refused to pay tribute to the brigands who controlled the African states. While no formal American declaration of war existed, Congress allowed Jefferson to use the Navy to defend American interests in the region. Maryland native Stephen Decatur led a rescue of the crew of the *Philadelphia* and succeeded in burning the ship. This event has often been used as justification for executive action without a formal declaration of war. It must be noted that Jefferson informed Congress of the situation and acted while Congress was out of session. Congress responded by authorizing the Navy to attack Barbary shipping and protect American commerce.

Meanwhile, the British continued to pester American merchant vessels following the Revolutionary War. A controversial treaty authored by John Jay provided a short respite of naval conflict between the United States and Great Britain. Washington, Adams, and Jefferson attempted to forestall potential war with the British. Madison continued a cautious course when he assumed office in 1809, but continued insults by the British navy and problems on the frontier with British-supported Indian tribes persuaded Madison to ask for a declaration of war. Congress granted his wish in June 1812. In matters of war and peace, the president could request action, but it was up to Congress to decide whether to take it.

The Founders, as a rule, wanted to avoid entanglement in foreign wars, which meant avoiding foreign alliances. In September 1796, Washington published a public letter to the American people. This document, now labeled his "Farewell Address," outlined Washington's view of the future of the United States. He cautioned against "permanent alliances with any portion of the world," but believed in extending American commerce. The United States should maintain a position of neutrality and avoid European entanglements as much as possible. This, Washington suggested, was the best safeguard for American liberty.

In 1823, President James Monroe issued through his annual message to Congress a series of resolutions that make up what is now called the Monroe Doctrine. Written primarily by his Secretary of State, John Quincy Adams, the resolutions reinforced the Founders' preference for neutrality in European affairs. Monroe argued that European and American systems of government were inherently different, a fact that bound America to steer clear of European domestic concerns. In return, Europe should stay out of the Western Hemisphere, where it might interfere with America's preference for neutral trade.

## Wisdom of the Founders

"Every true friend to this Country must *see* and *feel* that the policy of it is not to embroil ourselves, with any nation whatever; but to avoid their disputes and their politics; and if they will harass one another, to avail ourselves of the neutral conduct we have adopted."

**—George Washington, 1796.**

So great was the American tradition of avoiding entanglement in European politics that the first United States president to visit Europe during his period in office was Woodrow Wilson in 1919. The United States did not become involved in a permanent alliance system with European powers until the North Atlantic Treaty Organization (NATO) in 1949. While the Founders would be gratified to find that the United States is strong, they would be alarmed at how we have become a global policeman with an international web of alliances and troop commitments. The Founders had a narrower, simpler, humbler, or more reasonable definition of American interest.

## "No Taxation without Representation!"

Students are familiar with this battle-cry from the Revolution. The history of American patriots resisting oppressive taxation makes a great story. Yet, the taxes that American patriots resisted during the Revolution were far lighter than those Americans pay today. What would the Founding generation say about the current American tax system?

Before the Revolution, John Dickinson believed Parliament could indirectly tax the colonies through trade, but direct taxes under the colonial system of representation, which allowed for local assemblies but not representation in Parliament, were unconstitutional; indeed, such taxes were subversive of the British constitution. "Virtual representation," as the British called it, the idea that the colonists were "virtually represented" because voters in Britain similar to the colonists had elected members, was not real representation and did not preserve the rights of Englishmen.

When Dickinson began work on the Articles of Confederation in 1776, he was acutely aware of American resistance to taxes, particularly excise or consumption duties. The Articles denied Congress the ability to tax the people directly. States could levy taxes, and some, such as Massachusetts, did so quite substantially, particularly after the war, but the central government was running out of money and the states did not want to contribute. Subsequently, nationalists, such as Hamilton, crafted a series of proposals by the early 1780s that would essentially have usurped taxing power from the states. Initially, his ideas had little support, but as the central government went further into debt, interest in creating a central financial authority grew. Taxing power was high on the docket at the Constitutional Convention in 1787.

As long as taxes were assessed equally, there was little opposition at the Constitutional Convention to granting Congress the power of direct taxation. The Constitution mandated that "all duties, imposts, and excises shall be uniform throughout the United States." Hamilton, as first Secretary of the Treasury, actually opposed direct taxes, such as property taxes. He believed that not only were such taxes unconstitutional, but they would be difficult collect. Instead, he preferred luxury taxes, such as taxes on liquor. His plan was approved by Congress, but resistance soon followed.

The federal tax on whiskey hit western farmers hard, because it cut into the profitability of turning unsold crops into liquor. Farmers along the frontier began harassing tax collectors. One was tarred and feathered in Pennsylvania. This loose "rebellion" allowed Washington and Hamilton to showcase federal power. Washington personally commanded a volunteer militia and marched towards Pittsburg. When they couldn't find anyone who took part in the "rebellion," the militia rounded up twenty men as an example. One of them died in prison, but the others were quickly released or pardoned.

While Federalists claimed victory, this was an embarrassment to the federal government. Western Americans were still unwilling to pay the excise tax, and when threatened, communities hid or sheltered suspected "rebellion" participants and laughed at the show of "force." It also helped galvanize opposition to the new central authority. Jefferson and others used these western patriots to their advantage and eventually gained control of the federal government.

Jefferson's election in 1801—and Madison's in 1808 and Monroe's in 1816—signaled that Americans were tired of Hamiltonian economics, particularly its taxes. All federal taxes during Jefferson's administration were either reduced or eliminated; federal spending was cut and the debt halved; frugality reigned. Before taking office Jefferson declared, "I am for a government rigorously frugal and simple...." He and the leaders of Congress followed suit.

Jefferson had a history of being sympathetic to tax rebels—indeed he and the Founding generation were tax rebels. After Shay's Rebellion in

1786, another protest against taxes, Jefferson asked, "What country can preserve its liberties, if its rulers are not warned, from time to time, that the people preserve the spirit of resistance?" Resistance to unjust taxes marked the Founding generation. It is a generation that would disagree with Vice President Joe Biden that it's a "patriotic duty" to pay taxes. On the contrary, an American's patriotic duty is to defend liberty, and that means limiting the taxing power of the Federal government to a minimum.

## Who said that's unconstitutional?

Look for the following phrase in the Constitution: "The Supreme Court shall have the power to declare legislation unconstitutional and will be the final arbiter on all constitutional questions in the United States." Can't find it? That's because it doesn't exist. Members of the Founding generation believed the Supreme Court would, and should, eventually use this power as an ultimate check over the executive and legislative branches, but they did not foresee the power being used for partisan political purposes, nor the possibility of "legislation from the bench"—in other words, the Supreme Court weighing in on matters outside of its jurisdiction. Americans are now accustomed to this type of judicial review for two reasons: one, because of some creative and unconstitutional—and unfortunately precedent-setting—actions by a member of the Founding generation, John Marshall; and two, because Congress has declined to impeach judges who behave unconstitutionally.

Aggressive judges dominated the early American court system under the Constitution. The first Supreme Court justices were all ardent centralizers, and they often took advantage of opportunities to increase federal power at the expense of the states. In addition to their duties on the Supreme Court, early justices were required to serve on the lower circuit courts. Some of these justices, particularly Maryland native Samuel Chase, made a habit of using the bench for political attacks.

To Jeffersonian Republicans, who were his targets, his activities were both infamous and impeachable, and when Jefferson and the Democratic-Republicans moved into power in 1801, Chase became the first and only Supreme Court justice to be impeached by Congress. The Constitution stipulates that federal judges can be impeached and removed from office for "Treason, Bribery, or other High Crimes and Misdemeanors." Using the bench to target Republican partisans for prosecution certainly seemed an abuse of office, but in a masterful move Chase's attorney argued that Chase had not committed an "indictable" crime and could not be removed from office. The Senate accepted this narrow definition of "high crimes and misdemeanors" and did not convict him. Chase stayed on the bench.

Shortly before the Chase debacle in the Senate, the Supreme Court issued one of the most important decisions in United States history, *Marbury v. Madison*. William Marbury had been appointed to a federal court position (justice of the peace in the District of Columbia) by John Adams in 1800. Then Secretary of State John Marshall (now chief justice of the Supreme Court) neglected to deliver Marbury's commission to him, and without it Marbury could not take office. When Jefferson became president in 1801, he was certainly not going to let Marbury, a partisan Federalist, hold a court position. Marbury sued the government, namely the new Secretary of State James Madison, for denying his appointment. The Supreme Court took the case in 1803.

Marshall, who introduced the majority and minority opinion system to the Supreme Court, issued the "majority decision." Among other things, it stated that "it is emphatically the province and duty of the judicial department to say what the law is." This became the doctrine of "judicial review"—a right the Supreme Court arrogated to itself. There was no federal law that required Madison and Jefferson to appoint Marbury to office, but Marshall, legislating from the bench, essentially made up such a law in his ruling. Thereafter, because of the Chase acquittal in the Senate, Marshall knew that further pronouncements (laws) from the bench could not result in impeachment. He, and every other Supreme Court justice, was immune from Constitutional authority unless he committed an "indictable" crime. Legislating from the bench for political purposes was not an indictable offense—or at least precedent had made it so.

Certainly others in the Founding generation viewed the power of judicial review and "legislation from the bench" differently. Washington believed that the president, through his veto power, had the right of refusal for constitutional questions. Jefferson and Madison, through the Virginia and Kentucky Resolutions of 1798, argued that the states possessed the power to nullify a federal law if the state deemed it unconstitutional. Jefferson insisted that the power of judicial review could not be found in the Constitution. He was right. During the ratification debates, Anti-Federalists warned that this power would be lifted from the Constitution and used to enlarge the power of the central government. Not enough of the ratifiers listened.

Marshall's precedent established that the Supreme Court could control the legislative destiny of the United States. Congress, the president, and the states, could henceforth be emasculated by unelected justices. Andrew Jackson, marginally from the Founding generation having served in the Revolutionary army as a thirteen-year-old boy, once remarked following a Marshall verdict, "John Marshall has made his decision, now let him enforce it." This example of executive intransigence has never again been followed. Since 1803, the Supreme Court has run roughshod over the Constitution with little opposition from the executive or legislative branches. If we were to ask Thomas Jefferson and James Madison what they thought of this sorry state of affairs, they would undoubtedly say that it is up to the people of the states to resist unconstitutional judicial (and federal) power.

## John Adams is a war-mongering scoundrel!

The Founding generation considered the first amendment guarantee of freedom of speech, freedom of the press, and freedom of assembly and petition to be essential to the American republic. As with other provisions in the Bill of Rights, the First Amendment acts to help define the limits of the federal government.

The origins of the right to free speech can be found in English common law. Both the Magna Charta of 1215 and the English Bill of Rights of 1689 outline the right of free speech. Without this liberty, Americans would not have been free to print and produce documents denouncing the king and Parliament before the Revolution. Most of the best works of the Revolution appeared in newspapers or pamphlets. Patriots issued repeated legislative petitions and communicated by circular letters. Silence the press and the right of free speech, and the American Revolution would never have happened.

The right to a free press was put to the test in 1798. Republican partisans had been printing challenges to John Adams and the Federalist Party, particularly over the brewing war with France. Federalists in Congress believed the Republican papers were engaged in slander, if not treason, and passed the Sedition Act in 1798 to silence newspaper editors and others who stirred up opposition to the Federalist Party.

One such newspaperman, Matthew Lyon of Vermont, was arrested in 1798 under the Sedition Act. Lyon had emigrated from Ireland to Connecticut in 1765. He was trained as a printer but worked on a farm in the American colonies until the onset of war with Britain in 1775. He first organized a militia company in his new home of Vermont, and later took a commission as a Second Lieutenant in the famed Vermont Green Mountain Boys regiment headed by Ethan Allen. He served with distinction and was captured with Allen during a failed assault on Montreal. Lyon left the army in 1778. He founded the town of Fair Haven, Vermont, and started several successful businesses, including two newspapers. He served in the Vermont legislature for seventeen years and was elected to the United States House of Representatives as a Democratic-Republican in 1796.

Federalists in Congress loathed Lyon. In 1798, Roger Griswold of Connecticut attacked him with a chair, forcing Lyon to defend himself with a pair of tongs. Lyon had apparently spit on Griswold during a previous exchange of words. He never denied it, and Lyon became the first House member to be brought up on ethics charges. The charge: "gross indecency." The Ethics Committee recommended censure, but the house as a whole rejected the motion. Federalists were undeterred and continued to push for his departure from Congress.

They had their chance under the Sedition Act. When Federalists discovered that Lyon had been using his newspapers to disparage Adams and the Federalist Party, they had him arrested. He was sentenced to four months in prison and a $1,000 fine (roughly $17,000 in 2007 dollars). Federalist James Bayard of Delaware introduced a resolution to expel Lyon from the House, calling him "notorious" and "seditious," a man of "a depraved mind, and wicked and diabolical disposition." Lyon, however, had the last laugh. The people of his district re-elected him while he was in prison—he is the only member of Congress to have been elected while incarcerated—and Lyon cast the deciding vote in favor of Thomas Jefferson in the bitterly contested 1800 election (an electoral vote tie had thrown the election into the House of Representatives). After Jefferson took office, he pardoned Lyon, but Lyon decided against another term and retired from public life.

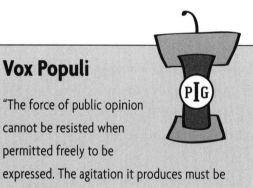

## Vox Populi

"The force of public opinion cannot be resisted when permitted freely to be expressed. The agitation it produces must be submitted to. It is necessary to keep the waters pure."

**—Thomas Jefferson, 1823.**

The new Congress, now controlled by Democratic-Republicans, simply let the Sedition Act expire in 1801. Federalists had lost both Congress and the White House in 1800 due in large part to popular opposition to the Sedition Act.

The Constitution does not stipulate that the press has to be fair. It simply has to be free. Early American newspapers were neither fair nor unbiased. Newspaper editors openly and frequently displayed their partisanship. The Founding generation, with a few Federalist exceptions, did not expect the press to be "fair and balanced" and certainly would have opposed any legislation (like the Sedition Act, which the Founding generation undid) that would allegedly make it so.

## Give me my welfare!

"The Congress shall have the power to lay and collect taxes, duties, imposts, and excises, to pay the debts and provide for the common defense and general welfare of the United States...." (Article 1, Section 8 of the United States Constitution.)

The "general welfare clause" is one of the most misunderstood phrases in the Constitution. What is "the general welfare of the United States?" Ask many Americans today and they would probably respond with, "The government needs to provide jobs"; "The government should provide medical care"; "The government should guarantee workers a minimum wage"; "The government should provide for the poor"; "The government should rebuild our fraying infrastructure." All of these "demands" on government have been fostered by an incorrect reading of the Constitution, or more accurately, by not reading the Constitution. Perhaps 90 percent of what the federal government does is actually unconstitutional—and it's all due to an expansion of government power under the guise of the "general welfare."

## No Pork in the Constitution

The Constitution does not authorize the government to take money from the treasury for "internal improvements," let alone welfare and other government programs, such as the gargantuan spending projects of Franklin Roosevelt's New Deal, Lyndon Johnson's Great Society, or Barack Obama's and George W. Bush's "stimulus package" and bailouts. The Founding generation would have rejected outright all pork-barrel projects, funding specific communities, as utterly unconstitutional.

The general welfare clause was lifted directly from the Articles of Confederation. The text from that document reads, "All charges of war, and all other expenses that shall be incurred for the common defense or general welfare" should be taken from the common treasury of the United States. As a confederation of independent states, the phrase "general welfare" was intended to cover anything that benefitted the union as a whole, such as military hardware for the common defense. Targeted items such as piers, canals, or harbors were not considered the "general welfare" of the union because they would benefit one state or community at the expense of the other states.

At the Constitutional Convention in Philadelphia, Gouverneur Morris of Pennsylvania attempted to expand federal power for internal improvements by placing a semi-colon between "excises" and "to pay" so that Article 1, Section 8 of the Constitution would read in part: "The Congress shall have the power to lay and collect taxes, duties, imposts, and excises; to pay the debts and provide for the common defense and general welfare of the United States. . . . " Roger Sherman of Connecticut discovered Morris's tactic and removed it before the draft reached the floor for debate. The power to tax and raise money for "the common defense" and the "general welfare" was meant to carry the same meaning as it did under the Articles of Confederation, as James Madison affirmed when he said that the general welfare clause was not a blank check for "indefinite power." Even the most fervent proponent of an "elastic" Constitution, Alexander Hamilton, did not believe the Constitution authorized the federal government to spend money for internal improvements.

As president, both James Madison and James Monroe vetoed legislation that would have used federal money for internal improvements. In 1817, Congress presented Madison with a piece of legislation known as the "Bonus Bill." The bill would have used the "bonus" money from the chartering of a new Bank of the United States for building infrastructure through an expansion of the "general welfare" clause. Madison argued in his veto message that Congress was expanding its powers beyond "the defined and limited [powers] hitherto understood to belong to them." They were perverting the Constitution. Five years later, Monroe reluctantly vetoed the Cumberland Road Bill because he thought the bill "implies a power to adopt and execute a complete system of internal improvements," a power that could be "granted only by an amendment to the Constitution and in the mode prescribed by it."

The central government does not exist to provide a paycheck, a job, a road, health care, charity for the indigent, or a minimum wage. The Founders believed these to be individual responsibilities, and they would not have viewed the transfer of responsibility from individuals to the government as a sign of progress.

# Part II

★ ★ ★ ★ ★

# THE MEN

T homas Carlyle once wrote, "History is the essence of innumerable biographies." What follows are pocket biographies of some of the most important of the Founding Fathers. The first six, the "Big Six," are the most well known of the generation: George Washington, John Adams, Thomas Jefferson, James Madison, Benjamin Franklin, and Alexander Hamilton. The next group is the "Forgotten Founders," and while some may be recognizable names, like Patrick Henry, John Marshall, and John Hancock, Americans would be hard pressed to give much detail about their lives. Others in this group have, unfortunately, been virtually erased from most modern American history books. Our understanding of politics, government, and society has suffered because of it.

Certainly, a list of twenty men does not do the generation justice, and there were other worthy members who were excluded due to space. The twenty I chose represent different sections and states—eight were from Virginia, four from Massachusetts, two from New York, two from Pennsylvania/Delaware, one from South Carolina, one from North Carolina, one from Connecticut, and one from Maryland—but they had much in common, and all led "politically incorrect" lives. With few exceptions, they were second, third, or fourth generation Americans, not recent immigrants, and were strongly colored by their long thinking of themselves as English in language, religion, and political understanding. Though they launched a revolution, they were men of overwhelmingly conservative convictions, diligent about preserving ancient liberties, and not interested in creating any new doctrines. The Founders, with the exception of John Marshall and two men omitted from this work, James Wilson and Gouverneur Morris, believed the federal government did not have the power to coerce a state. Of course, Marshall was one of the most powerful men in the generation, but the

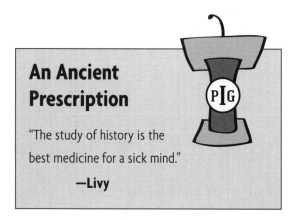

**An Ancient Prescription**

"The study of history is the best medicine for a sick mind."

**—Livy**

exceptions do not make the rule. The Constitution was a compact among the states, and the states retained their sovereignty. To a man, the Founding generation did *not* view the United States as a consolidated government and did *not* believe in expansive federal power. These men believed in individual liberty and thought the main objective of good government was the preservation of life, liberty, and property. That's it. Some had differing views as to how to ensure that objective, but none would recognize the modern federal government. Several demanded a bill of rights as a way to guarantee limited government before they agreed to support the Constitution, and others, even with that guarantee, still opposed the Constitution because they thought the government it created was too powerful. The freedoms of speech and the press, the right to religious liberty, the right to keep and bear arms, the right to trial by jury and due process, the right to life, liberty, and property, and the right of state sovereignty were so important that Richard Henry Lee, one of the forgotten Founders, thought Virginia should secede from the Union if the Bill of Rights failed adoption. The Founders all recognized that throughout history government had been the enemy of life, liberty, and property, not the protector. Modern Americans, it seems, have forgotten that and need a reminder.

The twenty men on the list were mostly statesman rather than politicians. A politician is an individual who "buys" votes through patronage or promises, and several of these statesmen preferred retirement to politics (Washington foremost among them), and only served when chosen. They didn't actively "campaign" for their "jobs." In fact, politics was not a job. They were planters, merchants, and businessmen first, and many held political appointments throughout their lives, but only because they were well respected men of their community. It was their duty to serve, not their passion or "career" choice, and they warned against the dangers of career politicians. Getting fat off the government was looked down upon. Ambitious men were not to be trusted with power, and previous political office did not constitute a qualification for a higher office. It could be helpful, but often the outsiders were more respected than the insiders.

Of the twenty men I discuss, fifteen owned slaves, and three of those men, John Hancock, Samuel Adams, and Benjamin Franklin, were from the North. Yet no one on this list, including the Southerners, thought the international slave trade should continue, and many thought slavery was an inherited evil, though they could not agree on a remedy for it. The fact that many of these men owned slaves should not denigrate their achievements. Slavery was a fact of life in eighteenth-century America. What is remarkable

## Wisdom of the Founders

"The most effectual means of preventing the perversion of power into tyranny are to illuminate, as far as practicable, the minds of the people at large, and more especially to give them knowledge of those facts which history exhibits, that possessed thereby of the experience of other ages and countries, they may be enabled to know ambition under all its shapes, and prompt to exert their natural powers to defeat its purposes."

**—Thomas Jefferson, 1779.**

about these Founders—and what links them in continuity with us—is what they achieved to pass on: a tradition of liberty, a tradition that now, naturally, includes all Americans regardless of race.

One other interesting side note: when Most Americans think of the Founders, they think of men who were remarkably well educated—and that is true. They were the best educated generation of statesmen our country has ever had. Yet when you look at how they were educated you discover that every man on this list had at least some element of home-schooling in his background, and several of the most famous members were entirely homeschooled. Most of them entered college in their mid-teens and had finished law school by their early twenties. Franklin was entirely homeschooled; Jefferson was admitted to the College of William and Mary at sixteen and was graduated at eighteen; and George Mason learned in his uncle's library. The Founding Fathers are, in their own way, an advertisement for homeschooling and a reproach to the modern education system. It should be part of every American's education to learn about them.

★ ★ ★ ★ ★

# "THE BIG SIX"

## Chapter Four

# GEORGE WASHINGTON

On 15 January 1783, General George Washington stood before his officers in a moment of crisis. His men had toiled and suffered for months with little pay, and Congress did not appear willing to ante-up. Washington could sense the growing possibility of mutiny. In a basic wooden structure that the men called "the Temple," Washington reasoned with his subordinates to avoid "any measures which...will lessen the dignity and sully the glory you have hitherto maintained...." As the men anxiously listened to his words, Washington thought they were unconvinced by his plea for patience. He began reading a letter from a sympathetic member of the Congress that explained the difficulties the government faced in discharging its war debt. The army would be paid, this member assured, after the Congress resolved other pressing financial matters. The letter was barely legible and the aging Washington had trouble reading it without stumbling. He paused, removed his glasses from his pocket, and said: "Gentlemen, you must pardon me. I have grown gray in your service and now find myself going blind."

In those two sentences, Washington captured his men. Captain Samuel Shaw wrote of the moment, "He spoke—every doubt was dispelled, and the tide of patriotism rolled again in its wonted course. Illustrious man!" Washington connected with the men as a human being, a patriot engaged in the same struggle, and the army and its general were entwined. His

## Did You Know Washington:

- Was largely homeschooled
- Believed God saved the Revolution
- Was regarded, almost universally, as the greatest man of his generation

closing statement echoed in the room: "You will, by the dignity of your conduct, afford occasion for posterity to say, when speaking of the glorious example you have exhibited to mankind, had this day been wanting, the world had never seen the last stage of perfection to which human nature is capable of attaining."

Washington was the first American hero, and without doubt is the most important man in American history. Contemporaries described him as a giant among men in both physical stature and character. He stood over six feet tall and weighed 190 to 200 pounds. His frame exuded strength; his countenance was firm but agreeable. Men wished to emulate him and would enthusiastically follow him to the end, and the women of Virginia society called him charming, sincere, and chatty—an amusing companion, though sometimes impudent in his conversation. They lined up to dance with him. Jefferson described him as the finest horseman in the country. He commanded respect and admiration from both his countrymen and foreign visitors. Without George Washington, the United States would not exist.

## The first American hero

George Washington was a fourth generation American, born on 22 February 1732 in Westmoreland County, Virginia, to Augustine Washington and Mary Ball. His father was a respected man of the community and owned a small plantation between Bridges Creek and Popes Creek, Virginia. Augustine Washington died in 1743. This forced young George Washington to spend much of his youth with relatives, including his half-brother Lawrence and his wife, Ann Fairfax, at their Potomac River estate, Mount Vernon.

Washington did not have a formal education, though by modern standards he would be considered extremely well educated. His father and brother were his primary tutors. Washington studied history, theology, and mathematics, including trigonometry, and had a great interest in drafting, map-making, surveying, and agriculture. His mother instructed him in discipline and morals and helped craft Washington's character. Washington in time would become the quintessential Southern gentleman planter.

While at Mount Vernon, Washington had contact with the most prominent members of Virginia society, including the powerful and influential Fairfax family. He befriended George William Fairfax, and the two adventurous youths embarked on a month-long adventure in 1748 that took them into the heart of the Virginia wilderness. One year later, at seventeen, Washington was appointed the county surveyor for Culpeper, a job that carried the spirited and energetic young man to the farthest reaches of the Virginia frontier. Though Washington is well known for being a man of Virginia society, his experience on the frontier and his athletic and bold personality earned him the respect of even the most rugged Americans. He was a man among men.

## Books They Don't Want You to Read

*George Washington: A Biography.* 7 vols., by Douglas Southall Freeman (New York: Charles Scribner's Sons, 1951). While Freeman is better known for his work on another Virginian, Robert E. Lee, his Washington biography is the best, most comprehensive—and most politically incorrect—study on the subject.

Lawrence Washington died in 1752 and bequeathed Mount Vernon to George Washington. This allowed Washington to establish himself in Virginia society. So did military service. The governor appointed Washington as district adjutant for southern Virginia. Washington had a passion for military service and a gift for leadership, qualities that led to his first major military assignment.

In 1753, Governor Dinwiddie commissioned the twenty-one-year-old Washington to carry an ultimatum to the French demanding they vacate lands on the frontier that were claimed by the British. Washington had to march more than one hundred miles through wintery swampland to find the closest French fort. As expected, the French refused to meet Governor Dinwiddie's demands. Washington had to make much of the return journey on foot after his horses gave out. He was shot at, nearly drowned, and almost froze to death, but successfully delivered the French response, a report that stirred animosity in both the colonies and in England.

Washington was commissioned a lieutenant-colonel in the Virginia militia in 1754 and given orders to reinforce the British presence along the Ohio River. He had 150 men, a force too insignificant to capture a French fort or make much of an impact along the wild frontier. When Washington arrived near present day Pittsburgh, he was informed that the French had overwhelmed a detachment of British soldiers and had occupied Washington's intended destination. Washington moved slowly, built a defensive position called Fort Necessity, and ultimately engaged a French scouting party in a surprise attack, a battle which resulted in the death of the French commanding officer. The French counterattacked and forced Washington to agree to terms. He was tricked into signing a document that, unknown to him, stated the French commander had been "assassinated." This false admission of guilt helped jumpstart the French and Indian War.

Washington accepted an appointment as General George Braddock's aide in 1755 and accompanied the British in an effort to capture Fort Duquesne. The expedition proved to be a disaster. The British were ambushed and routed. Washington had two horses shot out from under him and four bullets passed through his jacket. Braddock was killed, and Washington led what remained of the British forces home. Later that year, Washington was appointed commander of all Virginia militia and charged with defending the Virginia frontier from the French, but most especially from Indians. He served with distinction, and though outnumbered and with little food, supplies, or ammunition, was able to keep marauding Indian tribes at bay. After the British captured Fort Duquesne in 1758, Washington resigned his commission and returned to Mount Vernon. He married wealthy widow Martha Custis in 1759 and spent the next few years as a planter, enjoying the social life of aristocratic Virginia.

## The Revolution

Washington's political career spanned several decades. He was a member of the Virginia House of Burgesses, a justice of the peace of Fairfax County, and a vestryman. His faithful adherence to his civic duty won him the admiration of his peers. By the 1760s, Washington had grown increasingly suspicious of the British. He had witnessed their arrogance firsthand during the French and Indian War and now chafed at their restrictions on colonial trade. He supported non-importation of British goods and served as the chairman of a 1774 meeting that adopted George Mason's Virginia Resolves, a set of contentious grievances against the crown and Parliament.

Though he had been a conservative supporter of the king, Washington increasingly believed that Britain intended to saddle the American colonists with an "arbitrary" government, a government that would not be bound by the rights of Englishmen. He wrote in 1774, "I think I can announce it as a fact, that it is not the wish or interest of that government [Massachusetts], or any other upon this continent, separately or collectively, to set up for independencey; but this you may at the same time rely on, that none of them will ever submit to the loss of those valuable rights and privileges, which are essential to the happiness of every free state, and without which, life, liberty, and property are rendered totally insecure." Washington was the first example of the conservative revolutionary. He did not favor independence until the British appeared unwilling to compromise.

He was appointed as one of Virginia's delegates to the First Continental Congress and was selected to command a group of independent

Virginia militia companies in 1775. He once again donned a uniform and became an active proponent for the military preparation of the colonies should compromise fail and matters lead to war. By the time Virginia sent him to the Second Continental Congress in 1775, fighting had taken place at Lexington and Concord, and Washington was chosen to help organize an army and fortify New York City.

## A Humble Commander

"But lest some unlucky event should happen unfavorable to my reputation, I beg it may be remembered by every gentleman in the room that I this day declare with the utmost sincerity, I do not think myself equal to the command I am honored with."

—**George Washington, 1775, on accepting command of the Continental Army.**

Washington wore his blue uniform to every session of the Congress. This has often been construed as an ambitious power-play, but Washington already commanded several militia companies in Virginia and because of his military experience in the French and Indian War had been selected by the Congress to help prepare colonial defenses. He believed the colonies and Great Britain were in a state of war. Why not dress the part?

John Adams nominated him to command the newly created Continental Army. The decision was partly political and partly practical. Washington was from Virginia, and the other candidate, John Hancock, hailed from Massachusetts. By selecting Washington, the Congress ensured that the fight against the British would be a colonial struggle and not an isolated war in Massachusetts, and it concurrently chose the best military mind in the colonies for the job. Washington humbly accepted and refused a salary, asking only that the Congress repay his personal expenses made on behalf of the army at the end of the war. His unpretentious nature has been construed by some modern historians as insincere, a pose. Yet, when relaying the news of his appointment to his wife, Washington displayed the same humility.

One has to question why Washington would be disingenuous to Martha Washington. He would have nothing to gain from such a move.

Washington inherited an army that was little more than a rag-tag militia, and was faced with the daunting task of defeating the best-trained and equipped army in the world. He experienced problems of supply, pay, morale, discipline, and political intrigue against him throughout the war. The early years of the conflict were the worst. Most of the men who held Boston in 1775 were eager to return home when their terms of enlistment expired, and Washington complained that the New England militia took provisions without service and had an unchecked avarice. "There is no nation under the sun," he wrote, "that pays more adoration to money than they do." Of course, by nation he meant New England. This difficulty never faded. Some of his greatest "blunders" during the war can be attributed to bad morale and expired enlistments. He rarely had a unified veteran army to place in the field.

After a masterful campaign in Boston in 1776 that forced the British army to evacuate that city, Washington moved south to fortify New York. He had roughly 10,000 men and was instructed to defend sixteen miles of coastline against 30,000 British troops and 100 warships. He did not have a navy or many experienced officers, and the Continental Army suffered setback after setback in New York as the

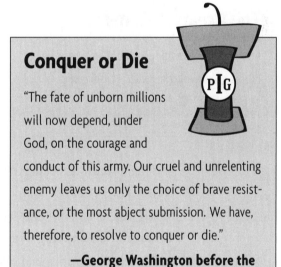

## Conquer or Die

"The fate of unborn millions will now depend, under God, on the courage and conduct of this army. Our cruel and unrelenting enemy leaves us only the choice of brave resistance, or the most abject submission. We have, therefore, to resolve to conquer or die."

**—George Washington before the Battle of Long Island, August 1776.**

British regulars and their Hessian mercenaries overwhelmed the undisciplined and undersupplied American forces.

As his army melted away during 1776 due to desertions and casualties, Washington began to formulate a plan of prudent and calculated strikes within an overall strategy of attrition, of wearing the enemy down. By late 1776, he had only 5,000 men at his disposal. Washington crossed the Delaware River into Pennsylvania. The British decided not to pursue him, but to divide their army and settle into winter quarters throughout New Jersey. This worked to Washington's advantage.

His most successful selective strike occurred on Christmas Day, 1776. The army crossed the Delaware River under the cover of darkness during an ice storm and surprised a Hessian regiment at Trenton. His troops fought a determined battle and killed or captured the entire Hessian detachment. This single blow rallied his men, and after a later success at Princeton, forced the British to evacuate New Jersey. He led two strikes on the British in the fall of 1777, one at Brandywine Creek and one at Germantown, Pennsylvania; neither was a victory, but Washington showed resilience and resolve, and, more important, the French were now paying attention to the American War for Independence. He settled at Valley Forge, Pennsylvania, in the winter of 1777 and faced his most difficult task as a commanding officer, keeping the army together during a brutal and unforgiving winter.

★★★★★★★

## The Greatest General

A common toast among American troops during the Revolution was: "Washington or No Army!"

Meat and supplies had often been short, but the shortages that winter of 1777–78 were the worst. Many of the men were shoeless, dressed in rags, and starving. The frigid cold and paltry living quarters amplified their suffering. Washington empathized with the men and feared the result of such misery, but, remarkably, desertions decreased as the suffering grew more intense. His men were supremely dedicated to both Washington and the cause. Washington also had to keep the larger picture in view: winning the war. When one junior officer pleaded with

Washington for a furlough to see his fiancé, claiming she would "die" if he didn't go, Washington refused, and responded, "Oh no; women do not die for such trifles." When the captain asked what he should do, Washington is reported to have said, "Why, write to her to add another leaf to the book of sufferings."

Washington demanded more disciplined training for his men, and they emerged from Valley Forge hardened and better prepared than at any time in the war. Unfortunately, continued problems of supply dogged his efforts at victory, while long-awaited French military involvement acted as a sedative rather than a stimulant. The army plodded through three more years of virtual inactivity. Washington had hoped, initially, that French reinforcements would lead to a quick victory, but when that victory did not materialize he fell back on his strategy of simply wearing out the British; though there was a great danger that his own men would wear out first. He wrote in 1780, "We have no magazines, nor money to form them; and in a little time we shall have no men.... The history of the war is a history of false hopes and temporary devices, instead of system and economy."

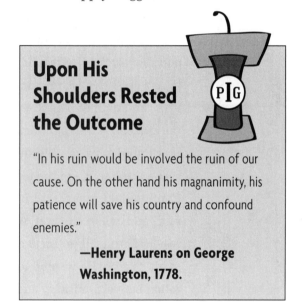

**Upon His Shoulders Rested the Outcome**

"In his ruin would be involved the ruin of our cause. On the other hand his magnanimity, his patience will save his country and confound enemies."

**—Henry Laurens on George Washington, 1778.**

The tide turned in 1781. The French made a daring move and captured the British navy at the mouth of the Chesapeake Bay, and a combined Franco-American force led by Washington trapped Lord Charles Cornwallis at Yorktown, Virginia, in September 1781. This was the last major military engagement of the war. Washington emerged as the hero of Yorktown and the savior of independence. He marched triumphantly into

New York City on 19 April 1783 and gladly resigned his commission shortly thereafter. He retired, on the verge of personal bankruptcy, to a dilapidated Mount Vernon, convinced that only Providence had saved the Revolution. At 51, he was also determined never again to enter public life.

His voluntary retirement was unprecedented in the annals of history. Washington could have marched into New York and taken over the government. His reputation ensured that the people would support him. Most victorious generals in history had sought political power from their exploits. Lucius Sulla, Julius Caesar, Oliver Cromwell, William of Orange, and Frederick the Great of Prussia had all used their battlefield success to seize power. Washington was consciously different. He was the American Cincinnatus. The Roman farmer Cincinnatus was called to duty by the citizens of the republic to act as dictator during two emergencies. He was found plowing his fields, and returned to his farm once he had secured the safety of the republic. Virginia appointed Washington to the Continental Congress while he was "plowing his fields" at Mount Vernon, and when the war was over, he returned to his plantation and resigned from all political appointments, even his position as vestryman at his church. He wanted to secure American liberty by ensuring a separation between military and civil power.

## The American Cincinnatus

"Having now finished the work assigned me, I retire from the great theatre of Action; and bidding an Affectionate farewell to this August body under whose orders I have so long acted, I here offer my commission, and take my leave of all the employments of public life."

—**George Washington, 1783.**

## Duty calls

When the people of Virginia called on him to serve in the Constitutional Convention in 1787, Washington at first refused, but he was finally persuaded by the same call of duty that led him to accept the command of the Continental Army in 1775. The Convention unanimously elected him president. His presence and support for the Constitution alone helped silence some opposition to it, and the delegates to the Constitutional Convention surely had him in mind when constructing the executive branch, because they knew the new government would depend on his involvement.

He responded to his unanimous election as president in 1789 with a sense of dread. "My movements to the chair of government will be accompanied by feelings not unlike those of a culprit, who is going to the place of his execution." Washington had the perfect disposition for the job. In sharp contrast to modern politicians, he did not campaign for, nor actively seek, power. There were no signs extolling "The Office of the President Elect." He believed God had intervened in the cause of independence and now believed only Providence could predict the outcome of his new role as president.

> Such being the impressions under which I have, in obedience to the public summons, repaired to the present station, it would be peculiarly improper to omit in this first official act my fervent supplications to that Almighty Being who rules over the universe, who presides in the councils of nations, and whose providential aids can supply every human defect, that His benediction may consecrate to the liberties and happiness of the people of the United States a Government instituted by themselves for these essential purposes, and may enable every instrument employed in its administration to execute with success the functions allotted to his charge. In tendering this

homage to the Great Author of every public and private good, I assure myself that it expresses your sentiments not less than my own, nor those of my fellow-citizens at large less than either. No people can be bound to acknowledge and adore the Invisible Hand which conducts the affairs of men more than those of the United States. Every step by which they have advanced to the character of an independent nation seems to have been distinguished by some token of providential agency; and in the important revolution just accomplished in the system of their united government the tranquil deliberations and voluntary consent of so many distinct communities from which the event has resulted can not be compared with the means by which most governments have been established without some return of pious gratitude, along with an humble anticipation of the future blessings which the past seem to presage. These reflections, arising out of the present crisis, have forced themselves too strongly on my mind to be suppressed. You will join with me, I trust, in thinking that there are none under the influence of which the proceedings of a new and free government can more auspiciously commence.

He had confidence in his own abilities and had gladly risked his fame and fortune as the commander of the Continental Army, but the war also displayed the darker side of political life, and Washington was unsure that he could quell the factionalism, bickering, and pettiness of politics.

Washington almost died before his first term began. He became ill, possibly with a bout of anthrax poisoning, and struggled to regain his strength. Once healthy, he tackled the mundane but important tasks assigned to him by the Constitution. With the help of his Secretary of War, Henry Knox, Washington began to shore up Indian relations and solidify the defensive capabilities of the new United States. He refused a salary, though Congress appropriated him one. He accepted the title of "Mr. President," turning aside the more flowery suggestions offered by Vice President John Adams. Above all, Washington wanted the United States to be respected on the international stage, and that required, in his view, a strengthening of government.

Washington determined to surround himself with bright, able individuals. He chose

## Books They Don't Want You to Read

*The Presidency of George Washington*, by Forrest McDonald (Lawrence: University Press of Kansas, 1974). This is an excellent and concise study of Washington as president.

his good friend from Virginia, Thomas Jefferson, as Secretary of State, and two former military subordinates, Henry Knox and Alexander Hamilton, as Secretary of War and Secretary of Treasury respectively. Washington believed he was better prepared for foreign and military affairs than anyone in the United States, so Jefferson and Knox essentially became glorified secretaries. Washington was also aware of his limitations and let Hamilton run the new Treasury department with little interference. This helped lead to Jefferson's resentment and later resignation.

When bitter disputes arose between Jefferson and Hamilton over the proper power of the new central government, Washington asked both men to compromise. They did on the matters concerning the federal government's assumption of state debt and on the location of the new national capital, but could not come to an agreement over Hamilton's proposed economic system, which included a central bank. Washington tried to mediate and believed he was acting in the best interest of the United States by siding with Hamilton. His relationship with Hamilton grew closer, while Jefferson began to distance himself from the first president, and by 1793 Jefferson had resigned his position and was back at Monticello in retirement.

Without Jefferson around to retard the increasing centralization of the government, Washington gravitated toward a more aggressive approach to federal power. His reaction to the Whiskey Rebellion of 1795 showed the extent he was willing to go to limit internal discord. When farmers in the western part of Pennsylvania resorted to violence to protest Hamilton's excise tax on distilled spirits, Washington personally led a militia of 10,000 men to the troubled region in an unprecedented display of American force. The "rebellion" turned out to be little more than a minor disturbance, and most of those involved were protected by their friends and neighbors, but Washington seized the moment and insisted that the farmers had to pay the tax. Jefferson said after the event that "an insurrection was announced and proclaimed and armed against, but could never be found."

Actually, a group of Democratic-Republicans were pegged as the instigators of the "rebellion," and Hamilton used the event as a political ploy to crush opposition to the Federalist Party in Pennsylvania. This was his, and the Federalists', chance to show that a standing army was necessary to prevent internal disruption. Washington also capitalized on the moment and placed blame on renegade groups determined to resist federal authority. The federal "smack-down" had the desired effect. Democratic-Republican societies ceased operation, and Federalists gained control of Congress following the 1794 elections.

In foreign policy, Washington wished for the United States to remain neutral in European affairs. He issued a Neutrality Proclamation in 1793, a questionable move constitutionally, but one that was designed to keep the United States out of foreign conflict. Washington believed the United States should remain a peaceful trading partner with the rest of the world. When presented with John Jay's controversial "Treaty of Amity, Commerce, and Navigation" with Great Britain in 1794, he hesitated to sign it for fear that the United States would be dragged into the international conflict between the French and the British. Southerners also denounced the treaty as purely sectional, claiming it would only favor Northern commercial interests at the expense of the rest of the country, and that it kowtowed to the British. Hamilton insisted it was the best treaty they could hope for, that it resolved remaining disputes between the two countries, would ensure the peace and promote commerce, and urged Washington to support the measure. Washington sent the treaty to the Senate for ratification and it took effect in 1796, but it remained a contentious issue.

Washington almost decided against a second term in 1792. He told Jefferson that he was feeling the effects of age, and that both his mind and body were beginning to fail him. Finally his sense of duty and the international difficulties confronting the United States obliged him to accept a second term, but it would be his last. He looked forward to retirement, even though he understood that some would suggest he was leaving because of falling popularity and a tarnished image. He had not escaped eight years as president without political and personal attacks, even from one-time friends and associates. Regardless, Washington believed he left the United States on firm ground both internationally and domestically.

On 19 September 1796, Washington issued a farewell address to the United States. The open letter to the public appeared in newspapers across the country and is perhaps Washington's most famous public doc-

## First in the Hearts of His Countrymen

"First in war, first in peace, and first in the hearts of his countrymen, he was second to none in the humble and endearing scenes of private life. Pious, just, humane, temperate and sincere; uniform, dignified and commanding, his example was as edifying to all around him, as were the effects of that example lasting. To his equals he was condescending, to his inferiors kind, and to the dear object of his affections exemplarily tender. Correct throughout, vice shuddered in his presence, and virtue always felt his fostering hand. The purity of his private character gave effulgence to his public virtues."

— **Henry "Light Horse Harry" Lee, 1799.**

ument. In it, Washington covered the most popular political topics of the day. He warned against political parties and factionalism, urged his successors and those in Congress to maintain a strict construction of the Constitution and use amendments when necessary to alter its limitations, cautioned against excessive government borrowing, and insisted on morality through religion. These guidelines, in his estimation, were the only way to maintain the republic. He argued, in addition, that permanent foreign alliances were dangerous to the future security of the United States and threatened American sovereignty. Washington's farewell message is something that our president and congressmen should commit themselves to study.

## The last years

Once Washington retired to Mount Vernon in 1797, he hoped, as in 1783, that it would be for the last time, but when the French threatened war with the United States in 1798, Washington again answered the call. President John Adams appointed Washington lieutenant-general and commander-in-chief of American forces. Washington demanded that Hamilton be named second in command with full authority over the army. Adams resisted, but Washington won the war of wills, and Hamilton began the process of organizing an army. At sixty-six, Washington wanted to act as little more than a figurehead and desired Hamilton to complete the difficult tasks of administration. Fortunately, Washington would not have to lead the army against France.

As tension with the French subsided throughout 1798 and 1799, Washington settled into a routine at Mount Vernon. He never fully recovered financially from the Revolution, but during his last years in retirement almost achieved self-sufficiency at his estate. The problems of caring for and maintaining slaves weighed on him financially. Though selling off some of his slaves might have alleviated his problems, he abhorred breaking apart families and refused to participate in the slave traffic. He supported the gradual abolition of slavery, but thought a forced end to the institution would only create more evil than good. Washington believed slavery to be an inefficient and paternalistic institution and thought it would end naturally. Thus, though unsatisfied with the economic and moral ramifications of the institution, he continued as a slaveholder until his death. He manumitted his slaves in his will.

Death came quickly and suddenly in December 1799. Washington had spent two days outdoors in foul December weather. He caught a cold that soon turned to a severe case of laryngitis and swelling of the throat. Washington had trouble breathing and instructed his personal physician to administer bloodletting. This process had worked for his slaves and he firmly believed in its therapeutic effects. When his condition grew worse, Washington prepared for the end. Because of the extreme loss of blood, he was too weak to fight his oncoming demise, but Washington reassured those around him that he was not afraid. He died peacefully on 14 December 1799 with his wife at his side, just two years after leaving the presidency. The great hero proved mortal, but his legacy would endure.

## The Washington effect

Washington established several important precedents while president. Until 1940, no president sought more than two consecutive terms in office. He could have remained president for life. The Constitution did not impose term limits on the executive, but Washington was always mindful of preserving the office of the president from any connotations of monarchy. No one in the Revolutionary generation dared break his precedent of serving no more than two consecutive terms.

He also added a famous line to the oath of office. The Constitution stipulates that the president must take the following oath or affirmation before taking office: "I do solemnly swear (or affirm) that I will faithfully execute the office of President of the United States, and will to the best of my ability, preserve, protect, and defend the Constitution of the United States." Washington attached the phrase "so help me God" to the end of the oath, an addition that remains. Washington would not have trusted anyone who did not call on Providence for assistance in executing the powers of the president.

Though Washington gravitated toward Hamilton in the final years of his administration, he maintained that the Constitution should be followed literally and strictly. He believed Congress should have the ultimate authority on most political matters. He issued the first Proclamation of Thanksgiving, and began the process of delivering the "State of the Union" address to Congress in person. This precedent was ignored for more than one hundred years, until it was revived by Woodrow Wilson. In his own "State of the Union" addresses Washington did not make any grand requests for appropriations. He simply asked Congress to "consider" measures that he deemed important. They were not required to act on his suggestions.

Perhaps his most important legacy, however, was not in the executive office; it was in the example of his character. He was idolized by succes-

## A Tribute from One Virginian to Another

"On the whole, his character was, in its mass, perfect, in nothing bad, in few points indifferent; and it may truly be said, that never did nature and fortune combine more perfectly to make a man great, and to place him in the same constellation with whatever worthies have merited from man an everlasting remembrance....These are my opinions of General Washington, which I would vouch at the judgment seat of God, having been formed on an acquaintance of thirty years...."

**—Thomas Jefferson, 1814.**

sive generations for his honor and integrity, qualities that have rarely been matched, particularly in the federal government. More monuments have been erected for George Washington than any other American. Inevitably, politically correct historians have tried to tarnish him because he was a slaveholder, because he was venerated in the Confederacy during its own war of independence (with his image on the Confederate States Seal), and because he was, allegedly, "not very smart," or "too ambitious," or "sort of a boob," or a "racist, Indian hater." But better, and more accurate, was the view of "Light Horse Harry" Lee, Robert E. Lee's father, who served with Washington: "Possessing a clear and penetrating mind, a strong and sound judgment, calmness and temper for deliberation, with invincible firmness and perseverance in resolutions maturely formed; drawing information from all; acting from himself with incorruptible integrity and unvarying patriotism; his own superiority and public confidence alike marked him as the man designed by Heaven to lead in the great political as well as military events which have distinguished the era of his life." That is how Washington should be remembered, because that is true to the Washington of history.

Chapter Five

# THOMAS JEFFERSON

F ew figures in American history are studied or debated as frequently as Thomas Jefferson. A colleague once remarked that American history and American politics are simple: you are either a Jeffersonian or a Hamiltonian. He might be right. Little has changed in two hundred years. Modern political ideology has blended elements of both men, but in substance, Americans can be split into two distinctive camps that have nothing to do with party affiliation: you either believe in a government of restraint or a government of action. Jefferson did not have the military record of Washington or the political stature, at least at first, of his fellow Virginian Patrick Henry, but his legacy, while not always correctly interpreted, has had a more lasting impact on American political life than most men in the Founding generation.

Jefferson was born on 13 April 1743 at his family plantation called Shadwell. His father, Peter Jefferson, earned his way into Virginia society through perseverance and marriage. The Jefferson clan arrived in the colonies around 1677, and like Washington, Thomas Jefferson was a fourth generation American. Jefferson's mother, Jane Randolph, was a member of one of the most powerful families in Virginia. Peter Jefferson ensured social standing for his children through his union to Jane and by conducting himself as a Southern gentleman. He made the first accurate

## Did You Know Jefferson:

- Called Virginia his country
- Supported secession and nullification
- Would have vetoed all federal domestic programs of the last one hundred years

map of Virginia, helped survey the boundary line between North Carolina and Virginia, and served as a burgess and county lieutenant for Albermarle. When Peter Jefferson died, he bequeathed Thomas Jefferson 2,750 acres of land and an established place in the community.

Thomas Jefferson obtained a rigorous education in his youth. He studied the classics, particularly the histories and philosophy of Greece and Rome, French, and mathematics. Jefferson grew attached to the land in his youth and developed an affinity for Virginian society that continued throughout his life. He entered the College of William and Mary in 1760 at sixteen and was graduated at eighteen. This was not uncommon at the time; young men with talent rose quickly through the formal education "system" and began their careers. To that end, Jefferson studied law, and continued his study of the classics under George Wythe, the first and only law professor in Virginia at the time. Jefferson had a natural talent for legal work, but little appetite to apply it in court. He

## Jefferson: An Aristocratic Democrat

"Men by their constitutions are naturally divided into two parties: 1. Those who fear and distrust the people, and wish to draw all powers from them into the hands of the higher classes. 2. Those who identify themselves with the people, have confidence in them, cherish and consider them as the most honest and safe, although not the most wise depositary of the public interests. In every country these two parties exist, and in every one where they are free to think, speak, and write, they will declare themselves. Call them, therefore, Liberals and Serviles, Jacobins and Ultras, Whigs and Tories, Republicans and Federalists, Aristocrats and Democrats, or by whatever name you please, they are the same parties still and pursue the same object. The last one of Aristocrats and Democrats is the true one expressing the essence of all."

**—Thomas Jefferson, 1824.**

was admitted to the Virginia bar in 1767, but never practiced law after 1775.

In 1772, Jefferson married a beautiful widow, Martha Wayles Skelton; she died ten years later. Jefferson was a devoted husband, and the marriage produced six children, two of whom lived to adulthood. The loss of his wife buried Jefferson in a deep, lasting depression, and he promised that he would not marry after her death. He never did.

Shortly after their marriage, Jefferson and his wife moved to Monticello, where all their children were born. Monticello became his passion; his happiest occupation was building and perfecting his mountain-top plantation. By 1775, he owned close to 10,000 acres and between 100 to 200 slaves, and with both came the debt and financial concerns that often plagued Southern planters. Jefferson maintained meticulous records of plantation life, from the activities of his slaves to the temperature, foliage, and migratory patterns of birds and wildlife. He was a naturalist and scientist with a passion for education. This pursuit of learning led him to charter the University of Virginia in 1819, a project he had envisioned since at least 1800. He wanted his college to be "temptation to the youth of other States to come and drink of the cup of knowledge and fraternize with us." Even more important, Jefferson wanted his fellow Virginians to be educated in their own state, to be free from the corruption of the "dark Federalist mills," such as Yale, Harvard, and Princeton. The University of Virginia, he believed, would perpetuate the agrarian order of Virginia. He listed the founding of the institution as one of his most important contributions to his state.

## Books They Don't Want You to Read

*The Founders and the Classics: Greece, Rome, and the American Enlightenment*, by Carl J. Richard (Cambridge: Harvard University Press, 1994). Liberals would like you to think that the American Founders were students of the French *philosophes* and subscribed to their doctrines of *égalité*. Richard destroys that myth.

## Patriot

In the years leading up to the Revolution, Jefferson gained political experience as a member of the Virginia House of Burgesses. He was renowned less as an orator than as a writer. His *A Summary View of the Rights of British America*, written in 1774, justified American grievances against the crown on the basis of their common, natural rights as Englishmen.

Jefferson emphasized that life and liberty were granted through God, and though the "hand of force may destroy, [it] cannot disjoin them." As in the case of the later Declaration, the *Summary* was aggressive but conservative. Jefferson begged the king in the spirit of "fraternal love" to check the oppressive acts of Parliament and maintain harmony throughout the empire. The colonists, who had carved a life for themselves through their own blood and toil and were of right Englishmen, had legitimate concern with the belligerent and unconstitutional acts forced upon them. Jefferson maintained the colonies were granted freedom of trade through "natural right" and demanded that taxing power be vested in the colonial legislatures. He was not a separatist in 1774. Jefferson believed the colonies could no longer suffer through the "slavery" of oppressive and unconstitutional government, but he preferred peaceful reconciliation to separation.

Though elected as an alternate, Jefferson spent little time in the Continental Congress before May 1776. He was appointed the commander of the Albemarle militia and organized his county's

## Rule Britannia... If Britannia Rules Well

"Believe me, dear Sir: there is not in the British empire a man who more cordially loves a union with Great Britain than I do. But, by the God that made me, I will cease to exist before I yield to a connection on such terms as the British Parliament propose; and in this, I think I speak the sentiments of America."

**—Thomas Jefferson, 1775.**

defense, but he did not see military duty during the war. In June 1776, Congress elected Jefferson—along with John Adams, Benjamin Franklin, Roger Sherman, and Robert Livingston—to draft a declaration of independence. The Declaration was, in the words Jefferson's biographer Dumas Malone, the document that justified the "secession of the colonies from the Mother Country." In Jefferson's mind, the colonists were acting within their sovereign, natural rights as Englishmen to resist tyranny.

Those sovereign rights were to be exercised by the sovereign states. The Declaration affirms that the colonies "are, and of Right out to be, FREE AND INDEPENDENT STATES...and that as FREE AND INDEPENDENT STATES, they have full Power to levy War, conclude Peace, contract Alliances, establish Commerce, and to do all other Acts and Things which INDEPENDENT STATES may of right do." The emphasis is in the original, and the use of the plural, "independent states," is not an accident. When Jefferson referred to his "country" he always meant Virginia, and it was this idea that the colonies were free and independent states, united by common interest, that later made Jefferson such an ardent proponent of limiting the power of the Federal government and reaffirming the rights of the states.

During the Revolution, Jefferson served in the Virginia House of Delegates until he was elected governor in 1779. He helped draft the first constitution for Virginia in 1776, a document that created a bicameral legislature with an independent executive and a declaration of rights. This constitution would be the model for the United States Constitution.

In 1779, he authored a bill for establishing religious liberty, the "Virginia Statute for Religious Freedom," a document that he believed to be his most important contribution to his state. The bill, which did not pass until 1786, with James Madison as its champion, is often used to illustrate Jefferson's distaste for established "religion." But Jefferson and every other American in the eighteenth century understood established religion to mean an established church, such as the Church of England. The bill was meant as an abettor, not a hindrance, to freedom of religion in the state.

The war took its toll on Jefferson, as it did on everyone else. In 1781, the British occupied Richmond. Benedict Arnold's "American Legion" of British loyalists sacked the Governor's House, Jefferson's home as governor. The following year Jefferson's wife died, and his own health was uncertain. From 1781, his last year as governor, to 1783, the last year of the Revolutionary War, Jefferson retired from public life and devoted himself to writing *Notes on the State of Virginia.* The *Notes* is the fullest expression we have of Jefferson's views on philosophy, education, science, and politics. He believed that his beloved Virginia needed improvements, and he openly discussed them, but he also understood that his freedom and individuality were only possible because of the rigid structure of the old order of Virginia life, an order that had been defined from the earliest settlers to Virginia and perpetuated by the moral, geographical, legal, and political boundaries of his state. In plain terms, tradition allowed freedom, not just for Jefferson the aristocrat, but for the members of his community regardless of status. The *Notes* explicitly recognized and defended this maxim.

> "In God's name, from whence have they derived this power (dictatorship during the Revolution)? Is it from our ancient laws? None such can be produced. Is it from any principle in our new constitution (of Virginia), expressed or implied? Every lineament of that expressed or implied, is in full opposition to it. Its fundamental principle is, that the state shall be governed as a commonwealth. It provides a republican organization, proscribes under the name of *prerogative* the exercise of all powers undefined by the laws; places on this basis the whole system of our laws; and, by consolidating them together, chuses [SIC] that they shall be left to stand or fall together,

never providing for any circumstances, nor admitting that such could arise, wherein either should be suspended, no, not for a moment. Our ancient laws expressly declare, that those who are but delegates themselves shall not delegate to others powers which require judgment and integrity in their exercise."

After accepting his election as a delegate to the Congress of the United States in 1783, Jefferson authored the bill that ceded Virginia's western lands, which extended from the Ohio Valley to the Mississippi River, to the new central government, quite possibly the most substantial act of generosity in American history. Since the early stages of the Revolution, Jefferson had envisioned this territory as room for American expansion, for the creation of new states, as equal and sovereign as the other American states. Jefferson also determined that the western territory should be free from slavery. If early western land legislation had been drafted according to his wishes, slavery would have been forbidden in all western territory after 1800. As it stood, the Northwest Ordinance of 1787, a document modeled after Jefferson's designs, prohibited slavery in the territory until the said territory became a state. At that point the sovereign state could legislate for the institution as it wished. Jefferson owned slaves, but he could also see the potentially destructive nature of the system, thus his insistence on the exclusion of slavery in the territories and his attempted inclusion of a statement condemning slavery in the Declaration of Independence.

## Diplomat and secretary of state

Jefferson began his career as a diplomat in 1784 when he helped negotiate a trade agreement with Prussia; from 1785 to 1789 he was the United States ambassador to France; and from 1789 until his resignation in 1793 he was secretary of state. Jefferson was something of a Francophile; he liked the French and preferred them to the English, whom he thought arrogant and selfish. Although he thought America could continue to benefit from its relationship with France, it is a common misconception that Jefferson wanted to make the United States more like France. He did not. While he sympathized with the leaders of the early stages of the French Revolution, he was disgusted by the violence and turmoil of the Reign of Terror and was shocked and dismayed by the ascension of Napoleon Bonaparte to power. He admired French arts, but did not think much of their science or philosophy. Jefferson was born with an English mind; and educated English minds were molded by the classics of Greece and Rome; it was the classics, not the French *philosophes*, that framed his philosophy.

As Washington's choice for first secretary of state under the Constitution, Jefferson accepted, but not without reservation. He continued to long for retirement from public service, but believed duty required him to be a good steward of the new Constitution, and also to watch the designs of the potential "monarchists" who had gained control of the central government during his long absence in France. Jefferson developed a clearer picture of American political life during this period. He became convinced that some Americans were attempting to subvert the principles of the Revolution, consolidate power, and trample on American liberty. His fears appeared justified when Hamilton presented his First Report on the Public Credit and advocated the establishment of a Bank of the United States.

Jefferson wished to "preserve the lines drawn by the Federal Constitution between the general and particular governments as it stands at present, and to take every prudent means to prevent either from stepping over it." Hamilton's program overstepped these boundaries. Jefferson had long been suspicious of Hamilton. He thought Hamilton was generally a good man, but did not understand his infatuation with Britain and its system of government, including its corruption, which Hamilton simply accepted without demur.

Jefferson outlined his understanding of the Constitution in his challenge to the bank. Because chartering a bank or any other corporation was not a specific power delegated to the central government by the Constitution, the bank could not be created. Jefferson argued that Hamiltonianism "flowed from principles adverse to liberty, and was calculated to undermine and demolish the republic...." It meant, in short, an ever-expanding federal government which would of necessity be an enemy of freedom.

Jefferson faced an international crisis in his final year as secretary of state that underlined his differences with Hamil-

**Jefferson on Economic Stimulus Programs**

"I sincerely believe ... that the principle of spending money to be paid by posterity under the name of funding is but swindling futurity on a large scale."

**—Thomas Jefferson, 1816.**

ton. In 1793, the French appointed Edmond Charles Genêt as minister to the United States. Jefferson described him as a hothead, and Genêt created controversy when he attempted to commission Americans to act as privateers and seize British shipping; Genêt also publicly and repeatedly disparaged George Washington. Genêt wanted the United States to join France's war with Great Britain. Washington had no interest in another war with Britain. Neither did Jefferson, who eventually requested that the government of France recall Genêt recall from the United States.

In April 1793, Washington issued his famous Neutrality Proclamation. Jefferson supported neutrality, but thought Washington was overreaching his authority. Jefferson knew that Hamilton, the pro-British Federalist, was actually behind the proclamation. Jefferson urged Madison to challenge it, which he did. Madison argued that treaty-making was the sole responsibility of Congress, and that by issuing a "proclamation" of neutrality, the executive was seizing power not delegated to it by the Constitution and violating the principle of congressional oversight over questions of war and peace.

Madison and the Jeffersonian Republicans are generally seen as sympathetic to the French, while the Federalists were sympathetic to Britain. But what was really at stake was not a matter of sympathies but of Jefferson's desire to maintain a strict obedience to the Constitution and the limits it set on the executive, legislative, and judicial powers of the Federal government.

## Retirement and vice president

Because he was increasingly at odds with Hamilton and Hamilton's growing influence over Washington, Jefferson resigned as Secretary of State in 1793. At fifty-one (the same age as Washington when he "retired" in 1783), Jefferson believed he was leaving public service for good. He brought his family to Monticello. First and foremost, Jefferson was a traditional Virginia planter. He believed agrarian life, coupled with "the eye of vigilance," provided the best security against what he saw as the evils of centralization, consolidation, and urbanization.

Jefferson implemented a scientific rotation of crops, then a novel experiment, added a grist-mill and nail factory to make the plantation more self-sufficient, and expanded Monticello. Jefferson wrote in the *Notes* that towns were unimportant in Virginia because commerce could be conducted along rivers. In any event, the goal for the planter was self-sufficiency so that he didn't have to dirty his hands too much with the money-grubbing of the merchant class. The goal was to be a gentleman, and as one Virginian wrote in 1773, "The people of fortune...are the pattern of all behaviour here." Politics was a duty, but the plantation was center of his life.

Duty called again. Jefferson finished second in the 1796 presidential election, and accordingly, served one term as vice-president. He fulfilled his constitutional duties and even wrote the definitive manual on parliamentary practice in the Senate. His defining moment as vice president, however, was not in any official capacity. It was during the Quasi-War with France, when the Federalists, worried that French revolutionary ideas and agents were spreading to America, issued the Alien and Sedition Acts of 1798.

Jefferson responded by writing, in secret, the Kentucky Resolutions for the state legislature of Kentucky. The Constitution, the resolutions stated, is a compact among the states, and if the federal government, as the agent of the contracting parties, breached that compact by violating its delegated authority (as in the Alien and Sedition Acts), the states had a right to declare such acts null and void. Popular opposition to the Alien and Sedition Acts doomed the Federalist Party, which was defeated by Jefferson and the Republican Party in 1801.

## The presidency

Jefferson detested his time as president. He was elected by Congress in 1801 after the Electoral College returns ended in a tie between Jefferson and Aaron Burr. Hamilton, who considered Jefferson to be the safer man, prodded Federalists in Congress to vote for Jefferson. He was elected by one vote on the thirty-sixth ballot. Jefferson viewed his election as a second revolution, and though he did not desire office and considered his election more of a curse than a blessing, he never-

# Wisdom of the Founders

"I had rather be shut up in a very modest cottage with my books, my family and a few old friends, dining on simple bacon, and letting the world roll on as it liked, than to occupy the most splendid post, which any human power can give."

**—Thomas Jefferson, 1788.**

119

theless seized the opportunity to place his stamp on the executive branch. As the third president and the first of an opposition "party," Jefferson sought to downgrade the presidency and place it within its proper constitutional position.

Jefferson took office on 4 March 1801. In his first symbolic move, Jefferson walked to the capitol building rather than ride in a coach. He wanted to portray an image of humility and republican simplicity. Jefferson was many things, and enemies described him as cunning and petty, but no one could rightfully accuse him of ambition. He was setting an example that he hoped future presidents would emulate. The president was to be the faithful defender of constitutional powers, but nothing more, and show leadership in restraint.

## Wisdom of the Founders

"I am for preserving to the States the powers not yielded by them to the Union, and to the legislature of the Union its constitutional share in the division of powers; and I am not for transferring all the powers of the States to the General Government, and all those of that government to the executive branch."

**—Thomas Jefferson, 1799.**

The most famous line from his first inaugural address, "We are all Republicans, we are all Federalists," is often taken out of context. In the next sentence, Jefferson stated, "If there be any among us who would wish to dissolve this Union or to change its republican form, let them stand undisturbed as monuments to the safety with which error of opinion may be tolerated where reason is left free to combat it." In other words, we can get along, but if the Federalists would like to secede and create a monarchy, go ahead. Though we may not agree with you, we won't stop you.

Jefferson outlined his plans for government later in the address. He desired "peace, commerce, and honest friendship with all nations, entangling alliances with none; the support of the State governments in all their rights, as the most competent administrations for our domestic concerns and the surest bulwarks against antirepublican tendencies.... " Jefferson's belief in abiding by the letter of the Constitution, strictly limiting Federal power, and jealously guarding states' rights would have made him an opponent of Teddy Roosevelt's "Square Deal," Franklin Delano Roosevelt's "New Deal," Harry Truman's "Fair Deal," John F. Kennedy's "New Frontier," Lyndon Baines Johnson's "Great Society," George W. Bush's "Compassionate Conservatism," and Barack Obama's unprecedentedly massive expansion of federal spending and debt. Jefferson would also have warned against joining NATO or any other military alliance.

Jefferson's vision of government was simple: "A wise and frugal Government, which shall restrain men from injuring one another, shall leave them otherwise free to regulate their own pursuits of industry and improvement, and shall not take from the mouth of labor the bread it has earned." He wanted a government that paid its debts with "economy in the public expense, that labor may be lightly burdened." He wanted government "enlightened by a benign religion...inculcating honesty, truth, temperance, gratitude, and the love of man." He wanted a government that jealously protected the sovereignty of the people through election, and that understood that the people held the right to use the "sword of revolution where peaceable remedies are unprovided" against overreaching government. A government possessing these attributes "is necessary to close the circle of our felicities."

"These principles," Jefferson said in his first inaugural address, "form the bright constellation which has gone before us and guided our steps through an age of revolution and reformation. The wisdom of our sages and blood of our heroes have been devoted to their attainment. They should be the creed by which to try the services of those we trust; and should we wander from them in moments of error or alarm, let us hasten to retrace our steps and to regain the road which alone leads to peace, liberty, and safety."

## The Spirit of '76

"The spirit of 1776 is not dead. It has only been slumbering. The body of the American people is substantially republican. But their virtuous feelings have been played on by some fact with more fiction; they have been the dupes of artful maneuvers, and made for a moment to be willing instruments in forging chains for themselves. But times and truth dissipated the delusion, and opened their eyes."

**—Thomas Jefferson, 1799.**

Jefferson followed through. The federal debt was cut in half; taxes were reduced or eliminated, and appropriations were only given for specific purposes. Jefferson often personally answered the door to the executive mansion and worked in his slippers. One socialite described his appearance during this period as one that had "no pretensions to elegance, but it was neither coarse nor awkward, and it must be owned that his greatest personal attraction was a countenance beaming with benevolence and intelligence." He eliminated official state dinners, delivered his annual messages to Congress in written form rather than in person, and generally downgraded the importance of the executive office. Opponents, even those in his own party, called him inconsistent, and Jefferson did have to mold his persona to the office at times, but he believed he was following the prescriptions set forth in his first inaugural.

One example of his "inconsistency" occurred in 1807. During the previous six years of his presidency, Jefferson tried in vain to renegotiate the terms of Jay's Treaty. With a fresh outbreak of warfare between France and England, the United States was again in the crosshairs of the most powerful military forces in Europe, with both powers seeking to drag the United States onto its side, embargoing the other. Jefferson wished to remain neutral and avoid the "entangling alliances" that could wreck the United States. The path of neutral trade had been blazed by Washington and by Jefferson as the first secretary of state and now as president. The experience of the Revolution also played a role in his decision to remain neutral. The young United States was in no position to wage war against either power, but the British were making things difficult. They harassed United States merchants and impressed its sailors. Jefferson applied diplomatic pressure to no avail. Then the British struck.

In 1807, the USS *Chesapeake* was fired upon by the H.M.S. *Leopard* in American waters. This act of aggression dictated war, but Jefferson hesitated and chose commercial rather than military action. He refused to ask for a declaration of war and instead drew plans for the most controversial bill of his career. He ordered all British vessels out of American waters and asked Congress for an embargo against *all* international commerce. This plan had its origins in the American Revolution. Non-importation, the favorite tactic of the colonists against the British, worked before, and Jefferson believed an assault on British commerce would surly weaken the empire again.

Unfortunately, his plan backfired. The British had other commercial outlets, and the only victims of the embargo proved to be honest New England merchants (whom Jefferson didn't much care for) and Southern planters who needed some imported manufactured goods and British outlets for cash crops. Members in Jefferson's own party blasted the embargo as unconstitutional. Jefferson insisted the policy was the most effective way to maintain peace, and believed if it had more time to work the British economy

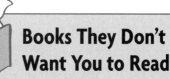

## Books They Don't Want You to Read

*The Presidency of Thomas Jefferson*, by Forrest McDonald (Kansas: University Press of Kansas, 1976). Like McDonald's book on Washington's presidency, his treatment of the Jefferson administration is concise, hard hitting, and non-PC.

would have been crippled. He never found out. Jefferson left office in 1809 with little support from his fellow Virginia republicans and a tarnished reputation made worse by the incessant attacks of an unfriendly press.

Historians often showcase the Louisiana Purchase as the crown jewel of Jefferson's inconsistency. After concluding a war with the British in 1802, the French received a large chunk of the North American continent through the Spanish. The territory and the prospect of a North American empire seemed intriguing to Napoleon Bonaparte, military dictator of the French "Republic." It terrified Jefferson. He remarked that if Napoleon were to control Louisiana and the Mississippi, "we must marry ourselves to the British fleet and nation." This conflicted with Jefferson's ideas of American independence and peaceful neutrality.

Jefferson sent a secret diplomatic delegation to France to gain the use of Louisiana and the Mississippi, but when the two-man team arrived in France, they were surprised by the offer: *all* of the territory for a steal, $15 million or what turned out to be roughly three cents an acre. The treaty was worked out without Jefferson's knowledge—they couldn't just pick up the "red-phone" and let him know—and they returned to the United States in 1803 and presented it to Congress and the president.

Congress had only authorized Monroe to spend $2 million for New Orleans and West Florida, so the increase in funds needed approval. Because it increased the public debt by nearly 20 percent, Jefferson's secretary of the treasury, Swiss-born Albert Gallatin, was forced to finance a deal he thought went against republican principles, and it did contradict republican ideals of independence because most of the stock used to finance the purchase were sold to foreign banks.

Jefferson also had to wrestle with the constitutionality of the measure. He did not think the Constitution permitted the United States to acquire territory. James Madison persuaded him otherwise, but for good measure Jefferson immediately went to work drafting a constitutional amendment that permitted the acquisition. When nary a soul confronted Jefferson on the constitutionality of the matter (even the staunch strict-construction-ist John Randolph of Roanoke supported the purchase at the time, though he later changed course) Jefferson considered the issue dead and did not follow-up. The Senate ratified the treaty with little debate.

On the one hand, Jefferson maintained American independence by steering clear of British attempts to hook the United States into an alliance against Napoleon, but on the other the treaty saddled the county with more debt than Gallatin or some other Republicans could stomach. It also laid the foundation for the sectional conflict of the mid-nineteenth century. But these problems appear more clearly in hindsight than they did at the time. Jefferson concluded that American independence was more important than any other issue and thought the Louisiana Purchase did more to augment republican principles than destroy them. Had he known of the future problems adding Louisiana would present, he may have pressed his case for a constitutional amendment more firmly and may have proceeded more cautiously. Either way, the case of "inconsistency" is only an issue if the diplomatic realities of the time and Jefferson's desire to remain independent are ignored.

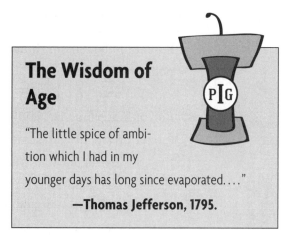

## The Wisdom of Age

"The little spice of ambition which I had in my younger days has long since evaporated...."

**—Thomas Jefferson, 1795.**

## The Jeffersonian tradition

Jefferson spent the final seventeen years of his life at Monticello living as a gentleman planter. He worked on various educational projects, including the foundation of the University of Virginia, and carried on extensive correspondence with his friends, both foreign and domestic. Jefferson was deeply in debt and died virtually broke. He sold his personal library of 10,000 volumes to the federal government following the War of 1812 in order to restock the burned Library of Congress and to gain much needed cash. Interestingly, although faced with a crushing financial burden, Jefferson continued to lend his less fortunate friends money, a policy he followed most of his life. He was benevolent to the end.

Jefferson died on 4 July 1826, the fiftieth anniversary of the Declaration of Independence, and just hours before John Adams, the only other former president who signed the document. This was a fitting end to his life. He instructed that his tombstone read simply, "Here was Buried Thomas Jefferson Author of the Declaration of Independence, of the Statute of Virginia of Religious Freedom, and the Father of the University of Virginia." He is buried under no grand monument, but a simple obelisk.

Jefferson remains an inspiration to Americans who revere liberty and states' rights and want a strictly limited federal government. Two of Jefferson's grandchildren served the Confederate States of America on just these grounds. His eldest grandson, Thomas Jefferson Randolph, was given a commission as a colonel in the Confederate army, while his youngest grandson, George Wythe Randolph, served as a brigadier general in the Confederate army and later as the Confederate Secretary of War. He also had numerous great-grandsons who served in the Confederate military. His family remained loyal to their "country" of Virginia and to Jefferson's conviction that "Rebellion to tyrants is obedience to God."

## Chapter Six

# JOHN ADAMS

Thomas Jefferson described John Adams as irritable and vain and a "bad calculator of the force and probable effect of the motives which govern men." On the surface, he was in almost every conceivable way the antithesis of Jefferson, though the two would find common ground later in life. They were from different sections and backgrounds, a fact that lent to their often bitter feuds, and they often viewed human nature and the world through different lenses. But Jefferson liked Adams personally and said in the same letter that "he is so amiable that I pronounce you will love him, if you ever become acquainted with him." Adams was one of the most quotable members of the Founding generation, rivaled only by Jefferson. At the same time, he was the most paranoid, egotistical, and backbiting member of the "Big Six." Benjamin Franklin once called some of his ideas insane, saying of Adams that he was "always an honest man, often a wise one, but sometimes, and in some things, absolutely out of his senses." Adams spent much of his time in politics engaged in personal battles and belittling those around him.

With the HBO mini-series *John Adams* based on the award-winning biography by David McCullough, Americans, it seems, have fallen in love with John Adams. They need a swift dose of reality. Adams was not a lovable man, and was in fact disliked by almost everyone in the Founding

## Did You Know Adams:

- Almost always played second fiddle to his contemporaries
- Was vain, egotistical, and insecure
- Married into a slave-owning family
- Considered virtue, morality, and religion to be the bulwarks of a free republic

generation. He was a patriot, served in a number of important positions in the Continental Congress, and was vice president and president of the United States, but he was always regarded by his contemporaries as a second-ranker—something that deeply annoyed him.

Adams was born on 30 October 1735 as a fourth generation American. His family settled in Massachusetts in 1636 and worked as independent farmers in the small community of Braintree for the next century. Adams's father, John Adams, married into the prominent Boylston family, a move that widened the social connections and prosperity of the Adams family. Adams was graduated from Harvard College in 1755 and considered a career as a minister. Most families in Massachusetts were of Puritan stock, and his father was a Puritan deacon. A similar career would have suited his family and community, but Adams had some reservations about Calvinism and after a short time as a school teacher, he decided to pursue the law. He remarked this choice did not "dissolve the obligations of morality or of religion."

His legal career proceeded slowly, but he took an active interest in town politics and legal affairs. Adams married Abigail Smith in 1764. Her father, the Reverend William Smith, was a slaveholder and a well respected man in the colony, and the marriage expanded Adams's social circle among the Massachusetts elite. Abigail and John would have six children. Their oldest son, John Quincy, also became president of the United States, in one of the most precarious elections in American history.

## The Revolution

Shortly after his marriage, Adams wrote a number of essays for the *Boston Gazette*, later published together as "A Dissertation on the Canon and Feudal Law," attacking the newly passed Stamp Act. Adams declared the act illegal and favored resistance, though he did not support the

Stamp Act riots or the violence that occurred against tax collectors. Adams was no extremist. As a lawyer, he defended the patriot John Hancock against charges of smuggling, but he also served as the defense attorney for British Captain Thomas Preston, the most important defendant in the "Boston Massacre" trial. Adams had Preston acquitted after he persuaded the jury that it could not be conclusively proven that Preston ordered his men to fire on the Boston mob.

## Character Counts

"Liberty cannot be preserved without a general knowledge among the people, who … have a right, an indisputable, unalienable, indefeasible, divine right to that most dreaded and envied kind of knowledge, I mean, of the characters and conduct of their rulers."

**—John Adams, 1765.**

Adams knew that in defending Preston he was risking "a Popularity very general and very hardly earned," but he believed it more important to prove that British soldiers could get a fair trial in a Massachusetts court. It also established him as a patriot who abjured violent protests.

Still, in contrast to Jefferson, Adams was ambitious, always conscious of his status in society, and concerned with what modern presidents call their "legacy." Adams believed "a desire to be observed, considered, esteemed, praised, beloved, and admired by his fellows is one of the earliest, as well as the keenest dispositions discovered in the heart of man." It was certainly true of Adams.

He was elected to the General Court of Massachusetts to represent Boston in 1771. Due to health concerns, he retired in 1772 and returned to farming, but the agrarian life did not suit him, and he was back in Boston within a year. He implicitly supported the Boston Tea Party in 1773—"the grandest event which has yet happened since the controversy with Britain opened"—and actively opposed the Coercive Acts of 1774. That same year, Massachusetts sent him as a delegate to the first Continental Congress.

Privately, Adams wished for separation from the crown, but he took cautious steps with a Congress that had not arrived at that solution. Adams helped draft a declaration of rights and supported the non-importation of British goods. He returned home disgusted with the results of the first Congress, but firmly resolved to keep pushing for separation. His running debate in the press with Tory Daniel Leonard under the pseudonym "Novanglus" provided both an intellectual and influential outlet for his patriotic views.

When he returned to the Second Continental Congress in May 1775, shots had already been fired at Lexington and Concord. The Congress needed to appoint a commander of all American forces, and Adams, recognizing that the other states were suspicious of New England, nominated George Washington. Washington, he hoped, would act as a unifying figure for the Southern states.

## Wisdom of the Founders

"Facts are stubborn things; and whatever may be our wishes, our inclinations, or the dictates of our passion, they cannot alter the state of facts and evidence."

**—John Adams at the Boston Massacre trial, 1770.**

Adams seconded Richard Henry Lee's call for independence from Great Britain on 7 June 1776 and served on the committee that drafted the Declaration of Independence. Jefferson was the primary author (Adams contributed little), but Adams was its greatest champion in the Congress. Jefferson later wrote that Adams was "its ablest advocate and defender against the multifarious assaults it encountered." Once independence was declared, Adams served on every important committee in the Congress and eventually was elected a commissioner to France.

By the time he arrived, the other commissioners had already secured French recognition of the United States and had agreed to a treaty of amity and commerce. Adams had little to do, but he often felt slighted by the French ministry, was suspicious of the French people, and took a tainted view of French foreign policy. As president, he often took a pro-British line—he had been the United States ambassador to Great Britain from 1785 to 1788—but he actually disliked the British as well, though he did feel they had shown him more respect than the French had.

Adams spent the war years overseas, not only in France, but as the American ambassador to the Netherlands. He helped nego-

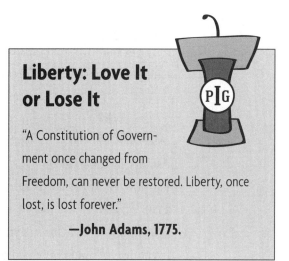

## Liberty: Love It or Lose It

"A Constitution of Government once changed from Freedom, can never be restored. Liberty, once lost, is lost forever."

**—John Adams, 1775.**

tiate the final peace treaty with the British, as well as a trade agreement with the Prussians, and became the first American minister under the Articles of Confederation to serve as ambassador to Great Britain. While in London, Adams wrote *Defense of the Constitutions of the United States of America.* The three volume work was intended as a defense of American institutions against attacks levied by the Frenchman Turgot. Adams did not deny that American political institutions mirror those of Great Britain, including in most states a bicameral legislature. Adams, however, expanded on the necessity of an upper house by arguing that those of wealth and status should be separated from the lower house in order to prevent them from dominating the government. He also advanced that every people must have "somebody or something to represent the dignity of the state, the majesty of the people, call it what you will—a doge, an avoyer, an archon, a president, a consul, a syndic. . . . " Certainly to his Republican enemies this seemed to indicate that Adams favored a monarchy.

Adams did little to dispel the notion. When The Jeffersonian Republican John Taylor of Caroline wrote his *Inquiry into the Principles and Policies of the United States* attacking Adams on this and other points, Adams responded in true form: "Remember, democracy never lasts long. It soon wastes, exhausts, and murders itself. There never was a democracy yet that did not commit suicide." It appears that Adams was, in fact, a closet monarchist; Jefferson surely thought he was.

## "His rotundity"

Adams returned to the United States shortly after the Constitutional Convention. He finished second to Washington in the Electoral College in the 1788 election and thus became the first vice president of the United States, a position he called "the most insignificant office that ever the invention of man contrived or his imagination conceived." He spent eight years in "this most insignificant office."

According to the Constitution, the vice president is the presiding officer of the Senate. Adams took this to mean that he should also participate in the debates, which he did with relish, antagonizing the senators by what they took to be his prideful, boorish manner. Because Adams would frequently interrupt other speakers to deliver lengthy lectures on political history, Senators believed that to avoid interruption they had to defend every statement they made by citing historical sources. This mad-

## From Battle to the Beaux Arts

"The science of government it is my duty to study, more than all other sciences; the arts of legislation and administration and negotiation ought to take the place of, indeed exclude, in a manner, all other arts. I must study politics and war, that our sons may have liberty to study mathematics and philosophy. Our sons ought to study mathematics and philosophy, geography, natural history and naval architecture, navigation, commerce and agriculture in order to give their children a right to study painting, poetry, music, architecture, statuary, tapestry and porcelain."

—**John Adams, 1780.**

dening process suited Adams. He believed—as did many of the early senators—that the Senate was an aristocratic body composed of the best men in society. They needed to display their learning and privilege. Adams also believed that American officials needed lofty titles in order to instill respect from the American people. This translated into a humorous and lengthy debate over the proper title for the president.

Titles such as "his elective majesty," "his mightiness," "his high mightiness," and others gave way to "His Highness the President of the United States and Protector of the Rights of the Same." Fortunately, the idea was defeated in the House, but Adams did not go down without a fight. When the bill returned to the Senate for consideration, Adams believed this issue to be a "great constitutional question." As a man who wore a sword to Senate sessions, Adams believed formality, titles, and executive deference had its place. If the United States developed into an elected monarchy, as Adams probably wanted at one point, senators would have a place of first rank in the government as a group of pseudo-courtiers.

Still, Adams languished in his vice presidential purgatory. He was miserable and thought the office did not suit his stature, but he cast twenty deciding votes in the Senate, more than his successors, and generally supported Federalist legislation. His conversion to a general support for monarchy seemed to be complete when he wrote and published *Discourses on Davila* in 1791. Jefferson believed the essays were a veiled

## Liberty's Foundation

"Statesmen, my dear Sir, may plan and speculate for Liberty, but it is Religion and Morality alone, which can establish the Principles upon which Freedom can securely stand....The only foundation of a free Constitution is pure Virtue, and if this cannot be inspired into our People in a greater Measure than they have it now, They may change their Rulers and the forms of Government, but they will not obtain a lasting Liberty. They will only exchange Tyrants and Tyrannies."

**—John Adams, 1776.**

attack on the growth of a republican opposition to Federalist legislation, and showed a desire for the stability of hereditary monarchy. But if that were the case, Adams's views were definitively of a kind where the monarch and the legislature might work in tandem while remaining separate institutions capable of checking each other's power.

Adams wrote *Discourses* out of a general fear for the escalating violence of the French Revolution. He thought the same spirit could infect Americans, and he implored them to arrest any sentiment that could be deemed contrary to the spirit of the American Revolution, an event Adams argued was nothing more than a conservative response to aggressive infringements upon life, liberty, and property. Adams believed a tyranny of one branch of government over the other would ultimately result in despotism. He wrote, "The executive and the legislative powers are natural rivals; and if each has not an effectual control over the other, the weaker will ever be the lamb in the paws of the wolf. The nation which will not adopt an equilibrium of power must adopt a despotism. There is no other alternative. Rivalries must be controlled, or they will throw all things into confusion; and there is nothing but despotism or a balance of power which can control them."

## If You Give Government an Inch…

"Nip the shoots of arbitrary power in the bud, is the only maxim which can ever preserve the liberties of any people."

**—Novanglus, a.k.a. John Adams, 1774–1775.**

## The insecure president

Washington retired in 1796, and Adams was elected second president of the United States. His arch political rival, Thomas Jefferson, became vice president. But it has to be said that Adams got along no better with his Federalist allies than with his Republican enemies.

Adams had a special disdain for Alexander Hamilton. He thought himself a superior man to Hamilton, but nevertheless sought Hamilton's approbation. So far was Hamilton from giving it that he tried to have Charles Pinckney elected over Adams in 1796, a move that did not endear him to the second president. Hamilton rarely spoke or wrote to Adams and had minimal influence in the new administration, but Adams's insecurity led him to believe that Hamilton, the former secretary of the treasury, conspired behind the scenes to reduce his authority and control the Cabinet and Congress. It is true the Cabinet and Congress solicited Hamilton's opinion, but they rarely followed his advice.

The new administration proved to be an exercise in stroking Adams's vanity. As president, Adams wanted to avoid war with France and England, and made solving that combustible international problem his top priority. Adams's policy was erratic. At first he tried to conciliate Thomas Jefferson and the pro-French Republicans. When that failed he encouraged the belligerence of pro-British Federalists in the Quasi-War against France of 1798–1800. Then he switched back and pushed for a diplomatic solution to end the undeclared war.

Meanwhile, Adams worried about an enemy within: the Jacobins who were infecting the country with the French Revolutionary creed though their Republican supporters, especially in the press. When the Federalist Congress passed the Alien and Sedition Acts, a series of laws intended to crush political opposition, Adams signed the legislation without reservation. The Sedition Act was an egregious violation of the Constitution that had the ironic effect of only increasing the vitriolic attacks of Republican newspaper editors against Adams and the Federalists. The Alien Acts were aimed at cleansing the United States from dangerous foreign "subversives," or those who voted Republican once they became citizens.

The acts were extremely unpopular and ruined the electoral prospects of the Federalist Party.

The presidential election of 1800 proved to be a humiliating embarrassment for Adams. Hamilton and other Federalists were convinced that Adams was unsuited for the job of president, and worked to defeat him. Adams finished third behind Jefferson and Aaron Burr. He wondered how a man of his stature could be so soundly defeated. In his mind, it had to be a conspiracy. He was out for revenge.

Believing that his cabinet betrayed him, Adams forced them to resign in bitter, temperamental, ranting interviews. Adams then took aim at the incoming Jefferson administration. He conceived and supported the Judiciary Act, a bill that allowed for the appointment of several new judges on the federal circuit. This provided Adams the opportunity to place Federalist judges in positions to thwart republican reforms. He then appointed his secretary of state, John Marshall, as Chief Justice of the Supreme Court, making the Court a Federalist bastion for three decades.

Adams left the new executive mansion in the District of Columbia a bitter man. He did not welcome the new president and was not gracious in defeat. Shortly after he retired to his farm in Massachusetts he wrote, "No party, that ever existed, knew itself so little, or so vainly overrated its own influence and popularity, as ours.... A group of foreign liars, encouraged by a few ambitious native gentlemen, have discomfited the education, the talents, the virtues, and the property of the country. The reason is, we have no Americans in America. The federalists have been no more Americans than the anties." He never again entered public life.

**An Unanswered Prayer**

Adams was the first president to live in the executive mansion in the District of Columbia. He wrote in 1800, "I pray Heaven to bestow the best of blessings on this house and all that shall hereafter inhabit it. May none but honest and wise men ever rule under this roof."

## Retirement

Perhaps the most interesting period of Adams's life was his retirement. He had served his country well during the Revolution, had been an able diplomat, and had occupied a position in the executive branch for twelve years, but he became more thoughtful and less erratic in his later years. After Jefferson's two terms as president, the Massachusetts farmer Adams and the Virginia planter Jefferson were reconciled and carried on an extensive correspondence that lasted until their deaths.

The historian Joseph Ellis views their correspondence as a purposeful exercise in history. It may have been so for Adams, who wanted to establish a reputation for posterity, but it is unlikely that Jefferson viewed it as such. In the correspondence, Jefferson's view of the past is consistent with what he wrote at the time, but Adams is clearly trying to repaint history in his own colors. But there was more to the correspondence than that.

They wrote to each other about history, the classics, religion, politics, and the fate of the union. Both feared for the future of American liberty. Adams wrote in 1812

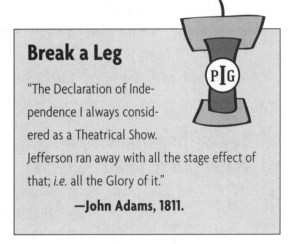

**Break a Leg**

"The Declaration of Independence I always considered as a Theatrical Show. Jefferson ran away with all the stage effect of that; *i.e.* all the Glory of it."

**—John Adams, 1811.**

that "the Union is still to me an Object of as much Anxiety as ever Independence was." A year later, he wrote to Jefferson that the Republic could be sustained only through "the general principles of Christianity [and] the general principles of English and American liberty." These principles were as "eternal and immutable, as the Existence and Attributes of God ... and ... as unalterable as human Nature and our terrestrial, mundane system."

Even in their newfound friendship, the two did not always agree. Jefferson wrote that there were but two views of government: "That every one takes his side in favor of the many, or the few, according to his constitution, and the circumstances in which he is placed." During the Revolution they were united, Jefferson said, but they had split in the 1790s when Adams took the side of the few. Adams vehemently denied this in a series of reserved but passionate letters, but the evidence is overwhelming that Jefferson was far more democratic in his beliefs than was Adams.

In the final years leading to his death, Adams lamented that he would not be revered like Jefferson, Washington, or Hamilton. He assumed this was his fate and tried to come to peace with it. But nothing would please the old curmudgeon more than finding that posterity has come to admire him after all.

Adams died on 4 July 1826, just a few hours after Jefferson. His last words were reportedly, "Jefferson still survives." Adams would be the only member of the Founding generation to serve just one term as president, and the only one-term president in American history until his son, John Quincy Adams, accomplished the same unimpressive feat from 1825–1829. He could rightly be called the father of the American navy—the first secretary of the navy, Benjamin Stoddart, was appointed during his administration and the navy was always one of his pet projects—but the blemishes on his political career are more prominent than the successes. Though he tried, he could never escape the notoriety of the Alien and Sedition Acts or the bungling diplomacy of the Quasi-War with France.

**Books They Don't Want You to Read**

*The Conservative Mind: From Burke to Elliot*, by Russell Kirk (Washington, D.C.: Regnery Publishing, Inc., 1986). Kirk includes a chapter on Adams and his impact on modern American conservatism.

Adams became the symbol of the New England Federalists, a group that became more sectional as Jeffersonian republicanism swept the United States almost unabated from 1800 to 1837. He was not a firm sectionalist, but he did believe the Northern vision of the United States was more in line with the true intentions of the Revolution. Adams thought that the republic could only survive with the guiding hand of an aristocracy—made up of those men with the "virtues and talents" to command votes—in a government of checks and balances. He argued that "the proposition, that the people are the best keepers of their own liberties, is not true; they are the worst conceivable; they are no keepers at all; they can neither judge, act, think, or will, as a political body." That might be the ultimate irony of Adams's life—the man who disparaged the people nevertheless yearned to be remembered, admired, and venerated by them.

## Chapter Seven

# JAMES MADISON

J ames Madison is perhaps the most enigmatic of the Founders. Patrick Henry called him a "theoretic statesman," a slap at Madison's character and reclusive nature. One Spanish ambassador said Madison was "full of subterfuges, evasion, and subtleties.... " Another contemporary described him as "studious" and "the master of every public question that can arise." He could defend either side of an issue and at times appeared inconsistent. His stubbornness and petulance often alienated him from others. He was slightly built, short, and preferred to wage political wars through surrogates, but could be a master with the pen. Madison was a Virginian, a Southerner, and a planter, but did not always mesh with men from his state. He has been called the "Father of the Constitution," but he almost led to its demise. He was almost forgotten by the time of his death in 1836, and his reputation was not revived until the 1920s. In many ways, Madison can be viewed as the champion of seemingly contradictory causes, but most important, he was a republican, a term that defined him throughout his life.

Madison was born on 16 March 1751 in Port Conway, Virginia, at his grandfather's plantation. He was, at minimum, a third generation American, and his father, James Madison Sr., owned a prosperous tobacco plantation called Montpelier. The family patriarch, John Madison, received a grant of more than 13,000 acres at the foot of the Blue Ridge

## Did You Know Madison:

- Was not the so-called "Father of the Constitution"

- Was the most inconsistent member of the "Big Six"

- Argued for states' rights and supported nullification

Mountains in 1653 and established the clan as a leading family in the region. James Madison spent much of his childhood studying the classics with the sons of other plantation families and enjoying the vigorous yet leisurely pace of plantation life. He was sent to Princeton in 1769, studied history and government, and was graduated in 1771. He considered a career in the ministry and continued at Princeton for another year while studying Hebrew, theology, and ethics.

After leaving Princeton, Madison fell into a state of deep depression. He was in poor physical condition and did not "expect a long or healthy life." His spirits were revived, however, by the coming conflict with Britain. He was elected to the Orange County Committee of Safety in 1775 and the following year served in the Virginia convention that drafted a state constitution. He assisted George Mason with the Virginia Declaration of Rights and actively pushed for religious toleration. Though he was from a proud Anglican family, Madison found religious persecution "diabolical." His new political career almost ended prematurely when Madison refused to participate in the jovial, liquor-filled social gatherings of the Virginia elite, and his community refused to return him to the Virginia legislature. He was in modern terms an antisocial "nerd" and the antithesis of Washington and other men of society.

Madison's father, a well respected man in Orange County, intervened and had him elected to the Virginia Council of State where he served under Patrick Henry and Thomas Jefferson. He spent most of the Revolutionary War in this capacity, but was elected to the Continental Congress in 1780, a move that honed his political skills and for a time placed him in the "nationalist" camp in the United States. He worked to strengthen central control over taxation and commerce and believed if the government did not undergo some type of reform, the Congress would "blast the glory of the Revolution." The fragility of central power under the Articles, a deep depression following the war, and political unrest led him to favor a stronger central government that was "not too democratic."

## "Father of the Constitution"

Madison has long been incorrectly labeled the "Father of the Constitution." He was one of its greatest champions following its passage and helped establish the general framework of the document, but he was not the single most important character in Philadelphia. Without the work of other notable members, namely Roger Sherman and John Dickinson, the Constitution would not have been approved at the Convention. And Madison almost did more to undermine the document than help it pass. The phrase "Father of the Constitution" is misleading in another way—it ignores the importance of the men who served their constituents in the thirteen state ratification conventions; they were as much the "fathers of the constitution" as anyone else because without them the Constitution would have been but a scrap of paper. Madison himself said the Constitution owed all its validity to the ratifiers.

Under the Articles of Confederation, Madison believed the states, through "majority factions," held too much power over the Congress. The states failed to comply with requisitions, neglected to adhere to or enforce treaties, did not respect the sovereignty of their sister states when it came to commerce, and ruined the financial system through excessive fiat (paper) currency. The United States was, in his opinion, the laughing stock of the world and as a whole lacked "faith and national honor."

He, along with other nationalists, began planning a new central government. The first step was the Mount Vernon Conference in 1785. This meeting between delegates from Maryland and Virginia at Washington's home helped build a commercial alliance between the two states and also led Madi-

## Books They Don't Want You to Read:

*Nullification, A Constitutional History, 1776-1833: Volume One: James Madison, Not the Father of the Constitution,* by Kirk Wood (Lanham, MD: University Press of America, 2008).

son to believe that commercial relationships could be forged regardless of the obstacles posed by the Articles of Confederation. Virginia invited delegates from all the states to attend a convention in Annapolis the following year to discuss further commercial cooperation.

At the Annapolis Convention Madison and Alexander Hamilton began landing decisive blows against the Articles, which led the two men to push for another convention to be held a year later in Philadelphia. This gave them time to prepare their *coup de grâce*. Madison coached the Virginia delegation before their arrival and crafted a series of resolutions that became known as "the Virginia Plan." If the other delegates had known that Madison planned to scrap the Articles and start over, they probably would not have attended. Madison set the agenda, but his agenda almost doomed the Union.

The Virginia Plan called for a bicameral legislature with proportional representation in both houses, a negative power over state laws, and the power "to legislate in all cases to which the separate states are incompetent or in which the harmony of the United States may be interrupted by the exercise of individual legislation." The last power later became the "necessary and proper" clause of Article 1, Section 8, but neither Madison nor Edmund Randolph, the man who presented his plan at the Convention, believed this gave the federal government indefinite powers (as Hamilton and John Marshall would later claim).

The other states immediately chafed at all three suggestions. Madison failed to consider that the states were more than just political jurisdictions. They were sovereign political communities, and had to be treated as such. Reducing their power through strictly proportional representation violated the foundation of the Union. This was not merely a "small state" against "large state" problem. It was a state sovereignty against a political centralization problem. This would have led to the adjournment of the Convention had cooler and more moderate men not stepped in. Madison was defeated, his nationalist program crushed by conservatives who wanted to provide the best government the people, through their state representatives, would approve, not the best government they could create or Madison could dream up.

Madison spoke almost every day during the Convention and as it drew to a close, became the irritating mosquito buzzing under the covers at night. He could not accept that *his* vision for a new constitution was being undermined by other members of the Convention. Madison remarked on practically every proposed correction or alteration to the document and often found himself at odds with the more conservative members of the Convention. In the end, the Constitution would have aristocratic checks on democracy as he intended, but his plan for Congress was dramatically altered; his vision of an executive chosen by the legislature was replaced with the state-dominated Electoral College system; there was implicit agreement on a bill of rights that would limit the powers of the Federal government more than Madison wanted; and his language was altered or eliminated throughout. In short, when the Convention ended, Madison returned to Virginia ready to defend a Constitution he originally argued against, one that explicitly maintained state control of the new central government.

Virginia was one of three states dominated by Anti-Federalists. Madison knew that ratification would not be an easy process, and he almost immediately began offering concessions to the powerful voices against ratification, namely Patrick Henry and George Mason. Madison was undergoing a conversion. He began using Anti-Federalist logic and rhetoric to defend the Constitution. Gone were his grand pronouncements of the necessity of centralization. He replaced them with explicit recognition of states' rights. "If the general government were wholly independent of the governments of the particular states, then, indeed, usurpation might be expected to the fullest extent. But, sir, on whom does this general government depend? It derives its authority from these governments, and from the same sources from which their authority is derived." In other words, the people of the states had the power in the new central government, not the people at large or the federal government itself. The states were still sovereign.

His participation in the *Federalist* mirrored this transition. Whereas Hamilton marveled at the new powers of the central government, Madison's contributions spoke of restraint. He wished to alleviate Anti-Federalist fears by enumerating what the government could *not* do. His most famous essay, *Federalist No. 10*, spoke of a need for a new central government to reduce the power of "factions." By that he meant men like Patrick Henry in Virginia, George Clinton in New York, and John Hancock in Massachusetts, who, in his estimation, wielded too much influence and created state factions that made the union under the Articles of Confederation a dead letter. But while the danger of factions drove his desire for a new constitution, his later essays explained the limited nature of federal power. For example in *Federalist No. 45*, Madison wrote that, "The State governments may be regarded as constituent and essential parts of the federal government; whilst the latter is nowise essential to the operation or organization of the former." Without the state governments, the federal government would cease to operate. He continued with his most definite statement of state power:

> The powers delegated by the proposed Constitution to the federal government are few and defined. Those which are to remain in the State governments are numerous and indefinite. The former will be exercised principally on external objects, as war, peace, negotiation, and foreign commerce; with which last the power of taxation will, for the most part, be connected. The powers reserved to the several States will extend to all the objects which, in the ordinary course of affairs, concern the lives, liberties, and properties of the people, and the internal order, improvement, and prosperity of the State.

Madison was a "nationalist," but a "nationalist" who believed in states' rights and a federal government limited to a few specific powers. It was one of the several ironies of Madison's life that by 1791 he was the recognized political leader of the Democratic-Republicans, the intellectual heirs of the Anti-Federalists who had opposed the Constitution because they feared it would endanger the rights of the states.

## The Federal career

Madison's political fortunes took an unexpected turn after the Constitution was ratified. He had appeased Anti-Federalists with the promise of a bill of rights. So he earnestly went to work on the first amendments to the Constitution. But Patrick Henry despised the little man from Orange County and worked to thwart his ambitions. Madison wished to take a seat in the first United States Senate. Under the original language of the Constitution, United States Senators were elected by the state legislatures, and since Henry controlled the legislature, he denied him a seat. Henry then gerrymandered the legislative districts in order to prevent Madison from being elected to the House of Representatives. Madison quite literally had to beg his neighbors to elect him—but it worked. Madison was sent to the House of Representatives and served there from 1789 until 1797.

He became the leader of the Anti-Federalists in the House. Madison regarded Hamilton's economic program as dangerous to individual liberty. He rallied against the "assumption scheme" (which had the Federal government assuming the debts of the states, rung up during the Revolutionary War) and considered the First Bank of the United States to be an unconstitutional act that benefited Northern capitalists at the expense of Southern agrarians. The apparent pro-British drift of George Washington's administration also drew his condemnation. Madison feared Washington's Neutrality Proclamation would establish a dangerous precedent, namely the removal of congressional power over matters of war and peace. While he desired American non-intervention in European wars, he also considered British violations of American sovereignty grounds for military retaliation. Madison and Hamilton debated the issue under pseudonyms through the press in 1792 and 1793. This issue, along with Jay's "Treaty of Amity, Commerce, and Navigation" with Great Britain in 1794, led to the final split between the Federalists and the Democratic-Republicans. The latter were led by Jefferson and Madison.

In 1794, at the age of 43, Madison married the widow Dolly Payne Todd, and three years later he retired from Congress to enjoy the life of a Virginia country gentleman. The Federalists had uncontested control of the government, and Madison had grown tired of the political battles of the early federal period. But when the Federalists passed the Alien and Sedition Acts, Madison and Jefferson took up their pens and assailed the legislation through the Virginia and Kentucky legislatures.

Madison secretly authored the Virginia Resolves, and though not as strongly worded as Jefferson's Kentucky Resolutions, he maintained the right of a state to declare federal legislation unconstitutional. Madison's reasoning was simple. The Union was a compact among the states that limited federal power, "as limited by the plain sense and intention of the instrument constituting the compact; as no further valid than they are authorized by the grants enumerated in that compact; and that in case of a deliberate, palpable, and dangerous exercise of other powers, not granted by the said compact, the states who are parties thereto, have the right, and are in duty bound, to interpose for arresting the progress of the evil, and for maintaining

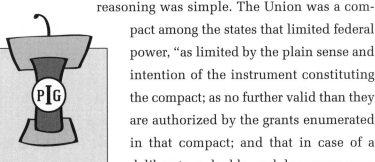

## If It Ain't There You Can't Do It

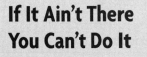

"I cannot undertake to lay my finger on that article of the Constitution which granted a right to Congress of expending, on objects of benevolence, the money of their constituents."

**—James Madison, 1794.**

within their respective limits, the authorities, rights and liberties appertaining to them." Though Madison would later deny that a state could nullify a federal law, he nevertheless in 1798 argued that states were the final arbiters of federal legislation. Unconstitutional legislation violated the compact and required state action.

After the Federalists were crushed in the 1800 elections and Thomas Jefferson was sworn in as president, he nominated Madison as Secretary of State. Jefferson

## Eternal Vigilance Begins at Home

PIG

"Perhaps it is a universal truth that the loss of liberty at home is to be charged against provisions against danger, real or pretended from abroad."

**—James Madison, 1798.**

had, in fact, preferred Madison to himself as the presidential nominee, so Secretary of State was the logical choice for his loyal friend. In foreign policy Madison and Jefferson preferred the application of economic muscle to military might, and their collaborative foreign policy followed this course through eight years. They believed firmly, from their experiences in the Revolutionary War, that refusing to import a belligerent country's goods was an effective weapon.

While it was Jefferson who took the lead in making the Louisiana Purchase and attempting to acquire Florida from Spain, it was Madison who denounced Britain's maritime policy of trying to prevent American ships from trading with France. John Randolph of Roanoke called Madison's protests "a shilling pamphlet hurled against eight hundred ships of war."

What followed was the most infamous measure of the Jefferson administration, the Embargo Act, which blocked all trade with Britain: an act that was arguably unconstitutional and a self-imposed sacrifice of American rights. When the embargo failed to cripple the British, Jefferson and Madison became hawks, advocating war against both the British and the French for their violations of American shipping rights, but they were blocked by Congress.

## The fourth president

Madison seemed the logical successor to Jefferson when the 1808 election rolled around, but there were those in Virginia, notably James Monroe, who mustered opposition to a potential Madison presidency. Still, Madison was elected, and to pacify his Virginia critics he selected Monroe to be his secretary of state. Madison's presidency was hobbled by war with the British and an anti-war movement in New England that led to talk of secession. Most American historians count Madison a failure as a president. But was he?

The War of 1812 began in part because Madison had allied the United States with Napoleon Bonaparte, embargoing trade with Britain and not with France. Many historians consider this a strategic error, characterizing Madison as incompetent, as Napoleon's dupe. It is true that Madison let his hatred of the British handicap his good judgment, but it is also true that he had plenty of reason to think he was justified in asking Congress for a declaration of war against Britain: Britain had been instigating Indian raids against American settlements on the frontier, it had been impressing American seamen into British ships, it had been seizing American cargo bound for France, and there were many war hawks within Madison's own party who believed the United States should kick Britain out of the continent by seizing Canada.

Without question, Madison made mistakes in his handling of the war, particularly in the early stages of the conflict. Factionalism and sectionalism created disaster on the battlefield. Incompetence reigned in the War and Navy departments, and the best American generals were not to be seen until the end of the war. Madison had to evacuate the District of Columbia and was humiliated when the battery he commanded was forced to retreat. The Founding generation believed it was their duty to be both the figurative and literal "commander-in-chief" of the armed forces. There were no Secret Servicemen to whisk the president to an underground bunker or awaiting getaway vehicle. He faced the enemy with the citizens of Washington, D.C.

Despite these early setbacks, the American navy performed well and won several impressive victories on the Great Lakes. Andrew Jackson and William Henry Harrison were made household names by their impressive victories over the Creek Indians and the Shawnee respectively. Jackson became a national hero with his victory at New Orleans in 1815. The United States defeated the British at Baltimore. and Winfield Scott led a crushing victory at Pittsburg. By the end of the war, the American military was a capable fighting force due in part to Madison's willingness to remove incompetent cabinet heads and help find men of talent in the army and navy. It must be remembered that this was the first major American war under the Constitution. The United States began the conflict with a small standing army and without the financial resources required to fight a large, European style conflict. The United States was over-matched from the beginning; and while the British did occupy American territory during the war, they gave it back after the Treaty of Ghent in 1814. Relations were stabilized, and Madison achieved a belated commercial victory when the British decided to cease attacks against American shipping. In fact, the United States and the British had a more cordial

## The Job of a President

"To hold the union of the States as the basis of their peace and happiness; to support the Constitution, which is the cement of the Union, as well in its limitations as in its authorities; to respect the rights and authorities reserved to the States and to the people as equally incorporated with and essential to the success of the general system...."

**—James Madison, First Inaugural Address, 1809.**

## Can a President Declare War?

Not according to the Constitution. Read Madison's statements on the issue in 1812. "Whether the United States shall continue passive under these progressive usurpations and these accumulating wrongs, or, opposing force to force in defense of their national rights, shall commit a just cause into the hands of the Almighty Disposer of Events, avoiding all connections which might entangle it in the contest or views of other powers, and preserving a constant readiness to concur in an honorable reestablishment of peace and friendship, is a solemn question which the Constitution wisely confides to the legislative department of the Government."

**—James Madison, 1812.**

relationship after the War of 1812 than at any previous time in the founding period. The United States showed a willingness to defend its sovereignty, and the British noticed and respected it.

Nevertheless, it did cause domestic trouble for Madison. At the Hartford Convention of 1815, New England Federalists proposed the idea of leading the New England states out of the union in protest at "Mr. Madison's War." Madison was annoyed by the Convention, though it came to nothing, and the Federalist Party dissolved from a sectional party into a nonexistent party soon thereafter.

If it was odd for Madison the dove to become Madison the war hawk, it was equally odd that though he vetoed a bank bill early in his administration, he signed a bill incorporating a second Bank of the United States in 1816. His argument justifying this apparent inconsistency was dubious. He noted that "precedent" authorized the Bank. As if to underline that stretching the Constitution had its limits, he vetoed an internal improvements bill because he believed such legislation to be unconstitutional. He argued such legislation required a constitutional amendment.

Was Madison inconsistent? In his own mind, no, though he conceded that the Bank was the one issue where he accepted Hamilton's economic program. Madison realized during the War that the lack of a central financial institution made waging war difficult. The Bank was the only option on the table. Madison believed that Congress's charter for the Bank had sufficient safeguards to keep it free from corruption. He was wrong. The bank created the economic climate that resulted in the Panic of 1819 (a severe depression), and was widely hated by Jacksonian Democrats. The Bank's charter expired in 1836, and it was not renewed.

## Death and legacy

Madison retired to his plantation in 1817 and rarely took part in political matters thereafter. He played a role in drafting the Virginia Constitution of 1829 and offered advice when solicited, but Madison became in many ways a forgotten figure after he left the executive office. Perhaps he preferred it that way. Years of political battles had left him tired and unenthusiastic about political life. He was in debt and had to sell off parts of his estate. He spent his last years working with the University of Virginia and the American Colonization Society (an organization that helped colonize free American blacks in Africa), as well as entertaining visitors and revising his papers. Madison was aware that his diary of the Constitutional Convention would be valuable and therefore prohibited its publication until after his death, so that any profits from it could be used to help support his wife and save his plantation. But he might also have wanted to delay publishing the notes because they reveal his inconsistency—and indeed, while in the public mind he was regarded as a champion of states' rights, in his last years he wrote privately against state sovereignty. He died in 1836, the last participant of the Philadelphia Constitutional Convention to meet his fate.

Madison penned a little note to his "Country" shortly before his death that read: "The advice nearest to my heart and deepest in my convictions is, that the Union of the states be cherished and perpetuated. Let the open enemy of it be regarded as a Pandora with her box opened, and the disguised one as the serpent creeping with his deadly wiles into paradise."

This statement captured his political career and legacy. Madison warned against the dangers of "factions" in *Federalist No. 10*, and continued to worry about the damaging effects of sectionalism and factionalism long after his retirement.

When South Carolina nullified a federal tariff in 1832, Madison was asked to defend nullification as the last living intellectual progenitor of the doctrine. He claimed that he never supported either nullification or secession, and while he had no sympathy for a "faction" of Northern states conspiring against the minority of the South, he could not agree with the remedy chosen by the people of South Carolina. He held "factions," North and South, abolitionists and secessionists, in contempt. Neither one "cherished" the Union.

In this regard, Madison was typical of his generation. He placed the Union above sectionalism and factionalism and believed each state and section should honor the compact among the states and do its best to uphold the commercial and military security the Constitution provided. To Madison, a "Unionist" was one who was willing to work for the good of the whole and resist attempts to favor one section or party over another. This also meant, as with the Virginia Resolves, that states should resist unconstitutional usurpations of power, because that too was part of the balance of power that made the union work. While Northerners viewed the War of 1812 as an affront to their prosperity, Madison believed he was asking for war to protect their interests and the interests of Southern and Western farmers. The end result of the war was actually a stronger commercial relationship with Great Britain, something that benefitted North and South.

Madison is difficult to explain. He was the defender of a Constitution that was, in significant ways, opposed to his original designs. He was a nationalist who initially favored vigorous central authority but later argued against its abuse and explicitly supported states' rights, only to begin tacking back to his original position towards the end of his life. He warned against a powerful standing army and navy but, following the War of 1812, supported strengthening both. He declared a central banking system unconstitutional but signed the bill authorizing the Second Bank of the United States. No one so straddled the Federalist and Republican traditions of the Founders as James Madison. Madison was inconsistent, nothing more or less, and his inconsistency is a virtually ignored part of his life. He was a republican, but the Left loves to use Madison as a defender of their principles. This makes illustrating his inconsistency all the more important.

## Chapter Eight

# ALEXANDER HAMILTON

T he columnist George Will wrote in 1992 that, "There is an elegant memorial in Washington to Jefferson, but none to Hamilton. However, if you seek Hamilton's monument, look around. You are living in it. We honor Jefferson, but live in Hamilton's country, a mighty industrial nation with a strong central government." George Washington is the most important man in American history and the personification of the American spirit, but it is Hamilton's vision that has been fulfilled in American history—the United States as a commercial superpower.

He was, as Jefferson recounted, the "Colossus to the anti-republican party," the man whose singular vision paved the way for a powerful federal government and the American financial system. But he, like the other founders, also believed firmly in liberty and limited government and would be shocked—and appalled—at the scope of government today, which has grown far beyond the boundaries he set for it.

John Adams enjoyed emphasizing Hamilton's undesirable beginnings. He was a bastard, born on 11 January 1757 to a beautiful French woman named Rachel Faucett (Lavien) and a Scotsman, James Hamilton, on the island of Nevis in the Caribbean. James Hamilton came from a noble bloodline, and Rachel was the daughter of a prosperous physician and planter on the tiny island. Though he possessed all the papers of nobility,

## Did You Know Hamilton:

- Favored a strong central government but recognized states' rights

- Is the Founding Father most responsible for America's economic system

- Did not believe in democracy, direct taxation, or a large government debt

- Wrote two famous attacks on the king and Parliament at the age of 17

James Hamilton was a shiftless speculator who ultimately went broke and deserted his family. Rachel and her two sons by Hamilton survived, but barely. She owned a retail store where young Alexander Hamilton learned credit, book-keeping, and wholesale and retail trade at his mother's knee. Rachel ensured that Hamilton had the best education she could provide, and it became apparent that Hamilton was bright and a quick learner. He studied the classics and learned Hebrew and French. Hamilton was a talented young man, everyone around him knew it, but his circumstances were hard.

## Books They Don't Want You to Read

*Alexander Hamilton: A Biography*, by Forrest McDonald (New York: W. W. Norton and Co., 1982).

Rachel died of fever in 1768, when Hamilton was eleven years old. Orphaned, he found work as clerk at an export-import firm. The poor boy dreamed of a higher social station, glory on the battlefield, and fame; and to achieve his goals, he continued to educate himself. His one familial treasure was his mother's books, classics, which a kindly benefactor had bought for him on the closing of his mother's estate. In 1772, the talented and industrious young Hamilton was "discovered" by the Reverend Hugh Knox, a Presbyterian minister and also publisher of a newspaper to which Hamilton contributed a story about a hurricane. Knox became Hamilton's mentor and helped raise funds to send him to the College of New Jersey at Princeton for a formal education. Hamilton bristled when the president of the school, John Witherspoon, would not let him work at his own (accelerated) pace, so he left Princeton and enrolled at King's College in New York (Columbia University), where he completed most of his degree in less than three years. Hamilton, however, did not devote as much time to his formal studies as other students did. Instead, he was captivated by politics and an independent study of military history.

# The Revolution

At only seventeen, Hamilton authored two pamphlets that caught the attention of the American Patriot community. His *A Full Vindication of the Measures of Congress* (1774) and *The Farmer Refuted* (1775) displayed an understanding of American and British political history matched only by men ten to twenty years his senior. Like others of the Founding generation, Hamilton pursued a cautious course toward independence. He warned against mob violence and maintained his allegiance to the crown despite his conviction that Parliament was exercising unconstitutional authority over the colonists. He wrote in *The Farmer Refuted* that "the origin of all civil government, justly established, must be a voluntary compact, between the rulers and the ruled; and must be liable to such limitations, as are necessary for the security of the *absolute rights* of the latter; for what original title can any man or set of men have, to govern others, except their own consent?" Parliament, in his estimation, was not governing by the consent of the governed.

Hamilton was too young to participate fully in the political campaign against the king. No matter. He preferred the military to debate, and he quickly caught the eye of American military commanders through his skill at drilling and the fact that he had helped raise and organize a New York militia company, in which he was elected captain, and had seen action, and performed well, in the early days of the war. General Nathanael Greene introduced Hamilton to Washington in 1776, a move that changed Hamilton's life. Washington was impressed with Hamilton's resolve and leadership, but most of all he was dazzled by Hamilton's skill with a pen. He promoted him to the rank of lieutenant-colonel and made him his personal secretary and aide-de-camp in 1777.

As both commander-in-chief of the Continental Army and de facto secretary of war for the Continental Congress, Washington had more business than he could handle personally. Hamilton organized and systemized his correspondence and in the process became a trusted advisor. He was not one to reserve his opinion. Though Hamilton yearned for military glory, Washington kept him to his desk. Hamilton complained privately about his assignment but worked diligently. His position allowed him contact with the most important men in the states, and allowed him to participate, if only informally, in major political and military discussions.

Hamilton believed as early as 1778 that the Confederation was inefficient and weak and needed reform. He championed representative government but believed that the central authority needed far more power. He also believed in the need for a central bank and a centralized financial system. In 1780 he pushed for a constitutional convention to amend or replace the Articles of Confederation. This was six years before the Annapolis Convention and seven before the Philadelphia Convention. Hamilton was remarkably consistent throughout his life, and he always had a "grand vision" for the United States. The historian M. E. Bradford called him a man with a penchant for the "everlasting glory" of the United States.

Hamilton resigned from Washington's staff in 1781. They were beginning to grate on each other's nerves. Hamilton thought Washington uncouth—the "most horrid swearer and blasphemer"—impatient, and temperamental; and Hamilton desperately wanted a field command. At last, with Washington's blessing, he was

## He Cannot Tell a Lie

Though Hamilton did not always have nice things to say about Washington, the same cannot be said in the reverse: "This I can venture to advance from a thorough knowledge of him, that there are few men to be found, of his age, who has a more general knowledge than he possesses, and none whose Soul is more firmly engaged in the cause, or who exceeds him in probity and Sterling virtue."

**—George Washington, 1781.**

given command of a light infantry battalion, shortly before the final siege at Yorktown. Hamilton captured a British redoubt during the battle. After the British surrender, he resigned his commission and returned to New York to begin life as a private citizen.

## The best government the country will permit

Hamilton was admitted to the bar after five months study in New York and was elected to the Continental Congress in 1782. He did little in the Congress, but his time there solidified his belief in the necessity of a stronger central government. He once called the Congress a "mass of fools and knaves" and did not soften his opinion after spending one uneventful year in that body. He continued to practice law after his retirement from Congress while organizing further support for a stronger central government. When Maryland and Virginia called for a convention at Annapolis to discuss commercial problems of the Articles of Confederation, Hamilton had himself appointed to the convention as one of two delegates from New York. This was his chance to push for a new governing document.

Only five states sent delegates to the Convention. Without a quorum, the twelve men in attendance, at the insistence of Hamilton, called for another meeting of all the states "to take into consideration the situation of the United States, to devise such further provisions as shall seem to them necessary to render the Constitution of the Federal Government adequate to the exigencies of the Union, and to report an act for that purpose to the United States in Congress assembled." This statement, of course, did not explicitly state that the next convention would draft a new constitution. In fact, very few men in the United States dreamed that the Philadelphia convention would take this course of action. But Hamilton had aligned with the nationalists from other states, and these men had a clear agenda to alter the powers of the United States government.

Hamilton's role at the 1787 Philadelphia Convention was largely insignificant. His vote was cancelled by the two Anti-Federalists in the New York delegation, and his home state was generally hostile to the idea of a stronger central government. He would therefore spend most of his time trying to convince the people of New York that a stronger central government was necessary for their future security and liberty. This was no easy sell. Today, Americans have come to believe that a stronger central government has been a positive good for the Union, that the Articles of Confederation were universally despised, and that men like Hamilton led crushing majorities in their respective states. Hamilton, in fact, was in the minority in his state—anti-Constitution men controlled the most powerful states in the Union: New York, Massachusetts, and Virginia—and many Americans, particularly in the Founding generation but even into the mid-nineteenth century, debated whether the idea of a stronger central government was a "positive good."

**Wisdom of the Founders**

"I have thought it my duty to exhibit things as they are, not as they ought to be."

**—Alexander Hamilton, 1802.**

For much of the convention, Hamilton remained silent or offered minor comments in relation to specific issues, but he did give one five-hour speech on 18 June 1787. He advanced that Americans should look to precedent and history rather than lofty political theory as the guiding hand for a new governing document. In that regard, he advocated a popularly elected (though muted through a sort of electoral college system) executive with a life term, a Senate chosen by state electors to similar life terms (both the governor and the senators could be removed for malfeasance), and a popularly elected assembly, serving three year terms. His model was obviously the English system of government adapted to American conditions, with an elected executive rather than a king and a senate rather than a House of Lords. "I believe the British government forms the best model the world has ever produced...," he wrote. "This government has for its object public strength and individual security."

Ultimately, Hamilton argued that a system of government that offered moderation between extremes—monarchy and pure democracy—offered the safest form of government. "We are now forming a republican government. Real liberty is neither found in despotism or the extremes of democracy, but in moderate governments—if we incline too much to democracy, we shall soon shoot into a monarchy." When the Philadelphia Convention completed its work in September 1787, no one did more to secure ratification of the new constitution in New York than Hamilton. His shrewd moves, including the threat of the secession of New York City should the document fail ratification, handcuffed a powerful Anti-Federalist cabal led by New York Governor George Clinton. Hamilton attempted to placate these men by assuring them that the states would still have the power to check the federal government if it overstepped its bounds. "The most powerful obstacle to the members of Congress betraying the interest of their constituents, is the state legislatures themselves... jealous of federal encroachments, and armed with every power to check the first essays of treachery.... Thus it appears that the very structure of the confederacy affords the surest preventives from error, and the most powerful checks to misconduct." To Hamilton, state sovereignty remained an integral part of the American political system.

These statements in support of states' rights appear out of place to the conventional interpretation of Hamilton as the prototypical "big government" guy. He was that, but "big government" in the eighteenth century was far different from "big government" in the twenty-first century. Hamilton never imagined a federal government that provided "welfare"

## If the States Go Down So Does Liberty

"The states can never lose their powers till the whole people of America are robbed of their liberties. These must go together; they must support each other, or meet one common fate."

**—Alexander Hamilton, 1788.**

to its citizens in the form of an income or medical care. And Hamilton's optimism about the power of the states was born from his own vision of the federation. Anti-Federalists, to their credit, insisted that the Constitution as written would eventually produce a federal "leviathan" that swallowed state power whole, but Hamilton could not foresee that because he could not imagine that the American love of liberty would degrade into welfare state, or socialist state, dependence.

During the process of ratification in New York, Hamilton, James Madison, and John Jay anonymously authored eighty-five essays in support of the Constitution under the title *Federalist*. Hamilton wrote fifty-two of the essays, and all three men wrote at an unprecedented clip. The essays appeared weekly, sometimes four per week, and each essay is around two thousand words. His passion for the limitless possibilities of the new government is evident from the first essay. "It will be … forgotten," he wrote in *Federalist No. 1*, "that the vigor of government is essential to the security of liberty; that, in the contemplation of a sound and well-informed judgment, their interest can never be separated; and that a dangerous ambition more often lurks behind the specious mask of zeal for the rights of the people than under the forbidden appearance of zeal for the firmness and efficiency of government." Hamilton believed that the new Constitution secured "the blessings of liberty" and the republican principles of the Revolution. Others disagreed firmly and loudly, but it was his passion for the new government, a government he called "the best that the present views and circumstances of the country will permit" that won the day and ultimately triumphed in the new republic.

## Secretary of the Treasury

Hamilton achieved victory over his Anti-Federalist foes with the final ratification of the Constitution in 1788. At the urging of James Madison, Washington chose Hamilton to serve as first secretary of the Treasury under the Constitution. Madison wished the treasury to be subordinate to the Congress; Hamilton had other plans. Hamilton became the most powerful person in the federal government and Washington's closest advisor for much of his administration.

Hamilton's financial plan involved assuming the federal debt acquired under the Articles of Confederation and the debt the states had accrued during the Revolution. Hamilton knew debt could have a tremendous impact on the government. He wrote in 1781 that "a national debt, if it is not excessive, will be to us a national blessing." The United States needed a line of credit, and a modest national debt (not the trillion dollar variety of the modern federal government) would provide a solid financial foundation. But his plan would also tax some states twice (principally Southern states). Virginia, for example, had already retired most of its Revolutionary War debt, but Massachusetts had not. Washington brokered a compromise that allowed the assumption of state debt in return for a promise to locate the new federal capital in the South—a poor bargain, but apparently Southerners wanted to keep an eye on the federal government.

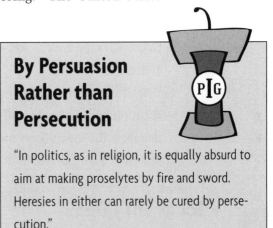

**By Persuasion Rather than Persecution**

"In politics, as in religion, it is equally absurd to aim at making proselytes by fire and sword. Heresies in either can rarely be cured by persecution."

**—Alexander Hamilton, 1787.**

Shortly after the "assumption scheme," Hamilton proposed a sweeping range of financial reforms that would ultimately centralize the financial system of the United States. This involved the creation of a central bank and a series of taxes and tariffs to provide revenue for the new government. Opponents immediately challenged the constitutionality of his "Bank of the United States." Jefferson wrote a lengthy articulation of the principles of strict construction of the Constitution in order to thwart the bank.

In his defense of the Bank, Hamilton advocated a loose interpretation of the Constitution. Hamilton wrote, "Every power vested in a government is in its nature sovereign, and includes by force of the term a right to employ all the means requisite . . . to the attainment of the ends of such power." In other words, Hamilton knew that the Constitution did not specifically authorize a bank, but believed the ends justified the means. Though Hamilton's economic system triumphed over its opponents at first, it was later defeated by the Jeffersonian Republicans and the Jacksonian Democrats until it was revived as the "American System" of Henry Clay, and ultimately implemented by the Republican Party in the 1860s.

Hamilton's financial system divided Americans as much as the Constitution had. Jefferson and Madison led the opposition party, the Republicans, while Hamilton and Washington led the Federalists. Much of Jefferson's support came from the South, and much of Hamilton's came from the North. Hamilton's taxes on whiskey and tariffs on imported goods were felt more acutely in the agricultural South; and Southerners suspected Hamilton's system of promoting urbanization and commerce, two trends that Jefferson and other Southerners feared. Hamilton was in many ways a traditional mercantilist who viewed government as the primary engine responsible for driving commerce and industry for the "national"

## Books They Don't Want You to Read

Hamilton's Curse: How Jefferson's Arch Enemy Betrayed the American Revolution—and What It Means for Americans Today, by Thomas J. Dilorenzo (New York: Crown Forum, 2008).

good. He loved the "corruption" of the British financial system, because he believed it was patronage and the government's encouragement of financial speculation that made the system work.

## Retirement and duel

After seeing his economic system through, Hamilton resigned as secretary of Treasury in 1795. He helped author Washington's farewell address and continued to be engaged in American politics, criticizing Jefferson's

## American Caesar

Jefferson wrote the following description of Hamilton in an 1811 letter to Benjamin Rush: "I invited them [Hamilton and John Adams] to dine with me, and after dinner, sitting at our wine, having settled our question, other conversation came on, in which a collision of opinion arose between Mr. Adams and Colonel Hamilton, on the merits of the British Constitution, Mr. Adams giving it as his opinion, that, if some of its defects and abuses were corrected, it would be the most perfect constitution of government ever devised by man. Hamilton, on the contrary, asserted, that with its existing vices, it was the most perfect model of government that could be formed; and that the correction of its vices would render it an impracticable government. And this you may be assured was the real line of difference between the political principles of these two gentlemen. Another incident took place on the same occasion, which will further delineate Mr. Hamilton's political principles. The room being hung around with a collection of the portraits of remarkable men, among them were those of Bacon, Newton and Locke. Hamilton asked me who they were. I told him they were my trinity of the three greatest men the world had ever produced, naming them. He paused for some time: 'The greatest man,' said he, 'that ever lived, was Julius Caesar.' Mr. Adams was honest as a politician as well as a man; Hamilton honest as a man, but, as a politician, believing in the necessity of either force or corruption to govern men."

affinity for the French, supporting a pro-British foreign policy, and disdaining his fellow Federalist John Adams.

He was commissioned as a major general in 1798 and charged with organizing a standing army for a possible war with France. As with all of his public assignments, he performed his duties energetically and faithfully. He used his influence to sway the 1801 presidential election for Thomas Jefferson. Hamilton wrote to key voters in the House of Representatives and insisted that Jefferson, though untrustworthy, was not as dangerous as Aaron Burr. Burr, naturally, resented being undone by his fellow New Yorker.

Hamilton never again served in a public capacity. He continued to denounce the Jeffersonians in the press, but supported Jefferson's acquisition of Louisiana in 1803. This proved to be a fatal decision. New England Federalists, led by Timothy Pickering, believed the purchase destroyed their chances of controlling the government. They concocted a plan to secede from the Union, but their scheme hinged on Vice President Burr. If he could be elected governor of New York, Burr would lead the state out of the Union and into a new Northern confederacy. Hamilton discovered the plan and threw his support behind the opposition candidates.

Burr lost by 8,000 votes and immediately questioned Hamilton's role in his defeat. Hamilton had apparently made some disparaging remarks about Burr's character, and though Hamilton denied it, Burr insisted on pressing the matter. He challenged Hamilton to a duel, and under the gentlemen's code, Hamilton had to accept. The date was set for 11 July 1804. Hamilton wrote before the duel that he intended to reserve his first shot and possibly his second, meaning that he had no intention of shooting Burr. For his own part, Burr never confessed he would miss Hamilton, though there is some evidence to suggest he did not mean to shoot him. Both men proceeded with their regular business. Hamilton wrote two letters to his wife and filled out his will.

The men met in New Jersey for their "interview" in the early morning of 11 July. Hamilton was allowed to fire first and apparently shot into the tree above, but Burr fired and hit Hamilton in the stomach. The .52 caliber bullet left a two inch entry wound, pierced his lung and liver and lodged in his spine. Hamilton knew it was mortal, and he suffered in excruciating pain for thirty-six hours before succumbing to his wounds. (Ironically, his son had been killed in a duel three years before, just yards from the spot where Hamilton was shot by Burr.) The vice president of the United States had shot and killed the former secretary of the Treasury, and though indicted for murder, never faced trial for it.

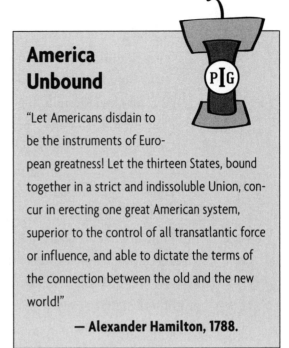

**America Unbound**

"Let Americans disdain to be the instruments of European greatness! Let the thirteen States, bound together in a strict and indissoluble Union, concur in erecting one great American system, superior to the control of all transatlantic force or influence, and able to dictate the terms of the connection between the old and the new world!"

— **Alexander Hamilton, 1788.**

Hamilton differed from other men in the Founding generation in one regard. Unlike many of the men who led the United States in the War for Independence, Hamilton was not a native of any particular state. He was a transplant and only came into wealth when he married Elizabeth Schuyler in 1780. The Schuyler family represented the interests of elite New Yorkers. As a first generation America, Hamilton did not have the same interests in the preservation of state authority as say Jefferson or John Hancock. The United States was his country, and he was one of the first Americans to display an attachment to a "nation" rather than a state.

## Legacy

The progressive Herbert Croly, often classified as one of the founders of modern liberalism, admired Hamilton because he championed a policy of "energetic and intelligent assertion of the national good." Liberals criticize Hamilton for his anti-democratic tone and his seemingly elitist attachment to an old social order, but some of them also see him as "their guy" for championing "big government" and a loose interpretation of the Constitution. There is a problem with this line of thinking. Progressives don't read the Founding generation carefully enough. No one in this generation, let alone Hamilton, could be "their guy." His statements on a range of issues contradict everything progressives stand for.

He was against direct democracy, a tactic the progressives carefully implemented in many states through referendum, initiative, and recall, and through the Seventeenth Amendment to the Constitution, the direct election of United States senators. Hamilton said in 1788, "It has been observed that a pure democracy if it were practicable would be the most perfect government. Experience has proved that no position is more false than this. The ancient democracies in which the people themselves deliberated never possessed one good feature of government. Their very character was tyranny; their figure deformity."

## No Radical He

"The passions of a revolution are apt to hurry even good men into excesses."

— **Alexander Hamilton, 1795.**

He supported individual gun rights. "The militia is a voluntary force not associated or under the control of the States except when called out; a permanent or long standing force would be entirely different in make-up and call." And he insisted that an armed citizenry was the only check on a standing army. "If circumstances should at any time oblige the government to form an army of any magnitude that army can never be formidable to the liberties of the people while there is a large body of citizens, little, if at all, inferior to them in discipline and the use of arms, who stand ready to defend their own rights and those of their fellow-citizens. This appears to me the only substitute that can be devised for a standing army, and the best possible security against it, if it should exist."

He believed direct taxation (such as an income tax or a direct property tax) to be a messy constitutional question and avoided advocating this type of tax even during the height of his power in the cabinet. He understood the states to be sovereign, arguing that they alone possessed the ability to check federal "misconduct." He argued a constitutional amendment was necessary for the federal government to finance internal improvements. He believed in the free market, and though a disciple of the old mercantilist system, would not have supported progressive regulation of industry and commerce.

He was a forthright opponent of the French Revolution, which was one reason why he was so ardently pro-British in his foreign policy, and a defender of a conservative social order. He believed in organized religion and near the end of his life created a Christian Constitutional Society to combat the worst elements of the "church of man."

Hamilton never believed, as progressives do, that man could perfect society. "I should esteem it the extreme of imprudence to prolong the precarious state of our national affairs, and to expose the Union to the jeopardy of successive experiments, in the chimerical pursuit of a perfect plan. I never expect to see a perfect work from imperfect man. The result of the deliberations of all collective bodies must necessarily be a compound, as well of the errors and prejudices, as of the good sense and wisdom, of the individuals of whom they are composed."

Far from being a liberal or a progressive, Hamilton, for all his belief in a strong central government, was an American conservative in the mold of a British Tory.

## Chapter Nine

BENJAMIN FRANKLIN

Other than George Washington, Benjamin Franklin was the most famous American of his generation. Any noteworthy activity in Philadelphia had his fingerprints, including the Declaration of Independence and the United States Constitution. Franklin was a philanthropist, entrepreneur, scientist, philosopher, diplomat, statesman, printer, and reluctant patriot whose morals and social activities were more in line with the "commoners" than men of society. He was called a "citizen of the world," a title that has its pitfalls and is out of place with other men from his generation, but he often called England his "home" and admired French society. Franklin provided humor, good will, and dignity to the important events of his time and is one of the most quotable men of the Founding generation. In contrast to the other "Big Six," Franklin never held a position in the federal government, but his contributions to American political and social life were, nevertheless, important. He championed compromise and resisted rash decisions. Without Franklin, the history of the early republic would be drastically different—less humorous, if nothing else.

Franklin was born in Boston, Massachusetts, on 17 January 1706 to Josiah and Abiah Franklin. His father had immigrated to New England around 1682 from Northamptonshire, England. His mother was the daughter of Peter Folger, one of the first settlers of Nantucket and an

**Did You Know Franklin:**

- Was "home-schooled"
- Wrote the most popular book in the colonies after the Bible
- Was the greatest American diplomat of the Founding Era

American Indian interpreter. Franklin was Josiah's youngest son and the youngest son of the youngest son for five generations. Josiah Franklin intended for his gifted son to enter the ministry and sent him to the prestigious Boston Grammar School, but as a poor soap and candle maker, he could not afford the fees and within a year transferred him out. Franklin worked with his father for a year or two and later was apprenticed at his half-brother's printing shop.

James Franklin, his brother, established the *New England Courant* in 1721, and young Benjamin learned every aspect of the printer's trade, even writing fourteen humorous letters under the pseudonym "Mrs. Silence Dogood" for the paper. When his brother was imprisoned for "seditious" language, Franklin ran the paper by himself. He also had access to a small library and read voraciously. The two brothers eventually had a falling out, and Franklin ran away to Philadelphia at the age of seventeen. Because he broke his apprenticeship, this made him a legal fugitive, and though he had little money and a poor appearance, he quickly found work in another printing shop. He acquired a circle of friends that included the royal governor of the colony. The governor convinced Franklin to travel to London to buy printing equipment on credit. After arriving in London in 1724, no letters of credit followed and Franklin was left to his own devices again.

He took another job in a printing house and saved enough money to buy a trip home. Franklin befriended a Quaker merchant on his return trip and worked at his Philadelphia shop learning the art of commerce. He formed a business partnership in 1728 with Hugh Meredith and bought *The Pennsylvania Gazette* in 1729. By the age of

## Indivisible Liberty

PIG

"They who can give up essential liberty to obtain a little temporary safety, deserve neither liberty nor safety."

**—Benjamin Franklin, 1775.**

twenty-four, Franklin had two illegitimate children and decided to settle down to arrest his "youthful passions." In 1730, he took a wife, Deborah Reed, through a common-law union. They had two children, and Reed proved to be a "good and faithful helpmate." She did not share Franklin's zeal for intellectual pursuits, but Franklin never complained and strove to make the marriage work.

His career took a decided turn for the better after his marriage. Franklin published the *Gazette* and ran a shop that traded in a variety of commodities, possibly including slaves. He acquired the contract for all Pennsylvania government printing and printed books, broadsides and other material. He lived a frugal and thrifty life. Franklin wrote that he not only wanted to lead a life of thrift and industry, he wanted to "avoid all appearances to the contrary." He dressed plainly and never appeared idle. This lifestyle eventually made him a household name in both the colonies and in Europe.

In 1732, Franklin began publishing a series titled *Poor Richard's Almanac*. His bits of wisdom made him the undisputed spokesman of the "common man" and exemplified the prudent and practical colonial spirit. The *Almanac* was second only to the Bible in popularity and "As poor Richard says" became a widely used phrase in the colonies. Bits of wisdom such as "Early to bed and early to rise, makes a man healthy, wealthy and wise," "Don't throw stones at your neighbours, if your own windows are glass," and "Haste makes Waste" have survived into the modern era. The *Almanac* is also a fine example of one of Franklin's important character traits: self-promotion. He made friends with the "right" people, always found time for the "right" activities, and was rarely in the minority on any given subject. Franklin was always described as honest, but he knew when to make the right moves and appear genuine.

His philanthropic ventures were also noteworthy. Franklin took an active part in virtually every public enterprise in Philadelphia. He organized fire brigades, helped establish nonsectarian churches, sponsored the creation of Pennsylvania Hospital, and helped found the University of Pennsylvania. He reformed police patrols and worked for better lighting on Philadelphia streets. He created the first circulating library in the colonies and helped broaden American scientific achievements through his own invention and exploration. He wrote about weather, earthquakes, geography, climate, agriculture, economics, and physics. He might have been the first to recognize Atlantic storms or "nor'easters" move against the wind. He was fascinated by electricity and developed a theory of lightning—by famously flying his kite—that led to the lightning rod. Franklin's inventions included a more efficient stove, a better clock, and bifocals. Because of his contributions to science, Harvard (1753), Yale (1753), and the College of William and Mary (1756) conferred honorary Master of Arts degrees, and Scotland's St. Andrews University (1759) an honorary Doctor of Laws degree. He established a Philadelphia debating club, urged the creation of an American Philosophical Society, and was ultimately accepted into the elite British Royal Society. "Dr." Franklin was the "American Sage" and the most respected man in the colonies in the pre-Revolutionary period.

## Cautious revolutionary

A productive public career followed his fame. Franklin became the clerk of the Pennsylvania assembly in 1736 and was the leading man in that body from 1751 to 1764. He served as postmaster of Philadelphia and eventually as deputy postmaster general for all the colonies. Franklin helped organize Pennsylvania frontier defenses during the French and Indian War and was elected a colonel of the Pennsylvania militia in 1757. He also favored a union of the colonies for defensive purposes and advanced an early design for such a union called the "Albany Plan" in 1754. His famous image depicting a severed snake representing the various colonies with the phrase "Join, or Die" has been called the first American political cartoon.

Franklin was an Anglophile who valued the role of the crown and sought its protection, and though he believed the North American colonies were a component of the British Empire, he thought administratively they were two separate entities. Parliament, in his estimation, had no right to impose taxes on the American colonies because American interests were not represented in that body, but he did not think violence was required or even justified to resist them. For a time, his fellow Pennsylvanians even considered him an agent of the crown and threatened to burn his house when Franklin implicitly supported the Stamp Act of 1765. But Franklin allayed their fears with a masterful performance before the House of Commons that questioned the legality of the measures. At once he was considered a firm colonial advocate.

In fact, from 1766 to 1770, the legislatures of Pennsylvania, Georgia, New Jersey, and Massachusetts chose Franklin to act as their colonial agent in London. He urged his American friends to exercise caution with the British, while defending the colonies in private conversations with his British friends, a group that ultimately included Edmund Burke and William Pitt. He often felt like a man stuck in a half-way house. He complained that people in England classified him as "too much of an American, and in America, of being too much of an Englishman." He thought the American colonists were "abusing the best constitution and the best King..." and believed they deserved punishment, but he longed to return to Philadelphia out of an "indelible Affection... for that dear country."

By 1770, Franklin was convinced that Parliament lacked the authority to legislate for the colonies. He encouraged

## No Handouts

"I think the best way of doing good to the poor, is not making them easy in poverty, but leading or driving them out of it."

**—Benjamin Franklin, 1766.**

peaceful resistance to "illegal" Parliamentary acts and wrote two political tracts that irritated anti-American forces in London. The second, "Rules by which a Great Empire may be reduced to a Small one," chastised Parliamentary practices in North America and was widely printed in both England and the colonies.

He also helped make public a series of letters written by Massachusetts Royal Governor Thomas Hutchinson that urged for the "abridgement of what are called English Liberties." After the letters were printed in Boston and London and Franklin admitted to his role in their "theft," he was brought before the Privy Council in London, denounced as a man of "no honour" who had made the term "man of letters" a "libel" statement and who had "forfeited the respect of societies and of men." His attempts to persuade British leaders that the end result of their coercive policies would be a long, disastrous war were in vain. He had arrived at a sad conclusion: independence was the only option to preserve the rights of Englishmen.

Franklin was a scientist, a philosopher, and a student of the English Enlightenment; he was also deeply conservative—a loyal subject of the crown who felt pushed into agitating for independence as the only way to preserve the true British constitution in America. He once wrote that the American Revolution was "a resistance in favour of a British constitution, which every Englishman might share in enjoying, who should come to live among them; it was resisting arbitrary impositions, that were contrary to common right and to their fundamental constitutions, and to constant ancient usage. It was indeed a resistance in favour of the liberties of England, which might have been endangered by success in the attempt against ours [America]." In other words, Franklin signed the Declaration of Independence because the crown and Parliament had ceased to respect the British constitution and the rights of Englishmen. It was a conclusion his own son William, the colonial governor of New Jersey, could not endorse, and father and son were never reconciled.

## The man in the fur cap

Upon returning to America in 1775, Franklin was elected to the Second Continental Congress. He drafted a proposal for a union of the colonies that was initially struck down, but later became the basis for John Dickinson's "Articles of Confederation and Perpetual Union." He served as Jefferson's editor on the committee that drafted the Declaration of Independence and as a member of the diplomatic team that presented the British with the ultimatum of independence before any further negotiations. He presided over the Pennsylvania Constitutional Convention of 1776 and placed his stamp on the new document. Franklin also established the new United States Post Office. But it was his role as minister to France from 1776 to 1785 that highlighted his long public career. Before he left, he lent around 4,000 pounds of his own money to the American government, the equivalent of roughly $500,000 in 2007 dollars.

Franklin was chosen to represent the United States in France because of his international fame and his relative familiarity with the French people. He was nearly seventy when he left the United States for Paris in 1776, and he was charged with arguably the most important political job in the Revolution: winning French recognition and support for American independence. The French greeted him in December 1776 with a hero's welcome. His unpretentious manners, plain dress, fur cap, charm, wit, and wisdom appealed to the French. It was the age of "reason," and Franklin persuaded the French that supporting the United States was a natural extension of French rational ideals. He promised them a return to a "Golden Age" when men lived simple lives of reason and leisure; America would be a new republic, the modern rival of the Greeks and Romans of classical antiquity.

He attended the French Academy of Sciences, entertained the leading members of French society, and visited the most important French *philosophes* of the day. He became a cult figure, a man whose *bon mots* were celebrated and repeated, whose picture hung in public buildings and private residences. John Adams, jealous of Franklin's stature, once remarked that "his name was familiar to government and people...to such a degree that there was scarcely a peasant or a citizen, a *valet de chambre,* coachman or footman, a lady's chambermaid or a scullion in a kitchen who was not familiar with it, and who did not consider him as a friend to human kind." King Louis XVI ultimately subscribed to Franklin's pitch that support for the United States would keep the English world divided and the war hounds of Britain away from their "natural enemy," France. Louis sent his money, his army, and his navy to help secure American independence. In the process, he deepened France's conflict with England, wrecked France's economy, and inspired a bloody revolution against his own rule, which led to a trip to the guillotine.

**Wisdom of the Founders**

"Our new Constitution is now established, and has an appearance that promises permanency; but in this world nothing can be said to be certain, except death and taxes."

—**Benjamin Franklin, 1789.**

The Continental Congress granted Franklin almost complete autonomy in France. He operated as an ad hoc "secretary of state" who handled almost all aspects of American foreign relations personally, including correspondence with British representatives and French officials. When peace finally arrived, Franklin brokered the deal that resulted in the Treaty of Paris of 1783. Independence would not have been possible without his diligence and charm.

Franklin moved easily in French society because he was a natural born diplomat, a man who learned to "sell" his craft years earlier and promote his cause with unmatched eloquence. He was a salesman and a shameless self-promoter who feigned humility when it suited his needs. This is not to call him disingenuous, though he once called himself an "amiable chameleon." He firmly believed in American independence; and though he genuinely liked the French people and French society, he knew his job was to secure the best "deal" for the United States. This, of course, is the job of every diplomat, but Franklin did it better than almost anyone in American history.

## The grandfather of the Republic

Franklin returned to the United States in 1785 and wished for retirement. He was seventy-nine, and he wanted to complete his *Autobiography*, a work he began ten years earlier but had not finished. Franklin instead was elected to the Executive Council of Pennsylvania and served for three years. Poor health began to derail his public activities, and he was originally not selected as a delegate to the Constitutional Convention in 1787. When his health improved, the Pennsylvania legislature unanimously elected him to serve, and though he was the oldest member of the Convention, he attended almost every session.

He did not play a prominent role at the Convention, but like Washington, served to lend authority to the proceedings. He had long favored a revision of the Articles of Confederation, for he believed that document did not provide a true "union." His consistent promotion of moderation led to one of the more famous events of the Convention. When it appeared that the Convention had broken into factions, Franklin rose and delivered a brief but powerful appeal for moderation and divine intervention. "We indeed seem to feel our own want of political wisdom, since we have been running about in search of it. We have gone back to ancient history for models of Government, and examined the different forms of those Republics which, having been formed with the seeds of their own dissolution, now no longer exist. And we have viewed Modern States all round Europe, but find none of their Constitutions suitable to our circumstances....I therefore beg leave to move—that henceforth prayers imploring the assistance of Heaven, and its blessing on our deliberations, be held in this Assembly every morning before we proceed to business...."

Franklin's appeal worked. Conservative men took control of the Convention and work moved forward. He lent his support to the easy naturalization of foreigners and believed all monetary bills should originate in the House of Representatives. He argued against a salary for the executive and a one-term limit. Above all, Franklin wished to avoid the problems Americans had faced twenty years earlier. If the powers of the government were not limited and defined, he feared the United States would be faced with tyranny and political unrest. He did not "entirely approve" of the Constitution as it stood in September 1787, but he urged its ratification "because I expect no better, and because I am not sure that it is not the best." He also understood that the Constitution was "likely to be well administered for a course of years, and can only end in despotism, as other forms have done before it, when the people shall become so corrupted as to need despotic government, being incapable of any other." He had no utopian visions for American progress or perfection. Always the practical sage, he accepted the best "possible" rather than the best "conceivable" society.

He led, for all practical purposes, a "retired" life after 1787. He entertained friends and admirers at his home in Philadelphia and took the time to revise his *Autobiography*. His mind never aged, and friends marveled at his detailed recollection of events many years earlier. He battled gout—once writing a satirical "conversation" with the disease—and chronic lung problems in his final years and died at the age of 84 in 1790. Twenty thousand people attended his funeral. In his twenties, he penned a humorous epitaph: "The Body of B. Franklin Printer; Like the Cover of an old Book, Its Contents torn out, And stript of its Lettering and Gilding, Lies here, Food for Worms. But the Work shall not be wholly lost: For it will, as he believ'd, appear once more, In a new & more perfect Edition, Corrected and Amended By the Author." His final stone simply read "Benjamin and Deborah Franklin."

Franklin's reputation has in many ways eclipsed his actual accomplishments and activities. One needs to look no further than the rumors of his sexual improprieties. His humor has been "rediscovered" in recent years through the publication of *Fart Proudly* and other essays on the more salacious side. It has become "cool" and "trendy" to like Franklin and think of him as a pure expression of enlightened eighteenth-century American society. Yet, Franklin only represented one element of that society, and a small one at that.

Philadelphia was a cosmopolitan city during Franklin's life and was much less imbued with the old order of society than any other American "metropolitan" area. Most eighteenth-century Americans still considered themselves to be Virginians or Bostonians or New Yorkers. Their state was their country. Franklin was wealthy and he lived in and among the elite of his community, but he was not a landed aristocrat like Washington or Jefferson. He cherished order and ultimately believed that a constitutional monarchy similar to Britain or France would best suit the United States. He was not an egalitarian, and before the war he worried that large numbers of immigrants

**Hope and a Nickel Will Buy You…**

What would Franklin think of "Hope and Change?" Let's see. "He that lives on hope will die fasting."

— **Benjamin Franklin, 1758.**

(non-English-speaking Germans in particular), would overwhelm the colonies. He craved fame and the "limelight." He hoped his *Autobiography* would perpetuate his fame after his death and keep his memory alive with that of the other Founding Fathers.

Franklin was, as the modern phrase has it, a "citizen of the world," but one who privately considered himself an Englishman. He publicly petitioned against slavery but possibly sold slaves and kept one in his home. He instructed men on how to seduce women and had two illegitimate children, but in his *Autobiography* recommended chastity. He favored form, wit, and humor in his public pronouncements, often at the sacrifice of content. He was not so much a man of contradictions as a man who accepted life as it was—and who was willing to defend America and its traditions of liberty to the end.

★ ★ ★ ★ ★

# "THE FORGOTTEN FOUNDERS"

## Chapter Ten

SAMUEL ADAMS

"Samuel Adams is a beer." This response appeared on an essay examination I gave a few years ago. While funny, it typifies what most Americans know about Samuel Adams; very little, if anything. Yet, Adams has been one of the more controversial and debated figures in American history. Some historians have classified him as little more than a demagogue, while others consider him to be one of the more important actors in the American War for Independence. Adams suffers from some of the same problems as Patrick Henry. He never had a major role in the federal government under the Constitution, and politically correct historians typically don't like champions of limited government. Adams fits that bill. He should be ranked above his cousin, John Adams, on a list of important Americans. In fact, it was Samuel who encouraged John to become more actively involved in the fight for independence.

Adams was born on 27 September 1722. He was a fifth generation American descended from Henry Adams, the first of the Adams family to arrive in the Massachusetts Bay Colony in the seventeenth century. His grandfather was a sea captain and his father, Samuel Adams the elder, was a deacon in Boston's Old South Church who owned considerable property and maintained a fine house in the city, along with a prosperous brewery. He also served in various elected capacities in his community and had a

### Did You Know Adams:

- Was a failure as a businessman, but a master polemicist

- Whipped up popular anger against the soldiers involved in the Boston Massacre—who were defended by his cousin John

- Believed in states' rights—and predicted sectional war if they were not respected

prominent role in society. Adams's mother was considered a woman of "severe religious principles."

Little is known of Adams's early life. According to family tradition, he attended the famous Boston Grammar School, and was admitted to Harvard in 1736 where he studied the classics. Though the faculty considered him a lazy student, he was graduated in 1740. He received a Master of Arts in 1743 and began the study of law. His mother persuaded him to abandon the pursuit, and Adams soon became a shiftless soul in search of a career. He started his own business, thanks to a large loan from his father, but went bankrupt. Adams then tried his hand at the brewery, though he did little to help the business. When his father died in 1748, he inherited most of his property, but tax obligations and poor financial decisions cost him most of the estate. He was married twice in this period, and had two children survive beyond the age of two. By his forties, Adams was living off the thrift of his second wife and the generosity of others. In short, in spite of his well-heeled rearing, Adams was irresponsible and unreliable. He once told John Adams that "he never looked forward in his life; never planned, laid a scheme, or formed a design for laying up anything for himself or others after him."

## Liberty above All

"The liberties of our Country, the freedom of our civil constitution are worth defending at all hazards: And it is our duty to defend them against all attacks."

**—Samuel Adams, 1771.**

But Adams was well known in his community as a writer, and while he did not possess his father's business acumen, he inherited his political talent and the ability to manage local affairs. He started a newspaper in 1748, *The Public Advertiser,* which quickly became the leading outlet for anti-Parliamentary sentiment in Boston. Adams dedicated the paper to the pursuit of liberty, and the crisis with Great Britain catapulted

Adams into the spotlight. For years he had worked with a group known as the "popular party" in Massachusetts politics, and when Parliament passed the Sugar Act and Stamp Act in 1764 and 1765 respectively, Adams and the members of the "popular party" had an issue to confront the more powerful "aristocratic party" led by future royal governor Thomas Hutchinson. He was elected to the Massachusetts legislature in 1765 and "stirred the pot" of resistance.

## Firebrand

Adams argued that both the Sugar Act and the Stamp Act were unconstitutional and called men like Hutchinson the "enemies of liberty." He authored a series of resolutions that declared, "All acts made by any power whatever, other than the general assembly of this province, imposing taxes on the inhabitants, are infringements of our inherent and unalienable rights as men and British subjects, and render void the most valuable declarations of our charter." Violence erupted in Boston when the Stamp Act went into effect. Hutchinson's house was destroyed by a mob; tax collectors were harassed and threatened with tar and feathers, and, to the British, Massachusetts appeared to be in a state of rebellion. Adams favored resistance but denounced the more violent protests and called them the result of the "mobbish" element in Boston. He appealed to English merchants to oppose the Stamp Act, claiming that the law would harm British commerce.

The economic pressure worked, and the Stamp Act was repealed in 1766. Adams was returned to the legislature in 1766 and served continuously until 1774. When the Parliament reasserted its taxing authority over the colonies through the Townshend Duties in 1767, Adams again led the opposition. He authored a "circular letter" that refuted Parliament's authority to tax the colonies. Adams insisted, as did most patriots, that the colonists were loyal to the crown, but they possessed all of the rights and privileges of Englishmen; therefore, without representation in the Parliament, which they did not have, taxes could not be levied without their consent. This unlawful and unconstitutional taxation abridged their rights as free Englishmen. Adams helped organize the Non-Importation Association and acted as the catalyst for anti-British sentiment in Massachusetts. As in 1765, Adams never openly supported violence, but he defended some violent resistance to the Townshend Duties in neighboring towns.

1770 proved to be the most violent year of the opposition to the British before the Revolution. The British sent four regiments of regulars to Massachusetts to enforce the Townshend Acts in 1768. This move was universally denounced in the colony. Adams had continued his assault of the British through anonymous letters in newspapers, possibly including a number of incendiary claims of rape and assault by British troops under the title of *The Journal of Occurrences*. Tensions reached a boiling point in 1770 when five Bostonians were killed by British soldiers. Adams labeled the event the "Boston Massacre" and along with other patriot leaders demanded that the British remove their troops from the colony. He informed acting royal governor Hutchinson that, "If you...have the power to remove *one* regiment you have the power to remove *both*. It is at your peril if you refuse. The meeting is composed of three thousand people. They have become impatient. A thousand men are already arrived from the neighborhood, and the whole country is in motion. Night is approaching. An immediate answer is expected. Both regiments or none!"

No retribution occurred, and after the trial and acquittal of the principal officers involved in the "massacre," tensions subsided. (Of course his cousin, John Adams, served as the defense counsel for the British soldiers.) The conflict over representation and taxation ebbed to its lowest level in years. Adams was returned to the legislature in 1772, but by significantly fewer votes than previous elections. He found this unacceptable. Adams continued his "full court press" against the British through the Boston newspapers. He authored no fewer than forty articles critical of the royal government in Massachusetts and the British in general. The tone also insinuated that the people of Massachusetts were being duped by the tranquility of the period and in short order would be made slaves by the British government.

Adams attempted to stoke the fires of opposition in 1772 with the creation of the Committees of Correspondence, which had the stated purpose of announcing "the rights of the Colonists and of this Province in particular as men, as Christians, and as Subjects; and to communicate the same to the several towns and to the world." He drafted a declaration of rights for the committee that emphasized the natural state of liberty, the rights of Englishmen, and American legislative independence from Parliament. Adams listed among these "natural rights...First, a right to life; Secondly, to liberty; Thirdly, to property; together with the right to support and defend them in the best manner they can." Adams argued in other writings that property, being the basis of a just society, created happiness. This is what Jefferson meant by, and how the other Founders understood, the phrase "life, liberty, and the pursuit of happiness" in the Declaration of Independence.

His perseverance finally bore fruit when patriot leaders in the colony obtained, through Benjamin Franklin, a series of letters written by Hutchinson that advocated the suppression of colonial liberty and, in

## When It Comes to Liberty, Never Give an Inch

Adams warned that liberty should be constantly guarded. "Instead of sitting down satisfied with the efforts we have already made, which is the wish of our enemies, the necessity of the times, more than ever, calls for our utmost circumspection, deliberation, fortitude, and perseverance. Let us remember that 'if we suffer tamely a lawless attack upon our liberty, we encourage it, and involve others in our doom.' It is a very serious consideration, which should deeply impress our minds, that millions yet unborn may be the miserable sharers of the event."

**—Samuel Adams, 1771.**

modern terms, the creation of a police state in Boston. Adams faithfully adhered to Franklin's wishes to keep the letters private, but the governor caught wind that the legislature possessed his letters and demanded to see them. The legislature refused and in short order printed them in the local press and circulated them in the committees of correspondence. Adams used this political capital as a "See, I told you so!" moment. He had been vindicated.

## Wisdom of the Founders

"All men have a right to remain in a state of nature as long as they please; and in case of intolerable oppression, civil or religious, to leave the society they belong to, and enter into another."

**—Samuel Adams, 1772.**

Adams participated in the Boston Tea Party of 1773. The Tea Act of that year essentially created a monopoly for the British East India Company by exempting it from an increased tax on tea. Adams declared that anyone caught selling the untaxed tea was an "enemy of America." When ten ships carrying the untaxed tea arrived in Boston harbor, the citizens of Boston refused to let the captains offload their cargo. Adams organized the resistance with the stated purpose of destroying the tea. On 16 December 1773, Adams gave the signal for the Boston Tea Party, after an all-day meeting of patriot leaders. "This meeting," he said, "can do nothing more to save the country." At that point, the men filed out of the meeting hall, disguised themselves as Mohawk Indians, gathered on the wharf, boarded the ships, and threw the tea into the harbor.

Parliament responded with the Coercive Acts of 1774. In typical fashion, Adams led the charge against these new violations of the rights of Englishmen. He determined that the only course was separation and independence and called for all the colonies to adopt measures of non-importation and resistance. The royal government almost immediately dissolved the legislature, but not before Massachusetts had selected delegates to the First Continental Congress. Adams was chosen to lead the group, and he was instrumental in securing the adoption of some of the more "radical" measures at the Congress, including the adoption of the Continental Association, a pledge of non-importation by all the colonies.

The British wanted Adams arrested as an enemy of the state. In April 1775, they attempted to capture him, along with John Hancock, on their march to Lexington. Adams, with the help of Samuel Prescott and William Dawes, evaded the army and reportedly said of the shots that day, "What a glorious morning for America!" War was at hand. He was elected to the Second Continental Congress, supported immediate independence, a confederation of the states, and the formation of independent state governments. He wrote in February 1776 that reconciliation was impossible. "The only Alternative is Independency or Slavery." He enthusiastically signed the Declaration of Independence and served in the Continental Congress until 1781 when he was elected to the Massachusetts legislature.

This is where many "progressive" histories of Adams trail off. They note his "workhorse" abilities at the Congress, his dedicated participation on the Board of War, and his noted support of George Washington, but neglect to mention his insistence on state sovereignty and limited central authority, or claim it is inconsistent with the "true" American

## A Call to Arms

"If ye love wealth better than liberty, the tranquility of servitude than the animated contest of freedom—go home from us in peace. We ask not your counsels or arms. Crouch down and lick the hands which feed you. May your chains sit lightly upon you, and may posterity forget that you were our countrymen!"

—**Samuel Adams, 1776.**

spirit. To them, he was quaint and amusing, and the champion of liberty before the war, but out of touch with the needs of the United States, and thus unimportant after leaving the Continental Congress. He had lost his role and influence. Now that liberty was achieved, the simple "demagogue" had nothing else to criticize and no issues to "incite" the populace. But Adams was always suspicious of a strong central authority, and in many ways, his time after the Continental Congress is more interesting than his activities leading to war with Great Britain.

## Anti-Federalist

Adams served as a delegate to the Massachusetts constitutional convention in 1779 and 1780 and used his influence to garner support for the new government. This led to his election in 1781, and he served in the Massachusetts legislature in various roles until 1788. He supported vigorous action against the participants of Shay's Rebellion in 1786, a revolt aimed at the oppressively high state taxes following the Revolution, including the recommendation to hand out death sentences. His reasoning: "In monarchy the crime of treason may admit of being pardoned or lightly punished, but the man who dares rebel against the laws of a republic ought to suffer death." In other words, Adams argued that republics, as elected governments, had greater legitimacy than a monarchy and therefore the laws should be applied more vigorously. The people had chosen the state government and should accept its laws.

When other states called for a revision of the Articles of Confederation, Adams accepted the idea in principle. He had signed the Articles of Confederation but thought the powers of commerce and defense could be enhanced. He did not anticipate the wholesale changes produced by the Constitutional Convention. He was selected as a delegate to the Massachusetts ratification convention, and though he played a minor role during the debates, he was one of the principal leaders opposed to the adoption of the Constitution without the addition of amendments. He believed the most pressing need was an amendment expressly clarifying the sovereignty of the states, the effect of which would be to remove "a doubt which many have entertained respecting the matter, and gives assurances that, if any law made by the federal government shall be extended beyond the power granted by the proposed Constitution, and inconsistent with the constitution of this state, it will be an error, and adjudged by the courts of law to be void." Adams argued states' rights should be explicitly maintained as "the strongest guard against the encroachments of power...." This demand appeared at the top of the Massachusetts list of proposed amendments. It is curious how it dropped to ten in the final version of the Bill of Rights.

Adams wrote to Virginian Richard Henry Lee in 1788 that when he entered the convention, "I meet with a national government instead of a Federal Union of Sovereign States. I am not able to conceive why the Wisdom of the Convention led them to give the Preference to the former instead of the latter." He believed a consolidated government was impossible in a territory as large as the United States. "Is it expected that the General Laws can be adapted to the Feelings of the more Eastern and the more Southern parts of so extensive a Nation?" he asked. "It appears to me difficult if practicable." Legislation attempting such amalgamation would necessitate a strong standing army and would produce the potential of "Wars and fighting" between the different sections. Prophetic? Adams argued that, on the other hand, a confederated government of sovereign states united under the principle of "mutual Safety and Happiness," and no more, would offer greater protection of liberty than the

**Virtuous, Informed, and Free**

"If Virtue & Knowledge are diffus'd among the People, they will never be enslav'd. This will be their great Security."

**—Samuel Adams, 1779.**

United States Constitution because the laws of each state were better adapted to "its own Genius and Circumstances."

Massachusetts ratified the Constitution by a slim majority, and Adams tried unsuccessfully to serve in the House of Representatives in 1788. He was elected lieutenant-governor of Massachusetts in 1789 and assumed the position of governor after John Hancock's death in 1794. He was elected as governor on his own in 1795 and committed to let the legislature conduct official business with little interference from the executive office. He received 15 Electoral College votes in the 1796 presidential election and was identified with the Republicans after his opposition to Jay's Treaty in 1795. Adams wrote Jefferson a warm letter of congratulations in 1801 for winning the presidency and expressed hope that the "ship will be rigged for her proper service." He died two years later at the age of 81.

Adams defended liberty and the rights of Englishmen throughout his life. Friends considered him a "priest in his religious observations" and a dedicated partisan of "Republican principles." He often followed an

## Never Submit

Adams had an interesting view of human nature. "The seeds of Aristocracy began to spring even before the Conclusion of our Struggle for the Natural Rights of Men, Seeds which like a Canker Worm lie at the Root of free Governments. So great is the Wickedness of some Men and the stupid Servility of others, that one would almost be inclined to conclude that Communities cannot be free. The few haughty families, think *They* must govern. The Body of the People tamely consent and submit to be their Slaves. This unravels the Mystery of Millions being enslaved by the few."

**—Samuel Adams, 1788.**

independent course and freely spoke his mind. In contrast to men like John Dickinson, Adams continually antagonized the crown and viewed talk of conciliation foolish, but he always believed he was fighting for the natural rights of Englishmen and the maintenance of the British constitution. He typifies most Americans in the Founding generation who regarded the states as sovereign political entities, and who jealously protected the rights of local sovereignty. Most of the men who favored the Constitution would not have supported it without limitations on its power, and Adams would not have voted for it if not for a guarantee of a bill of rights, the most important being a protection of state sovereignty.

So when savoring your favorite Sam Adams brew (mine is Irish Red), remember Adams as a resolute defender of American liberty.

## Chapter Eleven

# CHARLES CARROLL OF CARROLLTON

C harles Carroll of Carrollton has one of the more interesting stories of the Founding generation. He was one of the wealthiest men in the colonies in the eighteenth century, and like other members of the Southern gentry, he lived the life of a European aristocrat. But Carroll was Catholic, and while well respected by his fellow Marylanders, he could not vote or hold office before the War for Independence. Carroll is the founder of the conservative American Catholic tradition. He was a staunch patriot and signatory to the Declaration of Independence, and he pledged his fortune to the cause of independence. He served in the Maryland legislature and was the first United States Senator from Maryland, but like many of the Virginians among the Founding Fathers, he spent a good portion of his life "retired" at his plantation, committed to the further expansion of his lands. He was the last living signer of the Declaration.

The Carroll family had ties to the Irish nobility. The first Charles Carroll arrived in America in 1688 at the insistence of his father and the proprietor of the Maryland colony, Lord Baltimore. The Carrolls, as Catholics, faced persecution in England under the reforms of the Glorious Revolution of 1688. Maryland was founded under the idea of religious toleration and was "owned" by a Catholic, making it a natural destination. Charles Carroll the settler rapidly expanded his land holdings, and his son,

## Did You Know Carroll:

- Was the only Catholic to sign the Declaration of Independence

- Voted for Maryland to break from the crown before he signed the Declaration of Independence

- Devised the Electoral College system

## Books They Don't Want You to Read

*Charles Carroll of Carrollton: Faithful Revolutionary*, by Scott McDermott (New York: Scepter Publishing, 2005). While McDermott overplays Carroll's Catholicism, his book is a good, sound treatment of an unjustly neglected figure.

Charles Carroll of Annapolis, became a respected and wealthy man, despite the restrictions Protestants in Maryland ultimately placed on their Catholic neighbors.

Charles Carroll of Carrollton was born a "bastard" son of Carroll of Annapolis and Elizabeth Brooke in 1737. His father refused to marry his mother for many years because of reasons relating to the inheritance of his estate. But marry they eventually did, and Charles Carroll of Carrollton became the singular heir to his father's considerable fortune, which included landholdings totaling in the thousands of acres, a large contingent of slaves, and the family plantation named Doughoregan Manor. But this inheritance was not unconditional. His father was a stern patriarch who insisted that his son perform at a high level in his educational and societal pursuits. A poor showing could change his fortunes.

Carroll of Carrollton was educated at a secret Jesuit school called Bohemia Manor on Maryland's Eastern Shore, and then sent to St. Omers in Flanders to continue his studies. He received a fine classical education, and was well versed in the Catholic rebuttal of the Protestant Reformation. He finished near the top of his class and was sent to Paris to finish his education and then on to London to study law. Carroll did not return to Maryland until 1765. He took residence at Doughoregan Manor in that year and worked to "improve my own estate to ye utmost, and to remain content with ye profits a grateful soil and laborious industry will supply." Politics did not interest him initially, and Maryland law precluded Catholics from voting, but as the conflict with Great Britain intensified, Carroll, like many young men of his generation, was drawn into the debate.

He wrote several stinging letters to friends in England critical of the Stamp Act and its infringements on American liberty. Carroll advised one friend to sell his estate in England and move to America "where liberty will maintain her empire, till a dissoluteness of morals, luxury and venality shall have prepared the degenerate sons of some future age to secure their own" profit. Once the English constitution was dissolved, and Carroll believed it was rapidly moving in that direction, America would be the only place in the world to enjoy the freedoms Englishmen enjoyed. The Stamp Act broke the law, and as Carroll described it, "There are certain known fundamental laws essential to and interwoven with ye English constitution which even a Parliament itself cannot abrogate...." These included "privilege from birth of Englishmen of being taxed with their own consent: the definition of freedom is the being governed by laws to which we have given our consent, as the definition of slavery is the very reverse." Though he could not legally participate in colonial politics, Carroll had made his position clear: taxation without consent was illegal and violated the rights of Englishmen. The Stamp Act would bring, in his estimation, "political death... poverty and slavery."

How could a man who was barred from voting have such a vested interest in the "rights of Englishmen"? Simple. Carroll was the master of a ten thousand-acre plantation and quite possibly the wealthiest man in the colonies. He was descended from the nobility, and his grandfather had been active in English politics for years before the Maryland government, hostile to his attachment to Lord Baltimore, revoked his right to vote. England was, after all, a

## Books They Don't Want You to Read

*The Life of Charles Carroll of Carrollton 1737-1832 with his Correspondence and Public Papers.* 2 vols., by Kate Mason Rowland (New York: G. P. Putnam's Sons, 1898). This is a great politically incorrect treatment of the master of Doughoregan Manor. Available for free on Google Books.

## The Good Life

Doughoregan Manor is still home to the Carroll family and sits on more than 800 acres outside Baltimore. Until the 1990s, the family allowed the public to attend Sunday Mass in the small chapel built during Carrollton's life, but the Mass eventually attracted more worshippers than the chapel could handle.

Catholic country for much of its history. The barons who forced King John to sign the Magna Charta in 1215 were Catholic; every monarch in the early modern era until Henry VIII separated from the Church was Catholic. There was a strong Catholic tradition in England, and the Carroll family was a prominent part of it. And though Irish by blood, Charles *was* an Englishman because he lived and prospered under the English constitution. His hostility to the Stamp Act stemmed from a thorough understanding of the ancient rights of Englishmen—or what Patrick Henry called the "ancient constitutions." Like any other leader of the War for Independence, he ultimately believed that independence was the only way to ensure those rights. As early as 1764 he said the colonies "must and will be independent."

## Signer

Carroll remained attentive to his role as a planter for the next five years. He continued to question the legality of Parliamentary infringements on the English constitution in private letters, but his life was relatively quiet. He was married in 1768 to a cousin, Mary Darnall, and the two had seven children before Mary died in 1782. It was not until 1773, and a proclamation of new fees demanded by the Royal Governor of Maryland, that Carroll took his protests public. The Maryland House of Delegates had labeled the new fees "robbery," and Carroll said in a private letter that "War is now declared between Government and the People, or rather between a few placemen, the real enemies of Government, and all the inhabitants of this province." The rub was over the ability of an appointed royal official, in this case the governor, to issue fees by decree.

Shortly thereafter, a letter to the *Maryland Gazette* from "Antillon" grabbed Carroll's attention. "Antillon" proved to be the Maryland Attorney General, Daniel Dulany, a royalist, the most powerful man in Maryland politics, and member of a family who had long opposed the Carrolls. He was disdainful of the persistent attacks on the crown and Parliament and sought to defend royal authority. His letter set up a straw man, "First Citizen," which represented the irrational "people," against "Second Citizen," the rational and conservative adherent to government authority. Of course, many of the "people" were the very conservative and wealthy planters and merchants of Maryland, including Carroll. After the letter from Antillon appeared, Carroll struck back under the name "First Citizen" in the same paper. He was critical of "career politicians" like Dulany whose status was determined by their role in government. "Men under the basis of self-interest, and under personal obligations to Government, cannot act with a freedom and independency becoming a representative of the people." Disinterested statesmen like Carroll were the best safeguards against tyrannical authority.

Of course, no one knew, initially, that Carroll authored the response, but when word spread that it was a grudge match between the two most powerful families in the colony, the gloves came off. The two men exchanged written blows in the *Gazette* for months, and when the smoke cleared, Carroll had emerged as a leader in Maryland politics, and Dulany was shamed by his reckless personal attacks. Carroll, in true statesman-like fashion, wrote during one of the exchanges that when his opponent engaged in "virulent invective and illiberal abuse, we may fairly presume, that arguments are either wanting, or that ignorance and incapacity know not how to apply them." With his new fame, Carroll became involved in most of the activities leading to war with Great Britain. He went to the First Continental Congress as an observer and strongly supported the Continental Association of non-importation. He served on the Maryland Committee of Correspondence and was responsible for the enforcement of Maryland's boycott of British tea and other manufactured goods. It was Carroll who brokered the deal that led to the destruction of the *Peggy Stewart*, the ship that was burned during the height of the colonial tea protests. Carroll did not countenance mob action, but thought burning the ship was the best solution to avoid threats on both the captain's life—the captain had been an outspoken advocate of the Tea Act—and the lives of the fifty-three indentured servants in his cargo. The tea and his human cargo were unloaded before the ship was burned to the waterline.

In 1776, the Continental Congress appointed Carroll to serve on a three-man diplomatic team to Canada. The objective was to win Canadian support for independence and possibly form an alliance. Carroll was a natural choice for the mission. He was fluent in French and as a Catholic would be agreeable to the Catholic French Canadian population. The mis-

## The Pen Leads to the Sword

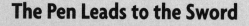

According to legend, Samuel Chase and Charles Carroll had the following verbal exchange in the early 1770s:

Chase: "We have the better of our opponents, we have completely written them down."

Carroll: "And do you think that writing will settle the question between us?"

Chase: "To be sure. What else can we resort to?"

Carroll: "The bayonet. Our arguments will only raise the feelings of the people to that pitch, when open war will be looked to as the arbiter of the dispute."

sion proved a failure, but Carroll had become both a star in his home state and in the Continental Congress. John Adams called him an "ardent patriot."

Carroll returned to Maryland more dedicated to the cause of independence after his disastrous effort in Canada. He wrote during the excursion that "My abilities are not above the common level, but I have integrity, a sincere love for my country, a detestation of tyranny, I have perseverance, and the habit of business, and I therefore hope to be of some service" to the cause. Carroll underestimated his role. He drafted the Declaration of the Delegates of Maryland in support of independence and voted to separate from the crown on 28 June 1776. Carroll's Declaration emphasized that "slaves, savages, and foreign mercenaries have been meanly hired to rob a People of their property, liberty & lives, guilty of no other crime than deeming the last of no estimation without the secure enjoyment of the two former." He was sent to the Second Continental Congress on 4 July 1776, and though he was too late to vote for separation in that body, he signed the engrossed copy of the Declaration of Independence on 2 August 1776.

He again returned to Maryland and helped craft the Maryland Constitution and Declaration of Rights. The Maryland Constitution was a model of conservative government, complete with separate powers and restrictions on popular sovereignty. Carroll devised the Electoral College system in the process, the same system that was adopted by the delegates to the Philadelphia Convention in 1787. He based his support for the new government on his knowledge of history and "insight into the passions of the human heart. . . . " Maryland extended a declaration of religious liberty to all Christians and required all office holders to be Christian. Catholics could now fully participate in Maryland politics, and because of Carroll's leadership, Maryland Catholics were one of the most passionate groups in support of independence during the war. They had a voice thanks in large part to the conservative revolutionary from Doughoregan Manor.

Carroll served in the Continental Congress from 1776 to 1778 and on the Board of War during the darkest years of the struggle. He was a resolute defender of George Washington, and the two men became close friends. When Washington resigned his military commission in 1783, Carroll had a place of honor beside the American Cincinnatus. The two men shared a conservative heritage and the disinterested ideals of the Southern planter. Carroll also opposed the confiscation of Tory land (land held by those who had remained loyal to the crown) and the enlistment of slaves into the American army without adequate compensation to slaveholders, and vigorously fought to maintain the conservative principles of the Maryland constitution while in the state Senate. He served in that body from 1777 to 1801.

## Mild Federalist

When several individuals began calling for a stronger central government in 1787, Carroll jumped on board. He was elected as a delegate to the Philadelphia Convention, but refused to attend because he wanted to keep an eye on the government in Maryland and ensure that the more democratic faction did not hijack the state. Though not elected to the state ratification convention, Carroll supported the Constitution because he believed it was the perfect mix of "the energy of monarchy, the wisdom of aristocracy with the integrity, common interest, & spirit of a democracy." Carroll, however, recognized that the government, even under the Constitution, was a "confederated Republic" and he remained in his Maryland Senate seat long after he retired from the federal government. Maryland was more his country than the United States. After the adoption of the Constitution, Carroll was sent to the first United States Senate by the Maryland legislature.

Though Carroll was the wealthiest man in the Union when he took his seat in the Senate, and was of aristocratic lineage himself, he opposed titles of nobility. He also opposed congressional salary increases and secret voting. He believed an elected seat was a duty rather than a station and feared the effect excessive compensation might have on the future of the government. If men could enrich themselves as public officials, what would stop the possibility of corruption? Carroll eventually supported efforts to centralize the banking and finance system and served on the Senate committee charged with hammering out the Bill of Rights. His activities in the Senate can be characterized as mildly Federalist. Carroll resigned his seat in 1792 in order to return to his business and plantation affairs. Interestingly, Alexander Hamilton considered him a leading candidate for president if Washington had chosen to retire in 1792. Carroll was unaware of Hamilton's design, but his conservatism and statesmanship were well admired traits among his compeers.

Carroll was defeated for re-election to his state Senate seat in 1801, a casualty of the Jefferson Revolution. He resolved never again to enter political life. His family had become a wreck during his continued absences. His wife was addicted to opium before her death and his son, Charles Carroll of Homewood, soon became a miserable alcoholic. Carroll tried to intervene to save his family, but more often than not, his efforts were futile. He invested in the Chesapeake and Ohio Canal Company and the Baltimore and Ohio Railroad and sustained a healthy, though conservative, return on his investments. As a prototypical planter, most of his capital was tied up in land and slaves. He usually owned 300 to 400 slaves at any given time.

His record as a slave owner and early abolitionist is a testament to his faith. He sold slaves, but avoided breaking up families, and he offered weekly religious instruction. He once presented a bill in the Maryland Senate for the gradual abolition of slavery which required all slave girls to be educated and then freed at twenty-eight so they could in turn educate their husbands and children. When several proposals for abolition failed, he joined the American Colonization Society, and in 1830 was elected president of that organization. Three older slaves kneeled at his bedside the night of his death, practicing the Catholic faith his religious instruction provided them.

Alexis de Tocqueville called Carroll a "European gentleman," and he was eulogized as the "last of the Romans" following his death in 1832. At 95, Carroll was the last remaining signer of the Declaration of Independence. He detested democracy, calling it nothing more than a "mob," and hoped that the spirit of civil and religious liberty fostered by the War for Independence would continue long after the passing of the Founding generation. Carroll personified the pious, conservative, agrarian, American tradition. He thought the government should be left in the hands of disinterested statesmen, men who accepted duty and did not seek power or the emoluments and patronage that office provided. His vision was good limited government free from corruption and civil or religious persecution. Carroll was a Catholic Southern planter, the type of man de Tocqueville said "provided America with her greatest spirits."

# Chapter Twelve

# GEORGE CLINTON

S tudents often ask if George Clinton of New York is any relation to Bill and Hillary Clinton. Both are "from" New York, and to students who have little understanding of even contemporary events, this is an obvious question. This answer, of course, is no, but it illustrates how little most students know about George Clinton (and also about Bill Clinton, who was born William Jefferson Blythe III).

George Clinton's ancestors had served the king during the English Civil War of the mid-seventeenth century and then supported the Glorious Revolution of 1688. Clinton himself was born in 1739 to Charles and Elizabeth Clinton of Ireland. His parents immigrated to New York in 1731 and established a farm in Ulster County. Clinton had no formal education, but his father provided his son with private tutors, and he was a bright student. The colonial governor of New York recognized Clinton's talent and, remarkably, appointed him clerk of the court of common pleas of Ulster County when Clinton was only nine years old. The expectation was that the young Clinton would assume the job once the senior clerk died. Clinton officially assumed the post in 1759, at the age of twenty, and he remained in the position for the rest of his life, a fifty-three-year tenure.

Like other frontier men of his generation, Clinton took part in the French and Indian War. At eighteen, he joined the crew of the privateer

## Did You Know Clinton:

- Vigorously opposed the ratification of the Constitution

- Served as Vice President of the United States under both Jefferson and Madison

- Was quite possibly the most popular governor in New York history

*Defiance* and served on a one-year tour in the Caribbean. When he returned to New York, he became a subaltern or junior officer in his brother's militia company and participated in the British assault on Montreal in 1760. He subsequently left the military and returned to New York to practice law. Clinton emerged as a leading colonial attorney, but augmented his profession with milling and surveying. After his marriage to Cornelia Tappen in 1770, he bought an estate overlooking the Hudson River. He was elected to the New York Assembly in 1768 and became an ardent defender of freedom of speech and freedom of the press. Clinton helped lead the patriot cause in the New York legislature, declared Parliamentary taxes unconstitutional, and stated in 1775 that "the time was nearly come, that the colonies must have recourse to arms, and the sooner the better."

This type of language led the people of New York to send him to the Second Continental Congress in 1775. He was also appointed brigadier-general in the New York militia. He supported Washington's appointment as commander-in-chief and hosted a dinner for him during Washington's trip north to Boston in 1776. While in Congress, Clinton reportedly wished for a dagger to be planted in the heart of George III, the "tyrant of Britain." He supported the Declaration of Independence but had to leave the Congress and attend to military matters before he could sign the document.

Clinton was charged with the defense of the Hudson River, but he was not an effective military commander. Though successful in raising enlistments, he lost Fort Montgomery and failed to prevent the British from burning the town of Esopus in 1777. He wrote to the New York legislature that he contemplated resigning because "I find that I am not able to render my Country that Service which they may have Reason to expect

### Books They Don't Want You to Read

*George Clinton: Yeoman Politician of the New Republic,* by John Kaminski (Lanham, MD: Madison House Publishing, Inc., 1993). The most recent and best biography on the subject.

of me." Some New Yorkers chaffed at his actions in defense of the cause. He confiscated loyalist property and, according to one eyewitness, was brutal in his treatment of anyone who resisted American independence. Clinton was commissioned brigadier-general in the Continental Army but left the military in 1777 after being elected governor of New York.

## Anti-Federalist governor

Clinton defeated Philip Schuyler—Alexander Hamilton's future father-in-law—for governor, and this set the stage for a political rivalry that lasted for the rest of his life. Schuyler was a wealthy and powerful New Yorker with connections to the "best" families in the state. Clinton was seen as a country bumpkin and an outsider. John Jay, future Supreme Court Chief Justice and author of three essays in the *Federalist*, wrote after the election that "Clinton's family and connections do not entitle him to so distinguished a pre-eminence." Still, the power in New York shifted to the second generation New Yorker from Ulster County. He served his state well during the war and managed state finances with success. His guiding hand in Indian policy, retributive treatment of Loyalists, and low taxes (in fact, New York freeholders did not pay taxes for eighteen years under Clinton), made him a popular governor, and he was reelected to the office for six consecutive terms.

Clinton developed a strong political following of young, like-minded men, mostly through patronage, and this group became outspoken opponents of a strong central government. The Articles of Confederation suited them well. New York had commercial advantages, and Clinton did not want a stronger central authority to erode his political power, nor did he want New York placed in a subservient position vis-à-vis other Northern states. But his motives were not purely personal. From the time leading up to the Revolution, Clinton believed the states offered the best protection for individual liberty, and like other Founding Fathers, Clinton considered his state to be his country.

When the Constitutional Convention wrapped up its work in September 1787, Clinton published a series of letters in the New York press under the name "Cato" challenging the proposed Constitution. He criticized it for consolidating the states into one general government which could not, in his estimation, protect the lives, liberty, and property of the people. In his third essay, Clinton wrote:

> The strongest principle of union resides within our domestic walls. The ties of the parent exceed that of any other. As we depart from home, the next general principle of union is amongst citizens of the same state, where acquaintance, habits, and fortunes, nourish affection, and attachment. Enlarge the circle still further, and, as citizens of different states, though we acknowledge the same national denomination, we lose in the ties of acquaintance, habits, and fortunes, and thus by degrees we lessen in our attachments, till, at length, we no more than acknowledge a sameness of species. Is it, therefore, from certainty like this, reasonable to believe, that inhabitants of Georgia, or New Hampshire, will have the same obligations towards you as your own, and preside over your lives, liberties, and property, with the same care and attachment? Intuitive reason answers in the negative.

Clinton, as governor, made a strategic error. He hoped to defeat the Constitution, but feared he might not have the votes at a state convention, so he delayed calling one. If, however, he had used his enormous influence to defeat the Constitution in New York *before* Virginia and Massachusetts made their votes, he might have swayed those states to join the Anti-Federalist camp.

The New York ratification finally met in June 1788. Clinton made his case succinctly: "Because a strong government was wanted during the late war, does it follow that we should now be obliged to accept of a dangerous one?" Civil liberties were not protected, he argued, and the document as written "would lead to the establishment of dangerous principles" endangering the rights of the states.

## Books They Don't Want You to Read

*The Anti-Federalist: Selected Writings and Speeches,* edited by Bruce Frohnen (Washington, D.C.: Regnery, 1999). Every student of the Constitution should read the Anti-Federalist papers in conjunction with the more famous *Federalist Essays.*

As in Virginia and Massachusetts, the New York convention demanded a bill of rights, and with the understanding that one would be added, the Constitution was ratified by five votes. In the end, Clinton reluctantly supported it, and the convention sent a circular letter to the other state legislatures calling for a second convention of all the states to address the need for constitutional amendments. This would ensure the "confidence and good-will of the body of the people." One delegate submitted a motion for New York to secede from the Union should these amendments not be added in a timely manner. Clinton fervently supported the addition of a bill of rights and believed an amendment protecting state sovereignty essential.

As governor of New York, Clinton was a pesky opponent of Federalists in the new central government and made a point of flaunting New York's state sovereignty (for example by issuing his own "Neutrality Proclamation" after President Washington had done so at the federal level). Despite his "Neutrality Proclamation," Clinton openly sympathized with the French in foreign affairs and befriended the infamous Citizen Edmund Genêt of France in 1793 after Genêt had irritated both Washington and

Jefferson by incessantly attempting to garner American support for France's war against England, Spain, the Netherlands, and the Holy Roman Empire. Genêt ended up marrying Clinton's daughter a few years later. Clinton decided to retire in 1795, and in his farewell address stated that he hoped "for an union of sentiment throughout the nation, on the *real principles of the constitution, and original intention of the revolution.*"

Clinton returned to the governor's seat in 1801 after being placed on the ballot to dissuade Vice President Aaron Burr from resigning his office and running for governor. No one trusted Burr, not even his old political allies, but he was still a force in New York politics. By nominating Clinton, the New York Republicans kept Burr off the ballot. But Clinton was ill, his wife had just died, and he considered another term an unbearable burden. He accepted the nomination only after continual prodding by his nephew and close friends; he was elected by a landslide.

## Books They Don't Want You to Read

*The Debates in the Several State Conventions on the Adoption of the Federal Constitution*, edited by Jonathan Elliot (Philadelphia, PA: J. B. Lippincot Co., 1891). Vol. II. If you want to know what Clinton or any other Anti-Federalist thought of the Constitution, read the state ratification records. Volume II in this series covers New York.

## Vice President Clinton

Jefferson and Clinton developed a warm relationship during the political struggles of the 1790s. Republicans viewed a Virginia-New York alliance as a necessary safeguard to their power at the federal level. When Burr created problems through his duplicity and his duel with Hamilton in 1803, he was dropped from the 1804 Republican ticket and replaced with Clinton. Clinton seemed a natural choice. He was a staunch Republican, a resolute defender of state's rights, and had fought alongside Jefferson against the Federalists. In 1804, with the reelection of Thomas Jefferson, he became the fourth vice president of the United States.

His relationship with Jefferson, however, soon grew tense, particularly when Jefferson and Madison supported a trade embargo against all foreign commerce. Clinton denounced the move because trade was the lifeblood of New York's economy. The people of New York sided with Clinton against Jefferson and Madison. Many prominent Virginians—like John Randolph, John Taylor, and James Monroe—agreed with Clinton and declared the embargo unconstitutional. This created an alliance between commercially minded republicans like Clinton and the agrarian "Quids" of the South.

With the 1808 election approaching, Madison appeared to be the frontrunner for the Republican nomination, but Randolph began floating a Monroe-Clinton ticket. The New York press called for an end to Virginian domination of the government, and Clinton harbored hope that he would be nominated as the presidential candidate. When it appeared that Madison would head the ticket, Clinton pressed his case more fervently. The New York Republican press noted his record as a general and statesman and his policy of non-interference in "mercantile transactions," while the Pennsylvania media championed Clinton's Anti-Federalism and his opposition to Federalist corruption. When the votes were finally counted, Clinton received only six electoral votes (of New York's 19 votes) for president, but easily secured the vice presidency.

As vice president for a second term, Clinton was openly hostile to Madison. He refused to attend Madison's inauguration, and because of illness was often absent from the Senate. His most important action as vice president took place in 1811 when he cast the deciding vote against the re-charter of the Bank of the United States. He called the measure unconstitutional in a short speech and voted to break a 17–17 tie. This would be his last major public act. Clinton died in office on 20 April 1812 at the age of 72.

## A states' rights patriot

When pressed by Hamilton during the state ratification convention in 1788 over his theoretical hostility to strong government, Clinton responded that he was "a friend to a strong and efficient government. But, sir, we may err in this extreme: we may erect a system that will destroy the liberties of the people." Clinton, in fact, did favor strong government, but not at the federal level. His eighteen years as governor of New York were a model of fiscal restraint, but Clinton favored public activity at the state level for education, internal improvements, and the promotion of commerce, science, and industry. Yet, he only advanced this agenda when state revenue reached a surplus, and the state accomplished that without direct taxation. In fact, his nephew, Dewitt Clinton, was responsible for the Erie Canal, built by the state without federal money. Clinton was not a friend of federal spending or federal power, but he did not fear the effects of state government. Like most Anti-Federalists, he was not an anarchist. Government had a purpose, and next to local government, state government was the most effective and responsive level of authority. It preserved the traditions and customs of the people.

This also illustrates another element of Clinton's Anti-Federalism. Clinton realized that the North and South had social, political, and economic differences. He was a Northerner and he feared a government dominated by the South. In 1787 he asked if Southerners would "be as tenacious of the liberties and interests of the more northern states, where freedom, independence, industry, equality and frugality are natural to the climate and soil, as men who are your own citizens, legislating in your own state, under your inspection, and whose manners and fortunes bear a more equal resemblance to your own?" He aligned with Southerners when necessary, but at one time courted Northern Federalists because of their similar interests in commerce and industry. Clinton believed climate and geography would never allow the North and South to have similar interests.

Clinton has often been described as an ambitious political thug, but he thought of himself as another George Washington, the disinterested soldier who resigned his command rather than seize power. He was certainly ambitious, but Clinton often asked for retirement, and only reluctantly agreed to return to political life. When he retired, for the first time, in 1795, he expressed satisfaction that he was "done" with the job.

In 1812, shortly after Clinton's death, Elbert Herring delivered a eulogy that called Clinton a "hero," a "patriot," and a "father of his Country." He had served in the Revolution, was an effective wartime and peacetime governor who favored republican frugality, was a leader against consolidation and a champion of civil liberties, and was vice president twice. Such a record deserves attention—more attention than he usually receives in American history textbooks.

**Chapter Thirteen**

# JOHN DICKINSON

John Dickinson, the "conservative revolutionary" as one biographer called him, is one of the most unjustly neglected figures of the Founding generation. Dickinson played a role in every significant event of his time, from the Stamp Act Congress in 1765 through the Constitutional Convention in 1787. For nearly forty years, Dickinson was one of the most respected men in both Pennsylvania and Delaware, even serving for a while as governor of both states concurrently. He took part in framing both the Articles of Confederation and the United States Constitution, both of which are stamped with his conservative ideas. It is no exaggeration to say that you can't really understand the American War of Independence without understanding John Dickinson.

He was born in 1732 at the family tobacco plantation in Talbot County, Maryland, to Quakers Samuel Dickinson and Mary Cadwalader. He spent most of his youth at the new family plantation near Dover, Delaware, an estate that covered six square miles. Dickinson was privately educated, and then studied law with a leading attorney in the Philadelphia bar. At 21, he traveled to London to complete his legal training, returned four years later, and established himself as one of the top lawyers in the American colonies. The people of Delaware recognized his talents, and in 1760 he was elected as speaker of the state legislature.

## Did You Know Dickinson:

- Was the "Penman of the Revolution"

- Served as governor of both Pennsylvania and Delaware

- Would have preferred the colonies to remain under the British crown—and yet was one of the most influential figures in achieving American independence

In 1762, the people of Philadelphia sent him to the Pennsylvania legislature where he became a fierce opponent of Benjamin Franklin and his attempts to place Pennsylvania under crown control. He believed the Penn family was corrupt and called the Pennsylvania constitution imperfect, but he did not believe that a new charter written by the king would be any better. His stand cost him his seat in 1764, but it showed Dickinson's willingness to oppose the popular will and the passion of the moment.

## "Penman of the Revolution"

Dickinson continued his political career as a pamphleteer, and in the process, became the "Penman of the Revolution," and the most recognized spokesman for colonial grievances against the crown. In 1765, he published *The Late Regulations Respecting the British Colonies . . . Considered*, a tract that took exception to the Stamp Act. Dickinson believed that the colonists needed to secure the help of British merchants in order to gain the repeal of the law, and he therefore outlined how the Stamp Act would be detrimental to their potential profits. His exposition of the subject led Pennsylvania to send him as a delegate to the Stamp Act Congress, held in New York in 1765.

Dickinson immediately emerged as a conservative leader, jealous of colonial rights but opposed to violent retribution. He drafted the Stamp Act Resolutions, a document that emphasized the "noble principles of *English* liberty" and the proper role of the colonists in taxation, where he unequivocally states "that all internal Taxes be levied upon the People *with their consent . . .*

### Books They Don't Want You to Read

*The Political Writings of John Dickinson, Esquire*. 2 vols., by John Dickinson (Wilmington, DE: Bonsal and Niles, 1801). If you want to know what Dickinson thought, go right to the source. Available for free on Google Books.

[and] That the People of this Province have... this *exclusive* Right of levying Taxes upon themselves." His work and principles became the basis of colonial resistance to unconstitutional Parliamentary acts. Even Whig members of the British Parliament relied on Dickinson's language to challenge colonial taxation. His genius was recognized on both sides of the Atlantic.

Two years later, Dickinson penned his masterpiece. In 1767, he began publishing a series of "letters" anonymously in the *Pennsylvania Chronicle* known as the *Letters from a Farmer in Pennsylvania to the Inhabitants of the British Colonies.* As in the case of the Stamp Act Resolutions, Dickinson challenged British authority over taxation in the colonies. He stated that his intention was to "convince the people of these colonies, that they are at this moment exposed to the most imminent dangers; and to persuade them immediately, vigorously, and unanimously, to exert themselves in the most firm, but peaceful manner for obtaining relief." He maintained that those engaged in the "cause of liberty... should breathe a sedate, yet fervent spirit, animating them to actions of prudence, justice, modesty, bravery, humanity, and magnanimity." This might seem out of line with a call for "firm" resistance, but Dickinson's conservative instincts always inclined him to preserve order and peace—while insisting on the rights of the colonists as Englishmen. Like Patrick Henry, he was at the vanguard of public opinion in 1767, but unlike Henry, he wished to extend the "olive branch" as long as possible.

His *Letters* became the toast of the colonies. The city of Boston thanked him in a public meeting, and Princeton granted him an honorary doctorate. He urged his fellow Pennsylvanians not to import British goods—a reversal from his position on the Stamp Act. The people of Pennsylvania returned him to the legislature in 1770, and from there Dickinson helped propel the events that led to the War for Independence. In 1771, he authored a Petition to the King in which he implored the crown to intercede on behalf of his majesty's colonial subjects. At the same time, he denounced some of the more violent actions undertaken in New England, a move that reduced his popularity in that section of the colonies. Dickinson showed a consistent attachment to conservative resistance.

Boston approached other colonies for aid in 1774 after again sparking violence, but Dickinson believed this imprudent and instead offered only "friendly expressions of sympathy." New England, he surmised, had destroyed any chance of conciliation, and he wanted to distance his native colony from such a policy. He was elected chairman of the Pennsylvania Committee of Correspondence and in 1774 served for a brief time in the First Continental Congress where he wrote the *Declaration and Resolves of the First Continental Congress*. These resolves carefully insisted that the colonists shared a common heritage with the people of England and as such retained all the rights and liberties of free Englishmen, including the right to "life, liberty, and property" and the right to participate in legislative councils. He defined the conflict as a contest over the rights of Englishmen and not a test of ideologies or philosophies. Most important, Dickinson wanted to restrain the potentially radical democratic sentiment emanating from some members of New England. The colonies were not pure democracies, and Dickinson hoped to keep it that way, even if a revolution were to take place, which by 1775 he considered inevitable.

He was returned to the Second Continental Congress in 1775, where he wrote the *Declaration of the Causes of Taking up Arms*, a petition that defended the right of colonists to resist the "tyranny" of the "aggressors" through force. "In our own native land," he wrote, "in defense of the freedom that is our birth-right, and which we ever enjoyed till the late violations of it—for the protection of our property, acquired solely by the honest industry of our fore-fathers and ourselves, against violence actually offered, we have taken up arms." But Dickinson also said the colonists would lay down their arms, if the British no longer violated the colonists' rights. "We shall lay them down when hostilities actually cease on the part of the aggressors, and all danger of their being renewed shall be removed, but not before." He followed this up with an "olive branch" petition to the king in July 1775. This document implored the king to intercede on behalf of the colonies and end the possibility of a "civil war." When the king and Parliament declared the colonies in a state of rebellion, Dickinson prepared for the war he hoped would not arrive but had helped bring about.

Dickinson had been elected colonel of the first battalion of militia raised in Philadelphia in 1775 and served as the chairman of the committee of public safety the year prior. Even while offering the "olive branch," Dickinson was actively preparing his colony for war. Congress began debate on a declaration of independence in June 1776, and Dickinson made clear his objection to such action. He still hoped for conciliation. When the document was finally presented to the Congress, he cast his vote against it—the vote was by states and not delegates—and he made one of the more brilliant speeches of his career. He did not oppose independence in principal, but he did not believe the colonies were ready to fight a war with England. They had not obtained any foreign

## Death Might Be Inevitable but Taxation without Representation Is Not

Dickinson called the maxim of "no taxation without representation" the most fundamental liberty of the English people. "To maintain this principle is the *common cause* of the WHIGS, on the other side of the Atlantic, and on this. *It is liberty to liberty engaged.* In this great cause they are immovably allied. It is the alliance of *God* and *nature*, immutable, eternal, fixed as the firmament of heaven."

**—John Dickinson, 1775.**

alliances and had not adopted a plan for a stronger "union." He later insisted that it was the timing and not the idea of independence that led him to vote "no." Dickinson retired from the Congress after his vote and took up arms against the British as a brigadier general in the Pennsylvania militia. But, before leaving in July 1776, Dickinson drafted a plan of union entitled "The Articles of Confederation and Perpetual Union," the general framework of which became the first governing document of the union of the States.

The British considered him a principal actor in the march to American independence and in December 1776 burned his Philadelphia home, Fairhill, in retaliation. He was forced to retreat to Delaware where he helped plan the defenses of his home region during the war. He served as a private soldier at the Battle of Brandywine in 1777, and in 1779 Delaware sent him back to the Continental Congress. His term in the Congress lasted two years, and in 1781, Delaware elected him president of the state. Pennsylvania likewise chose him to serve in the same capacity in 1782, so for two months, Dickinson served as the executive of two states. He resigned from his position in Delaware but maintained his office in Pennsylvania until 1785.

## The Convention

Dickinson retired to his Dover plantation in 1785. He was chosen the next year to act as the chairman of the Annapolis Convention, the meeting that led to the call for a new constitution. Delaware then chose him to lead the state delegation at the Philadelphia Convention in 1787, and it would be his brand of federalism that led to a new constitution. It could be argued that Dickinson was more important to the final document than James Madison. His contemporaries expected much from him. Illness prevented him from participating as fully as they hoped, but when present, he was a constant check on the slippery slope of reason and theory. He was directed by the powerful hand of British and American tradition, the only guide he had followed throughout his career.

He supported a new constitution for specific purposes, namely common defense, commerce, foreign affairs, and revenue. This position had been unchanged since he first opposed the Declaration of Independence in 1776. He was reluctant, however, to concede too much to a new central government. The states, in his estimation, had to remain sovereign, and he almost immediately suggested that each state have equal representation in the new government. This may be discounted as a ploy to protect his small state, but Dickinson called both Pennsylvania and Delaware home, and his other remarks suggest that he wanted to preserve the sovereignty of the separate states in order to ensure local customs, traditions, and order. He argued that liberty was grown and preserved by the local communities, not the central government, and these local communities would be the most vigorous agents for its defense. The history of both Rome and England had proven this, and now, he argued, the United States should follow the same path.

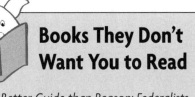

**Books They Don't Want You to Read**

*A Better Guide than Reason: Federalists and Anti-Federalists*, by M. E. Bradford (New Brunswick, NJ: Transaction Publishers, 1994). Bradford has a nice essay in this volume on John Dickinson's politics in addition to other fine selections on American politics of the Founding period in general.

As during the Revolution, he feared the excesses of democracy, and was especially worried about the masses confiscating the property of others through the vote. At the same time, he worried about the potential of an artificial aristocracy able to secure economic privilege if too much power was placed in the hands of the central authority. There had to be a median, and to Dickinson the perfect model was the English constitution adapted to American circumstances and conditions. He compared the Senate to the House of Lords and the House of Representatives to the House of Commons. He argued that the executive branch and Supreme Court should be restrained by both the Congress—most importantly the Senate—and the states, and he warned against constitutional "innovations" that had no historical precedent.

Dickinson signed the Constitution because he believed it provided the best form of republican liberty in the history of the world and later defended it in a series of letters published under the name "Fabius" in 1788. These nine essays rival the more famous *Federalist Papers* in substance and argument. In true form, Dickinson's letters were the median between the Anti-Federalist attacks on the Constitution and Hamilton's infatuation with a powerful central government.

## Wisdom of the Founders

"Experience must be our only guide. Reason may mislead us. It was not Reason that discovered the singular and admirable mechanism of the British Constitution. It was not Reason that discovered or even could have discovered the odd and in the eye of those who are governed by reason, the absurd mode of trial by jury. Accidents probably produced these discoveries, and experience has given sanction to them. This then was our guide."

**—John Dickinson, 1787.**

Dickinson believed that an affirmation of states' rights was inherent in the Constitution. He stated in essay nine, "America is, and will be, divided into several sovereign states, each possessing every power proper for governing within its own limits for its own purposes, and also for acting as a member of the union." Translation: the states are sovereign, and the federal government has specific, delegated powers. Those not listed are reserved to the states (as per the tenth amendment to the Constitution). A central government could never protect the liberty of the people without proper safeguards, among them being the sovereignty of the states.

## Retirement

Dickinson never again held public office after the Constitutional Convention. He spent his final years mostly in Delaware living the life of a planter. Though a slave owner, he proposed the gradual abolition of slavery in Delaware and thought state laws in relation to the institution should be reviewed. He broke with the Federalist Party when he determined they had violated the principles of the Constitution and the spirit of the union and became an independent supporter of the Jefferson administration until his death in 1808.

### A True Patriot

Jefferson wrote at the time of Dickinson's death that "A more estimable man or truer patriot could not have left us. Among the first of the advocates for the rights of his country when assailed by Great Britain, he continued to the last the orthodox advocate of the true principles of our new government, and his name will be consecrated in history as one of the great worthies of the Revolution."

Contemporaries described him as a man of honor, integrity, and character. His firm support of liberty led him to reluctantly accept a break with Britain in 1776, and his belief in the sovereignty of the states and the aristocratic checks of the Senate and the Electoral College fostered his support of the Constitution in 1787. Dickinson led a life of moderation, and was a man who pursued every means to achieve peace and liberty throughout his public career. His final words were, fittingly, "I wish happiness to all mankind, and the blessings of peace to all the nations of the earth, and these are the constant subjects of my prayers." This pious, conservative, liberty-loving, states' rights advocate seems out of touch with modern society. This might be why he is routinely ignored by left-leaning history professors.

## Chapter Fourteen

# ELBRIDGE GERRY

With the exception of James Madison, Elbridge Gerry is quite possibly the most complex character of the Founding generation. He was an important contributor to both the fervor leading to the Revolution and the Anti-Federalist crusade against the ratification of the Constitution in 1788. He served as governor of Massachusetts, as a member of the House of Representatives, and as vice president of the United States. Both admirers and critics alike charged him with inconsistency at one point or another—he simply declared that he was "independent" in mind and spirit—and it was this elusive and antagonistic nature that in many ways defined his life.

Gerry was born on 17 July 1744 in Marblehead, Massachusetts. His father, Thomas Gerry, settled in New England in 1730, and his mother, Elizabeth Greenleaf, was a native of Boston. Thomas Gerry established a merchant business in Marblehead and made enough money to send his son to Harvard College in 1759. Elbridge Gerry was an average student and was graduated in 1762. He then joined his two older brothers and his father in the family business, where he gained an appreciation for commerce and finance. Gerry was a small man with a broad forehead and a long nose. Contemporaries admired his integrity and attention to detail. He may have been something of a "ladies man," but he was also described as humorless and suspicious, qualities that don't always incite

### Did You Know Gerry:

- Thought the Constitution could produce a civil war

- Argued the Constitution infringed upon the liberties of Americans

- Gave us the word "Gerrymander"

attraction from the opposite sex. He remained a bachelor until the age of forty-four, when he married the daughter of a wealthy New York merchant, twenty-one years his junior.

The Gerry family became early opponents of the Stamp Act and Sugar Act in Marblehead, and their anti-British tone was influenced by the nature of their business, international trade, which was circumscribed by British regulations. Elbridge Gerry helped organize a boycott of tea in 1770, and he was elected to the Massachusetts legislature in 1772 where he met and befriended Samuel Adams. The two men corresponded extensively, and Adams considered Gerry an intelligent and trustworthy patriot. Gerry served in the legislature until it was shut down by the royal military governor Thomas Gage. He then served in the Massachusetts Provincial Congress, holding a seat in that body until being sent to the Second Continental Congress in 1776.

While in the Provincial Congress, Gerry was appointed to the Executive Committee of Safety. This group included Samuel Adams and John Hancock and was charged with the military preparedness of Massachusetts. On the night of 18 April 1775, the British attempted to capture Gerry while he was sleeping at a tavern. Though still wearing his night clothes, he escaped into a field and avoided capture. The War for Independence began the next morning at Lexington and Concord, and the men who fought the British that day benefitted from the preparations the Committee of Safety had made the weeks before. The Provincial Congress named Gerry the chairman of the Committee of Supply, a charge that made him almost personally responsible for the supply of the Massachusetts troops. Much of the work was conducted from the family business at Marblehead, and Gerry sank a good portion of his personal fortune into the cause.

Gerry took his seat in the Continental Congress on 9 February 1776. He was immediately elected to serve on the Treasury Board. He supported immediate independence from Great Britain, and had a gift for the politics of persuasion. He once wrote, "Some timid minds are terrified at the word Independence. If you think caution in this respect good policy, change the name." His work in the Continental Congress was invaluable to the cause, and his attention to detail on the Treasury Board served the group well. He was in Philadelphia on 4 July 1776 but was exhausted from his labors, left the city, and did not sign the Declaration of Independence until he returned in September.

Gerry's primary concern during the war was military supply. He often argued against profiteering and favored price-fixing on essential commodities, but the Gerry family prospered by selling military supplies, and Elbridge Gerry himself made a fortune on privateering (pirating) and heartily endorsed this type of activity. Gerry supported long-term enlistments during the war, but was openly distrustful of a standing military. He opposed both Washington and Franklin during the war, believing that Washington was unfit to lead the army and that Franklin had grown too attached to the French.

Gerry left the Congress in 1778 after a dispute arose over whether Massachusetts had provided its quota of supplies. He accused Congress of violating the rights of his state in the dispute, and though still nominally a member of the Congress, he stayed away from Philadelphia for three years and instead served in the Massachusetts legislature. He resumed his place in Congress in 1781. He took a special interest in the Northwest Territory (covering what would become Ohio, Indiana, Illinois, Michigan, Wisconsin, and part of Minnesota) because he had investments in the region. He also argued for a stronger commercial relationship among the states.

He returned to Massachusetts in 1786 and again took a seat in the state legislature. With a fortune in real estate and government securities, he retired from business in that year, married, and acquired Elmwood, a confiscated Loyalist estate. He refused to attend the Annapolis Convention in 1786 but was chosen as a delegate for the Philadelphia Convention in 1787, which he supported enthusiastically. Gerry's support for a stronger central government, though he had previously been an advocate for states' rights, was likely motivated by Shay's Rebellion in 1786—he detested democracy—and a fear of mob rule (some of his property had been destroyed before the Revolution by a mob). "The people," he said, "feel rather too much their own importance; it requires great skill in gradually checking them to such subordination as is necessary to good government."

## The "self-serving" politician?

When Gerry entered the Philadelphia Convention, he declared, "The evils we experience flow from the excess of democracy. The people do not want virtue, but are dupes of pretended patriots." In a typical Gerry turnabout, he initially supported Madison's Virginia Plan but quickly reversed course and became one of the most outspoken opponents of the document. While seeing a need for a central government that would help check democracy, he simultaneously feared that the proposed Constitution would reduce the power of the states, which in turn would reduce the power of men like himself who dominated the politics of their respective states.

He spoke over one hundred times at the Convention and consistently argued for a bill of rights, limited executive and judicial powers, and cautioned against unlimited federal power under the "necessary and proper clause" of the Constitution. Gerry believed Congress should have little power and the other branches of government even less. He fired off impressive salvos against a standing military and congressional control of the militia. His colleagues accused him of irascibility. One said he "objected to everything he did not propose." Gerry was often self-interested, and he proved that by advancing the idea that the new government assume both the federal and state debts, a good portion of which he held personally.

He did not sign the Constitution and shortly before returning home sent a letter explaining his objections to the Massachusetts legislature. He wrote that "the Constitution proposed has few, if any, federal features, but is rather a system of national government." With proper amendments, Gerry believed the government could be charged with the "preservation of liberty," but as it stands the liberty of the people "may be lost." He

## Mobocracy

Gerry debated the balance of democracy in the American republic. During the Constitutional Convention, he said, "Much depends on the mode of election. In England, the people will probably lose their liberty from the smallness of the proportion having the right of suffrage. Our danger arises from the opposite extreme. Hence, in Massachusetts, the worst men get into the legislature. Several members of that body had lately been convicted of infamous crimes. Men of indigence, ignorance, and baseness, spare no pains, however dirty, to carry their point against men who are superior to the artifices practiced." Gerry believed preventing mob rule was just as important as preventing monarchy.

thought that if the new Constitution were ratified, the state governments could be "altered as in effect to be dissolved." This, of course, would not be beneficial to the people of Massachusetts. Gerry did not attend the ratification convention. The document passed there by a slim margin only after the convention agreed to a demand for a bill of rights.

It might be true, as is sometimes said, that Gerry assumed the Constitution would not be ratified and that he would gain political capital from his opposition to it. But it is also true that Gerry displayed a consistent attachment to a "small republic" mentality. He feared both the tyranny of mob rule and the tyranny of distant arbitrary power. The people could be checked in Massachusetts through local or state action, but a powerful central authority with unlimited power would be more difficult to rein in. He could declare democracy the enemy and still favor local control because he always believed the natural ruling class, people like himself, would be in power. Thus, he insisted on state control of the militia and of elections, including those for the federal government.

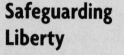

## Safeguarding Liberty

"It was painful for me, on a subject of such national importance, to differ from the respectable members who signed the Constitution; but conceiving, as I did, that the liberties of America were not secured by the system, it was my duty to oppose it."

**—Elbridge Gerry on the Constitution, 1787.**

He was elected to the House of Representatives for the first Congress in 1789, and though he supported a bill of rights, he argued early in the first session "that the vessel ought to be got under way, lest she lie by the wharf till she beat off her rudder and run herself a wreck on shore." He claimed he did not support parts of the Constitution but did not think calling for a second convention was wise. He reasoned, "If the Constitution which is now ratified should not be supported, I despair of ever having a government of these United States." Stability, even with reservations, was more important than changes at this point, but at the same time he wished for a speedy consideration of a bill of rights in order to entice North Carolina and Rhode Island to join the new government and remain in the Union.

He also shocked his fellow Anti-Federalists when he called for an "energetic government." Had he not attacked this prospect during and after the Philadelphia Convention? Gerry seemed to suggest that this was the government the states wanted—and if states' rights were protected with a bill of rights, it was the sort of government he would therefore support. When a bill of rights was finally presented to the Congress for approval, he supported the full list.

Gerry's waffling makes him a difficult man to peg. He supported Alexander Hamilton's Bank of the United States and the "assumption scheme" (of assuming state wartime debts) and appeared to be inclined toward the Federalist Party in the early sessions of Congress. He was, after all, a New England merchant, and the Federalists tended to favor that group. But he also supported an independent treasury commission separate from Hamilton's control and became increasingly suspicious of apparent Federalist attachment to the British.

He left Congress in 1793 after serving two terms and later supported John Adams for president in 1796. Adams returned the favor by sending him to France in 1798 as part of a three-man diplomatic team charged with avoiding war with France. The French foreign minister, Talleyrand, only wished to negotiate with Gerry, a man he considered an ally because of his "republican" principles, and told the rest of the delegation that they would need to "pay" for diplomatic correspondence. Gerry and Talleyrand worked in secret to reach a diplomatic compromise. When word reached the United States of his unilateral negotiations, Adams recalled him, and Gerry fell into disgrace, at least among the Federalists, as the whole episode became public (as the "XYZ Affair"). Gerry, along with Jefferson and Madison, was now considered at the top of the Federalists' public enemy list.

No matter. He was soon running as a Democratic-Republican for governor of Massachusetts. He did not win until 1810 and though he had a relatively quiet first term, he exacted political revenge on the Federalists of his state by rigging the legislative districts (from which we get the word gerrymandering) to give the Republicans crushing majorities in the Massachusetts legislature. The Federalists responded with several attacks in the press, and one Federalist threatened to burn his house and tar and feather him. Gerry retaliated by providing a list of more than 200 newspapers that he claimed libeled him. He asked for a revision of libel laws to make criticizing the governor a crime.

Gerry was defeated for re-election in 1812, but to honor his "good work" and to balance the ticket with a Northerner, the Republicans nominated him for vice president. Gerry received word of his selection in June shortly before the Congress declared war on Great Britain. Gerry was alarmed by the disunionist sentiment in his home state and warned President Madison that Federalists intended to obstruct the war effort—by violence, if necessary. His addition to the ticket did not help Madison carry Massachusetts, though Madison and Gerry won handily in the Electoral College. Gerry took the oath in 1813 and immediately declared the United States would acquire Canada. Gerry died before the war was over, in November 1814.

★ ★ ★ ★ ★ ★ ★ ★ ★ ★ ★ ★ ★ ★ ★ ★ ★

## Predicting Civil War

What did Gerry really want? He said during the Constitutional Convention, "Let us at once destroy the state governments, have an executive for life, or hereditary, and a proper Senate, and then there would be some consistency in giving full powers to the general government." But as the state governments were not to be abolished, nor did he really want them to be, he warned that state sovereignty needed some explicit recognition, otherwise: "Some people will support a plan of vigorous [central] government at every risk; others, of a more democratic cast, will oppose it with equal determination, and a civil war may be produced by the conflict." Gerry believed the states were still sovereign, but a failure to make this clear could lead to a war between the states, which, of course, it eventually did in 1861.

## Gerry vs. Mason

For all his political ambiguity, Gerry was recognized as a champion of the Anti-Federalist cause. One Anti-Federalist publication admired Gerry for his "manly" resistance to the Constitution, and another scolded supporters of the Constitution for their "indecent" attacks against Gerry and George Mason of Virginia. Without question, both men were fervent supporters of states' rights and a bill of rights to protect individual liberty, but the similarities stop there. Mason was a man descended from an ordered, agrarian society whose political "philosophy" was based on history and the code of a gentleman. States' rights and civil liberty, in Mason's view, protected Southern states from the designs of Northern capitalists and scheming centralizers; his philosophy was couched not in self-interest but in the interest of his society. Gerry, on the other hand, was a Northern capitalist, and one whose guiding principle was self-interest. Mason retired after the state

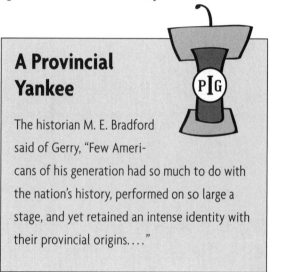

### A Provincial Yankee

The historian M. E. Bradford said of Gerry, "Few Americans of his generation had so much to do with the nation's history, performed on so large a stage, and yet retained an intense identity with their provincial origins...."

ratification convention in 1788 and never again served in any level of government. He was a planter, not a politician. Mason believed the Constitution only profited men who lusted after power, privilege, and patronage.

Gerry was actually one of those men, and it was to protect his own power, privilege, and patronage that he became an Anti-Federalist. He argued against the Constitution because he believed it would weaken his own power and influence in his state. Gerry's political flip-flops are most easily explained by his shifting personal interests. Gerry was a merchant who favored a different type of political economy than did Mason and the other Virginia planters, and unlike Mason he was an ambitious politician who never retired from public "service." Of all the Founding Fathers, Gerry is the one that modern politicians might most identify with.

## Chapter Fifteen

# JOHN HANCOCK

"Place your John Hancock on that line." We have all heard that phrase dozens of times, but you may have asked, who is John Hancock? Hancock was a wealthy merchant, a patriot, a president of the Continental Congress, a governor of Massachusetts, and a mild Anti-Federalist. He has been described by historians as a rogue smuggler, and as a vain and dim-witted demagogue. In that regard, he has prestigious company. George Washington and Samuel Adams are often described in similar fashion. John Hancock was more than a famous signature; he was an admirable man with an interesting, and in some ways politically incorrect, history.

Hancock was born in 1737 in Braintree, Massachusetts, the same birthplace as John Adams. His father was the pastor of the church at Braintree and his mother was a widow from the small community of Hingham, Massachusetts. They lived a comfortable life with at least one slave. Hancock's father died in 1744, so care of the boy fell to his wealthy merchant uncle, Thomas Hancock, proprietor of the "House of Hancock," a prosperous mercantile firm which imported manufactured goods and exported rum, whale oil, and fish. John Hancock and his mother moved into his uncle's home, Hancock Manor, on Beacon Hill in Boston. The house was the finest in Boston, possibly in the colony of Massachusetts, and was staffed by a number of servants and slaves.

## Did You Know Hancock:

- Was more popular in Massachusetts than John Adams or Samuel Adams

- Lived like an aristocrat, owned slaves, and was the wealthiest man in the North

- Was a smuggler

Hancock was educated at the Boston Grammar School and was graduated from Harvard in 1754. His uncle began grooming him for the family business, and in 1760 he was sent to London for an education in British trade. The House of Hancock obtained several profitable government contracts during the French and Indian War, and master John Hancock had a large expense account and a taste for European fashion and social life. He was young and wealthy and what Americans would call a "playboy" today. He loved fine wine, good parties, and was considered a charming ladies man. In 1763, Hancock was made a partner in the House of Hancock, and after his uncle died in 1764, he eventually inherited the firm, Hancock Manor, thousands of acres, two or three slaves, and close to 70,000 pounds (or roughly $10,000,000 2007 dollars). Hancock, at the age of twenty-seven, was now, by far, the wealthiest man in Boston if not all the colonies. This proved fortunate for the patriot cause, for Hancock would be one of the chief financiers of the early stages of the American War for Independence. Samuel Adams supposedly called him the "milch cow."

## "Treasonous" John Hancock

In contrast to most of the other prominent revolutionary leaders, Hancock did not have the gift of the pen, and was not a great speaker. But because of his personal connections through the House of Hancock, he was an important and respected member of his community. The Stamp Act riots that erupted in 1765 worried Hancock. He was a conservative business-man, worried that violence from the lower classes could be precipitated against any wealthy man, including himself. He gently urged his powerful friends, royal officials included, to reconsider the Stamp Act, but when the act was implemented against his warnings, Hancock decried it as unconstitutional. "I have a right," he wrote, "to the Libertys and privileges of the English Constitution, and as Englishmen will enjoy them."

He supported, in protest, the non-importation of British goods, and gave liberally to the patriot cause. Hancock eventually became allies with the more outspoken Samuel Adams, who groomed him for leadership in the cause of independence. While he served as a local selectman and in the Massachusetts government, he focused most of his energy on the House of Hancock and hoped that the British would refrain from any further hostile acts. But the Townshend Duties of 1767 sparked a furious response. He wrote to a London associate that the only choice left for Americans was to "unite & come under a Solemn agreement to stop importing any goods from England...." But this didn't stop him from continuing his thriving merchant business, sometimes clandestinely through smuggling.

## The Rebel Hancock

"If history has any proper concern with the individual qualities of Hancock, it may be doubtful whether, in these respects, distant generations will know exactly what manner of man he was. But, as a public man, his country is greatly indebted to him. He was most faithfully devoted to her cause, and it is a high eulogy on his patriotism, that when the British Government offered pardon to all the rebels, for all their offenses, Hancock and Samuel Adams were the only persons to whom this grace was denied."

**—William Sullivan, 1834.**

He was moving closer to the position that a breach with England was inevitable.

Hancock owned several ships and a wharf in Boston. In 1768, one of his ships, the *Liberty*, docked with a cargo of wine. Most of the wine was offloaded under the cover of darkness and therefore Hancock escaped paying the customs duty. When the customs officials boarded the next morning, they found a dead captain and only twenty-five pipes of wine, far less than the ship's capacity. One man who was locked up in the hold during the illegal activity was eventually bribed to tell his story. The British seized the *Liberty*, and Hancock was dragged to court under the charge of smuggling, the objective being to cut the life-blood of the patriot finances in Boston. He was represented by John Adams, and though only one witness could be found on behalf of the prosecution, the trial continued for five months. Hancock was eventually acquitted due to a lack of evidence, but he became a celebrity in Boston and the symbol of resistance to unconstitutional Parliamentary acts and abuse at the hands of royal officials.

Hancock was reelected to the Massachusetts General Court in 1769, and in 1770 was selected to head a town committee following the Boston Massacre. Hancock forced the royal governor to remove his troops from Boston through a false boast of "ten thousand men armed and ready to come into town upon his refusal." He was again the hero, the forceful negotiator who had bluffed his way to a strategic victory. The relative calm following the "Massacre" allowed him to again focus on business, but by 1773, the tension in Boston, particularly over the publication of the "Hutchinson Letters" (from the royal governor Thomas Hutchinson, advocating restrictions on colonial rights) and the Tea Act, was thick. Hancock had in fact led the charge against Governor Hutchinson in the General Court, and had enthusiastically supported the Boston Tea Party. When offered the chance to be the Massacre Day orator in 1774, he seized the opportunity to move the people toward independence. As a man predisposed for public glory, his star never shone brighter.

Shortly after the Massacre Day remembrance, the Massachusetts legislature was dissolved and in its place the citizens created the Provincial Congress in defiance of the royal authority. Hancock was chosen president of the Congress and elected chairman of the committee of safety with responsibility over the militia. He used his own money to help supply the famous Massachusetts "Minutemen" and the rest of the state militia in the months leading to war. Massachusetts elected him to serve in the Second Continental Congress in 1775, and politics was now his full-time occupation—he even gave instructions to sell his ships. Hancock's influence was so large in Massachusetts that the British government regarded Hancock and Samuel Adams as its chief enemies.

In April 1775, the British made their move on the Massachusetts rebels. They hoped to apprehend Hancock and Adams in Lexington and then march to Concord to seize the town arsenal and coerce the "illegal" state government, which had relocated there from Boston. When Paul Revere and William Dawes arrived in Lexington and informed Hancock that the "Regulars are coming out," he initially marched out to the Lexington green with the other militia, but was persuaded to flee north with Samuel Adams for the good of the cause. He evaded capture, and the war began with the shots fired in Lexington. But to the British, Hancock was now the leader of a military rebellion and had committed an act of treason.

With the rest of the Massachusetts delegation to the Continental Congress in tow and under a military escort, Hancock departed for Philadelphia shortly after the battle at Lexington and Concord to take his seat in the Congress. He was met by thousands of excited and enthusiastic people and ringing bells in New York and Philadelphia, and by the second week of the Congress, Hancock was elected president. He would serve continuously in that capacity until 1777. While there is some suggestion that he wanted to be commander-in-chief of the Continental Army, Hancock supported Washington's selection and called him a fine gentleman worthy of the role. Hancock, meanwhile, also took on the role of husband, marrying Dorothy Quincy in August 1775, at the age of thirty-eight.

## ★★★★★★★★ The Hancock Style

Hancock was never one for republican simplicity. A 1778 newspaper described his public appearances: "John Hancock of Boston appears in public with all the state and pageantry of an Oriental prince; he rides in an elegant chariot which was taken in a prize to the *Civil Usage* pirate vessel, and by the owners presented to him. He is attended by four servants dressed in superb livery, mounted on fine horses richly caparisoned; and escorted by fifty horsemen with drawn sabers, the one half of whom precede and the other follow his carriage."

Hancock was an able president and worked vigorously to shore up the Continental finances and supply for the military. He also helped create the first American navy, and the frigate USS *Hancock* was commissioned and named in his honor. Hancock also famously presided over the ratification of the Declaration of Independence in July 1776. The first copy was sent to the printer on 4 July and Hancock, as president of the Congress, was the only name to appear on the document. These broadsides were sent to all the states and Hancock sent a copy to George Washington with instructions for it to be read to his troops.

Along with most of the other delegates to the Congress, he did not affix his signature to the document until August. His was the largest because he was president, and possibly because he was vain, but he never said he signed large enough for King George to read it without his glasses (as the legend goes). This engrossed copy is the most famous copy of the Declaration, but was neither the first nor the only one produced.

★★★★★★★★

## "The Independent States of America"

If you think the Founding generation did not think the states were sovereign, think again. Upon receiving word that Rhode Island had ratified the Constitution in 1790, Hancock issued the following message to the Massachusetts legislature: "I congratulate you, Gentlemen, on the accession of another State to our Union; and am happy to say, that I am persuaded that the Wisdom and tried patriotism of the Citizens of Rhode Island will very soon compleat the Union of all the Independent States of America...."

Hancock had to flee Philadelphia with the Congress twice as president and by 1777 was worn out from the stress of two years of leading the group. He asked for a personal leave of absence in order to spend time with his family. He briefly returned to the Continental Congress in 1778, where he had been replaced as president by South Carolinian Henry Laurens. He was disappointed, but he remained for a time and signed the Articles of Confederation with the rest of the Massachusetts delegation, before he turned to what he believed was his true calling, state and local politics. His only foray into military life during the Revolution occurred in 1778 when he led a group of 5,000 Massachusetts militiamen against the British in Rhode Island. That expedition, however, proved a failure. He returned to Boston later that year and remained engaged in local and state politics for the remainder of his life.

## The governor

If nothing else, Hancock was wildly popular among the people of Massachusetts. While the leaders of Massachusetts questioned his sincerity and intelligence, the people called him a hero. Hancock was a wealthy and pretentious man, often a glory-seeker, and he continued to give lavish parties to local and foreign dignitaries, but to the people of his state, he was one of them, the man who had used his fortune to help the poor and destitute during the hardest days of the struggle for independence, and who had brought them to tears with his Massacre Day oration in 1774. He realized his power was in Boston, not Philadelphia, and as one biographer has labeled him, he was the gout ridden, five-foot-four-inch "Baron of Beacon Hill."

Massachusetts ratified a new state constitution in 1780, and Hancock was elected governor with 90 percent of the vote. The state elite could not understand his appeal, and Samuel Adams often complained of his subordinate status to Hancock. He was re-elected every year until 1785, when an attack of gout forced him to resign. The historian William Fowler called this "political gout," because Hancock seemed to disappear when the political situation in Massachusetts grew difficult. His resignation allowed him to miss the mess known as Shay's Rebellion in 1786. The Massachusetts economy was in shambles; heavy debt led the legislature to pile on high taxes, and the farmers who could not pay were often thrown in debtor's prison or had their property confiscated. Several formed a militia and led a revolt against the government. They were ultimately crushed by state forces, and many were captured, imprisoned, and sentenced to death.

Hancock used this to his advantage. He was re-elected governor in 1787 and pardoned or commuted the sentences of all those involved. He had once again come to the rescue of the people. He would be re-elected every year for the remainder of his life by crushing majorities. His health declined during this time, and he grew less interested in government, becoming more or less a figurehead. He had been elected to serve in the Confederation Congress in 1786, and was even chosen president, but he never showed up and resigned his seat due to his health.

When the Constitutional Convention was called in 1787, Hancock, due to his role as governor, was not selected as a delegate, but as a firm advocate of state authority, he questioned the need for a stronger central government and feared the result of political centralization. He was appointed to the state ratification convention and though he did not take his seat as president of the convention until its end (because of gout), he gave a speech in support of the Constitution in conjunction with a series of amendments demanded by the convention. The first in this list stated, "That it be explicitly declared, that all powers not expressly delegated by the aforesaid Constitution are reserved to the several states, to be by them exercised." Hancock gave his "assent to the Constitution in full confidence that the amendments proposed will soon become a part of the system. These amendments being in no wise local, but calculated to give security and ease to all the states, I think that all will agree to them." Such was his support, conditional. Massachusetts ratified the document by a slim majority even with Hancock's approval.

Hancock died in 1793 at the age of fifty-six. His funeral was a grand event. State dignitaries, including friends and former enemies, and Vice President John Adams joined in the procession. Bostonians lined to streets to see their governor one last time. No man was more respected in

## Mellowing with Age

In 1791, jealous little John Adams once said of John Hancock, "Yes, there is the place where the great John Hancock was born....John Hancock! A man without head and without heart!—the mere shadow of a man!—and yet a Governor of old Massachusetts!" Years later, he changed his tune, calling him "essential to the Revolution," and in 1818 he said, "Of Mr. Hancock's life, character, generous nature, great and distinguished sacrifices and important services, if I had forces, I should be glad to write a volume."

Massachusetts than Hancock, save perhaps George Washington. This is why his relative historical eclipse is so befuddling. One possible explanation is that Hancock was so devoted to his state and its politics rather than to the politics of the Union. Another is that he has been overshadowed by other Massachusetts politicians who were intensely jealous of him, men like Samuel Adams and John Adams. But without John Hancock the cause of independence might have failed in 1775.

# Chapter Sixteen

# PATRICK HENRY

It may seem curious to include Patrick Henry in a list of "forgotten Founders." His impassioned cry of "give me liberty or give me death!" is one of the more well-known phrases in American history, though it is quite possible that many Americans would think someone other than Henry said it. His name is more recognized than any other in this group, save perhaps John Hancock and Samuel Adams, and their fame comes from a signature and a modern brewing company. Henry has been the subject of several biographies and even a few children's stories. But most Americans could probably not list any of his accomplishments other than his famous speech. He has been virtually ignored by the modern historians and those who do discuss his life often focus on his status as an "inconsistent slave owner" or describe him as an unintelligent, smooth-talking, country-bumpkin demagogue. This is due, in part, to Henry's resolute defense of states' rights for much of his life and to Jefferson's unflattering description of the man. But if Dickinson was the "Penman of the Revolution," then Henry was the "Spokesman of the Revolution" and the man who in many ways made the Revolution possible.

Henry was from a typical Virginia frontier family. His father, John Henry, arrived in the American colonies around 1730 from Scotland, and his mother, Sarah Winston, was a second generation American whose father, a Presbyterian, moved to the colonies from Yorkshire, England.

## Did You Know Henry:

- Was a conservative
- Feared the effects of the Constitution and voted against it
- Was a practicing Christian

249

Henry's parents had modest means, but both were well-respected members of society. His mother was described as a woman of wit and social charm, and his father was a man of good character and education who served as a vestryman in the local parish church and as a colonel of the militia. He owned a small tobacco plantation on the South Anna River called Mount Brilliant. Patrick Henry was born there in 1736 and spent his youth under the tutelage of his father, who taught him to read Latin and appreciate the classic texts. His vigorous schooling was underscored by a hearty plantation life and the moral teachings of his pious minister uncle, the Reverend Patrick Henry, and his mother's favorite minister, the famous Samuel Davies, later president of Princeton University.

At the age of fifteen, Henry worked as a clerk at a local store. A year later, he opened his own store in partnership with his brother. The store failed, but the young Henry was soon married to Sarah Shelton. This union netted a dowry of six slaves and three hundred acres of poor land, so Henry returned to farming. Fire destroyed the young couples' home three years later, and Henry was forced to open shop again. Mounting debt and a large family led him to pursue a more lucrative career as a lawyer, and in 1760, he was admitted to the Virginia bar. His practice became one of the most profitable and well known in the region, and in three years he had managed 1,185 suits and won most of his cases.

## The Revolution

He purchased a plantation in Louisa County, Virginia, in 1764, and at twenty-nine was elected to the House of Burgesses from that county, taking his seat in May 1765 with the session already in progress. Henry waited only nine days before making an impact in the legislature. While most of the Tory members of the House were absent, Henry presented a series of resolves later known as the "Virginia Stamp Act Resolutions." He had shown a willingness to challenge the crown in 1763 during a famous constitutional dispute known as "the Parson's Cause" (in which the king had vetoed a law passed by the Virginia legislature governing the salaries of Anglican clergy in the colony), but the "Stamp Act Resolutions" trumped the "Cause" in both scope and substance.

Henry declared the Stamp Act unconstitutional and argued that only the colonial legislatures possessed the authority to tax the people directly. This resolve, the fifth, sparked the most debate, passed by only one vote, and was stricken from the record the next day. The other resolutions passed without much confrontation. But many conservative Virginians thought Henry's speech on the resolutions bordered on treason, particularly the last line where he famously said, "Caesar had his Brutus; Charles the First his Cromwell; and George the Third may profit by their example.... " Henry maintained that he was loyal the king—as long as the king and the British Parliament adhered to their ancient constitutions and recognized that the colonists possessed "all the liberties, privileges, franchises, and immunities that have at any time been held, enjoyed, and possessed by the people of Great Britain." Henry believed the Stamp Act infringed upon these rights.

The "Stamp Act Resolutions" stirred debate in other colonies and fired a warning shot at the British. The colonies would not lie prostrate and accept unconstitutional authority. Henry became the most popular man in Virginia, if not the colonies, from 1765 to 1770. As each aggressive act by the British Parliament moved the colonies closer to war, Henry solidified his power in Virginia. In 1774, the Virginia governor dissolved the House of Burgesses. Henry led the assembly to Raleigh Tavern in Williamsburg where the group adopted a call for a Virginia convention and asked for all the colonies to meet in a continental congress. At the first Virginia convention in 1774, Henry was chosen to lead the Virginia delegation in the First Continental Congress. He sided with the more radical elements in the Congress and supported a colonial declaration of non-importation of British goods. Henry was less inclined to make peaceful petitions to the king than were other delegates. He had already decided that the British government would never respect colonial rights under the British constitution. The colonies' only recourse was independence.

Henry and the other members of the Virginia convention decided to meet again in March 1775 at St. John's Church in Richmond. This meeting was held less than one month before the first shots of the Revolution were fired at Lexington and Concord, and Henry, through a passionate plea against the "illusion of hope," forced his fellow Virginians to face the facts: "The war is inevitable—and let it come! I repeat it, sir, let it come!" His speech, typically reproduced under the title "Give me Liberty, or Give me Death!" is often characterized as a radical articulation of revolutionary principles. But, in fact, Henry made his case not from any general "rights of man" but from what he regarded as direct violations of the British constitution. He outlined the measures the colonies had taken to forestall war, to no avail. "Our petitions have been slighted; our remonstrances have produced additional violence and insult; our supplications have been disregarded; and we have been spurned, with contempt, from the foot of the throne!"

The convention almost immediately adopted resolutions for mustering, training, and arming the militia of Virginia. Without Henry's impressive call for action, the convention might not have acted so quickly, particularly before shots had been fired. He was sent to the Second Continental Congress and was later appointed commander-in-chief of the Virginia militia, but many—including Washington—doubted his effectiveness as a military commander, and Henry resigned his commission in February 1776. He attended the third Virginia convention in the spring of that year and took part in the drafting of a new Virginia constitution and a Virginia declaration of independence. Even before the "United States" declared independence, Virginia, as a sovereign political entity, had already done so.

Henry was elected governor in 1776, and he served until 1779. He made lasting contributions not only to Virginia, but to the United States during this period. He sent George Rogers Clark on a military expedition into the western lands beyond the Appalachians in order to both clear the British and solidify Virginia's claim to the land. It worked. Virginia would control most of what was called the "Northwest territory" until ceding it to the United States in 1784. He also personally intervened and protected George Washington when there was a move to strip him of command. He retired to his plantation in 1779 and enjoyed the company of his second wife, Dorothea Dandridge (the two had eleven children between 1777 and 1799).

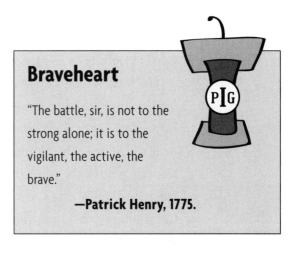

### Braveheart

"The battle, sir, is not to the strong alone; it is to the vigilant, the active, the brave."

**—Patrick Henry, 1775.**

## The Constitution

Henry could not stay away from politics. After only two years, he returned to the legislature and became a principal opponent of his onetime political ally, Thomas Jefferson. He was re-elected governor in 1784 and faced the most pressing financial crisis in Virginia's history. The war had destroyed the state's finances, and paper money created oppressive inflation. Henry favored restoring Loyalist land (ostensibly to raise revenue by taxing the Loyalists and requisitioning their tobacco) and offered veterans land grants in the western territory. Henry became increasingly suspicious of the Northern states during this period, as rumors swirled that they desired a treaty with Spain that would have surrendered American navigation rights on the Mississippi. Henry believed the agrarian South was under attack from Northern commercial interests. He retired from his fifth term as governor in 1786 and re-located his family to Prince Edward County in south-central Virginia.

The Virginia legislature decided to send delegates to a "Federal Convention" in 1787 and asked Henry to lead the group. He declined and made clear his opposition to creating a new, stronger central government over the states. The Virginia Ratifying Convention met in June 1788. Henry attended the convention and used every weapon in his rhetorical arsenal to defeat the Constitution. His opening remarks classified the Constitution as a "consolidated government instead of a confederation.... and the danger of such government is, to my mind, very striking." He questioned whether the work of the convention was valid. "The federal Convention ought to have amended the old system; for this purpose they were solely delegated; the object of their mission extended to no other consideration."

He took issue with the wording of the Preamble, namely the phrase "We the People...." He foresaw the effects of the phrase and to Henry, it smacked of consolidation. "The fate of...America may depend on this. Have they said, We the States? If they had, this would be a confederation. It is otherwise most clearly a consolidated government." Moreover, the people could not have created the new document, principally because "the people have no right to enter into leagues, alliances, or confederations....States and foreign powers are the only proper agents for this kind of government." "We the People," then was both improper and ille-

## The Limits of Government

"The Constitution is not an instrument for the government to restrain the people, it is an instrument for the people to restrain the government—lest it come to dominate our lives and interests."

**—Patrick Henry**

gal. He argued that a compact between the "people" and the government fundamentally altered the American system of government, and not for the better. In short, it would "oppress and ruin the people."

Henry characterized the Constitution as a document that would place power in the hands of a "tyranny." Even with the guarantee of a bill of rights (which Madison promised), Henry voted against ratification. In his closing remarks, Henry declared that the Constitution violated the principles of the Revolution. The colonies had revolted against a central government that failed to protect their rights; he saw no reason why the people of the states should now seek a new, powerful central government, with a standing army, that could impose a similar tyranny.

★★★★★★★★★

## "We the People"

Henry insisted that the preamble to the Constitution should have read "we the states" rather than "we the people," warning that "we the people" was not only inaccurate, and in fact illegal, but would create an un-American government that would trample on states' rights. He was prophetic. Daniel Webster and other "nationalists" in the mid-nineteenth century used the phrase "we the people" to justify their vision of a consolidated "nation."

## Red Hill

Henry ended his political career in the Virginia legislature shortly after the ratification convention, and retired to his plantation, Red Hill, in 1788. Henry had been the unequivocal champion of limited government and states' rights during the ratification debates, and he refused to serve under the Constitution. Yet, in the 1790s, things began to change as Henry grew suspicious of his former allies in Virginia. By 1798, Henry was a leading supporter of the Federalists in Virginia, a conversion that shocked even his own family. Why the sudden shift? Had he become a "big government" advocate? The answer is no, and there are two possible explanations for his apparent reversal.

The first is personal. The leading members of the new opposition party were Jefferson and Madison, two men Henry considered personal enemies. Jefferson called Henry "the laziest man in reading I ever knew" and believed Henry betrayed him in 1781 when he was under attack for his handling of the war in Virginia while governor. Henry never liked or trusted Madison. Henry despised Madison for his role in framing the Constitution and attempted to have him gerrymandered out of the new Congress in 1789; and he used his power in the Virginia legislature to block Madison from becoming a United States Senator from Virginia.

Neither Jefferson nor Madison wanted Henry involved in their new party, the Republicans (sometimes called the Democratic-Republicans), and both shunned him repeatedly, while at the same time courting Henry's long-time allies. This was, to them, political revenge. Federalists George Washington and John Marshall knew of the feud and attempted to bring Henry into the Federalist camp. Henry opposed the Republicans not because he liked the Federalists—he didn't—but because he considered the Republicans hypocrites. He warned them in 1788 of the disastrous effects of the Constitution they supported. "What must I think of those men, whom I myself warned of the danger of giving the power of making laws by means of treaty, to the president and senate, when I see these same men [Madison, for one] denying the existence of that power, which they insisted, in our convention, ought properly to be exercised by the president and senate, and by none other?"

The second concerned his fear of radical democratic theory. Henry admired the British constitution, and spoke reverently of it many times

## Wisdom of the Founders

"Suspicion is a virtue as long as its object is the preservation of the public good.... Guard with jealous attention the public liberty. Suspect every one who approaches that jewel."

—Patrick Henry, 1788.

during the Virginia ratification debates. When the leaders of the new Republican Party appeared to embrace the radical tenets of the French Revolution, "Liberty, Equality, Fraternity," Henry recoiled. Liberty he championed, but the French Revolution destroyed the social order of France through a bloody massacre and wanton destruction of property. To Henry, the American Revolution was never a war for radical theories such as "equality." It was fought to *preserve* "English" liberty and the old, agrarian, social order of Virginia. A "French Revolution" in America would be detrimental to liberty as he viewed it. For example, as governor, he fought against attempts to "separate" church and state, though he believed every man should have freedom of conscience. Henry was not a royalist, but he was a conservative who cherished the Virginia of his past, a society based on ordered liberty.

Henry died in 1799 of stomach cancer. He had just been elected to the Virginia House of Delegates as a "Federalist" but died before he could serve. He left behind an intellectual legacy that exists not in written documents, but in passionate speeches for liberty. Men without a written record are too often ignored by professional historians. Henry has suffered that fate. He said during the ratification debates that "The voice of tradition, I trust, will inform posterity of our struggles for freedom. If our descendants be worthy of the name of Americans, they will preserve, and

## Henry the Christian

"It cannot be emphasized too strongly or too often that this great nation was founded, not by religionists, but by Christians; not on religions, but on the gospel of Jesus Christ. For this very reason peoples of other faiths have been afforded asylum, prosperity, and freedom of worship."

**—Patrick Henry, 1776.**

hand down to their latest posterity, the transactions of the present times; and, though I confess my exclamations are not worthy the hearing, they will see that I have done my utmost to preserve their liberty...."

## Chapter Seventeen

# RICHARD HENRY LEE

No *Politically Incorrect Guide™* would be complete without a discussion of the Lee family. Robert E. Lee is the most conspicuous family member, but several Lees served Virginia and the American military with distinction before, during, and after the War for Independence, including Robert E. Lee's father, "Light Horse Harry" Lee.

Richard Henry Lee was a patriot, Anti-Federalist, and statesman from his "country," Virginia. He led the charge for independence in 1776 and was a powerful figure in Virginia political life. He served one term as president of the Continental Congress and was elected a United States Senator from Virginia immediately after the ratification of the Constitution. His role in the founding period is often overlooked due to his "personality" and the slapstick characterization of him in the musical *1776*. Lee was a Southern aristocrat, sometimes considered pompous and arrogant, but he was not a bumbling idiot. John Adams, in fact, called him a "masterly man," though "tall and spare." Excluding Lee from a list of Founding Fathers would be a travesty, for he was as important to the cause of independence as Jefferson, Adams, and Franklin.

Lee was descended from one of the oldest and most powerful families in Virginia. His great-grandfather, Richard Lee, was the first of the family to settle in Virginia and he served as the Attorney General and

## Did You Know Lee:

- Thought Virginia should secede from the Union if a bill of rights was not added to the Constitution

- Believed the Constitution could lead to a civil war

- Was the great-uncle of Robert E. Lee

259

Secretary of State for the colony and was a member of the king's council. His father, Thomas Lee, served in the Virginia House of Burgesses and as acting governor of Virginia. His mother, Hannah Harrison Ludwell, was a member of the powerful Harrison family of Virginia.

Richard Henry Lee was born in 1732 at the family plantation, Stratford. His brother, Francis Lightfoot Lee, and nephew, Henry Lee III ("Light Horse Harry"), would become American military heroes, but Richard Henry Lee was more like his grandfather, Richard Lee II, often called "Richard the Scholar." His service would be rendered in the political break with Great Britain and as a champion of the rights of Englishmen.

Lee was educated by private tutors and was graduated from the Wakefield academy in Yorkshire, England, in 1751. He received a solid background in the classics, government, and history, and in 1752, Lee returned to Virginia and practiced law. He began his public career in the Virginia House of Burgesses in 1757 and became a justice of the peace for Westmoreland County in 1758. He was a leader in the House of Burgesses, an ally of Patrick Henry, and an early opponent of Parliament's authority to tax the colonies. He wrote in 1764, one year before the infamous Stamp Act, that taxes imposed on the colonies without proper representation in Parliament were akin to an "iron hand of power" and a violation of the British constitution. "Surely no reasonable being would," he stated, "quit liberty for slavery; nor could it be just for the benefited to repay their benefactors with chains instead of the most grateful acknowledgments."

He was not in attendance in 1765 when Henry presented his famous Stamp Act Resolves to the House of Burgesses, but he

## Books They Don't Want You to Read

*Memoir of the Life of Richard Henry Lee and His Correspondence with the Most Distinguished Men in America and Europe: Illustrative of Their Characters and of the Events of the American Revolution,* by Richard Henry Lee (Whitefish, MT: Kessinger Publishing, 2007). If you want to know what Lee thought, go to the source.

agreed with him. Lee, along with several other Virginia gentlemen, attempted to force the Stamp Act collector to resign his appointment, and Lee later called the collector "an execrable monster, who with parricidal heart and hands," would "ruin...his native country." Lee organized the first non-importation association in the colonies, the basic structure of which later became the Virginia Association and Continental Association for the boycott of British goods. In contrast to the violent opposition to Parliamentary acts in New England, Lee chose boycotts and "persuasion" and never threatened tar and feathers or the destruction of property. His was a gentlemanly rather than a radical approach and based upon the constitutional rights of Englishmen, which his family had fought to preserve for generations.

The Townshend Acts of 1767 were, to Lee, an even graver injustice. He called them "arbitrary, unjust, and destructive of the mutual beneficial connection which every good subject would wish to see preserved." Lee began urging for colonial committees of correspondence, not unlike those which Samuel Adams suggested a few years later. He was present when the House of Burgesses was dissolved in 1769 and participated in the famous Raleigh Tavern meeting where the Virginia Association, which organized the non-importation of British goods, was agreed upon. As British violations of colonial sovereignty became more pronounced, Lee was more aggressive. He pushed his call for committees of correspondence in 1773, stating that such action should have been taken from the beginning of the conflict as a means to achieve "perfect understanding of each other, on which the political salvation of America so eminently depends." And in 1774, Lee, Henry, and Thomas Jefferson called for a day of fasting and prayer in protest of the closing of Boston Harbor. He called this action of Parliament the "most violent and dangerous attempt to destroy the constitutional liberty and rights of all British America."

Lee was elected as a member to the First Continental Congress in 1774, and he enthusiastically supported the adoption of the Continental

Association for boycotting British goods. By 1775, he was urging independence. The Fifth Virginia Convention followed his lead and declared Virginia independent from Great Britain in May 1776. They sent Lee instructions to present a series of resolves to the Second Continental Congress calling for the independence of all the colonies in order to form foreign alliances and establish a confederation for common defense. He presented the "Lee Resolutions" to Congress in June 1776. The language was clear: "Resolved, That these United Colonies are, and of right ought to be, free and independent States, that they are absolved from all allegiance to the British Crown, and that all political connection between them and the State of Great Britain is, and ought to be, totally dissolved."

Lee left the Congress one week later to participate in the formation of the new Virginia government, at that time a much more prestigious role than hammering out a formal declaration of independence. He had already laid the rhetorical groundwork for independence, and Jefferson copied much of Lee's language and that of George Mason's Virginia Declaration of Rights when he wrote the Declaration of Independence.

Lee later returned to Philadelphia and, along with his brother Francis Lightfoot Lee, became one of two Lees to affix his signature to the Declaration. Lee was an active participant in the Continental Congress, but was worn out by his duties and resigned his seat before the end of the war. He was re-elected to the Congress in 1784 and served as the president of that body from 1784 to 1785.

## Those who love liberty

As the clamor for a stronger central government grew more pronounced, Lee attempted to quiet discontent over the Articles of Confederation. Virginia was his native country, and though he could see that the powers of government under the Articles were often insufficient, he cautioned men to avoid granting "to Rulers an atom of power that is not most clearly and indispensably necessary for the safety and well being of Society." He opined that the central government should not have the power of "both purse and sword." Lee was offered a seat at the Philadelphia Convention of 1787 but declined because he believed it would be unconstitutional and improper to serve in both the Congress under the Articles of Confederation and a convention charged with altering the existing government. But when the Constitutional Convention concluded its work in September, Lee quickly became an outspoken opponent of the new government.

He wrote to George Mason in October 1787 that the Constitution would produce "a coalition of monarchy men, military men, aristocrats and drones whose noise, impudence and zeal exceeds all belief." Lee believed that the "commercial plunder of the South" and the possibility of "tyranny" or "civil war" would be the only results from the adoption of the Constitution as it stood, and recommended withholding "assent" until amendments protecting civil liberty were added. Later in a letter to Samuel Adams he said, "The good people of the U. States in their late generous contest, contended for free government, in the fullest, clearest, and strongest sense. That they had no idea of being brought under despotic rule under the notion of 'Strong government,' or in form of *elective despotism*: Chains being still chains whether made of gold or iron." Clearly, Lee believed the Constitution would turn the liberty-loving people of all states into slaves, bound by a government of elected tyrants whose sole purpose would be to glorify and enrich themselves. Lee understood free government to be limited government.

## Books They Don't Want You to Read

*Virginia's American Revolution: From Dominion to Republic, 1776-1840*, by Kevin R. C. Gutzman (Lanham, MD: Lexington Books, 2007).

During the months leading to Virginia's ratification convention in 1788, Lee penned seventeen letters entitled *Letters from the Federal Farmer to the Republican* that appeared in two pamphlets. They outlined his arguments against the Constitution and equaled the *Federalist* in depth. Taken as a whole, they are the best expression of Anti-Federalism outside of the ratification conventions. Lee expressed fear that the Constitution supplanted a federal with a consolidated government. "Instead of being thirteen republics, under a federal head, it is clearly designed to make us one consolidated government." He reasoned that such a system would render the people in the "remote states" vulnerable to "fear and force," and it would end in "despotic government." Lee conceded that parts of the government under the Constitution were sound, but without a bill of rights and strict limitations on government, the people would be subjected to the worst evils of power.

★ ★ ★ ★ ★ ★ ★ ★ ★ ★ ★ ★ ★ ★ ★ ★

## Author, Author!

The authorship of the *Letters from the Federal Farmer* has been an issue of historical dispute. Richard Henry Lee's most recent biographer, J. Kent McGaughy, concludes that the letters were written by New Yorker Melancton Smith. The famous American historian Gordon Wood offered the same conclusion in 1974. The esteemed American historian Forrest McDonald considers Lee to be their author. Lee's contemporaries believed he wrote the *Letters*, and Lee never denied writing them. Published anonymously, there will probably never be conclusive evidence about who wrote them, but Lee seems the most likely author.

The *Letters* emphasize that the Constitution is a compact among the states. If the states approved the Constitution, they were entering into an agreement, a compact, and Lee insisted that if the state governments ceased to exist, the federal government "cannot remain a moment" because it was the creation of the states; moreover, the federal government could not have any powers that were not expressly delegated to it by the people of the states.

Lee was elected as a delegate to the Virginia Ratifying Convention in 1788, but he did not attend due to poor health. Still, he privately pressured other delegates to consider amendments prior to ratification. Lee considered freedom of the press, frequent elections, and trial by jury vital for "*good*" government, for "the violation of these...will always be extremely convenient for *bad* government." He also believed state sovereignty offered a protection against "*arbitrary rule.*" If, however, the proposed amendments were not adopted by the new government within two years, Lee recommended that Virginia be "disengaged" from the ratification. Another word for "disengaged" is secession. When the Constitution was ratified by Virginia, Lee wrote, "'Tis really astonishing that the same people, who have just emerged from a long and cruel war in defense of liberty, should now agree to fix an elective despotism on themselves and their posterity!"

Through Henry's power in the Virginia legislature, Lee was elected to serve as a Senator from Virginia in 1789. His main focus during the early days of the Senate became the consideration and adoption of a bill of rights. He worked zealously to ensure that the bill of rights would be crafted according to the designs of the Virginia convention and criticized James Madison for his abridgement of the original list. Lee called the final list "mutilated and enfeebled" and concluded, "What with design in some, and fear of Anarchy in others, it is very clear, I think, that a government very different from a free one will take place ere many years are passed." He was sick for much of his time in the Senate and resigned his seat in 1792. Lee returned to his plantation, Chantilly, and died two years later at the age of 62.

## Virginian

Like his compatriots from his native state, Lee was first and foremost a Virginian and a Southerner. He once wrote to Samuel Adams that, "So extensive a territory as that of the U. States, including such a variety of climates, productions, interests; and so great differences of manners, habits, and customs; cannot be governed in freedom, unless formed into States sovereign sub modo, and confederated for common good." While in the Senate, he informed Patrick Henry that "The most essential danger from the present system arises, in my opinion, from its tendency to a consolidated government, instead of a union of Confederated States." He urged Henry to fill state offices with men who would firmly oppose encroachments on state power, for states were the only reliable safeguards against tyranny and the preservation of traditional order.

Lee believed the states should never be consolidated into an "American people" because they were, in reality, the people of the several states with different cultures and interests. He had led Virginia to independence in 1776 and from that point on he considered Virginia to be an independent, sovereign republic, his country. When his nephew Robert E. Lee supported the secession of his state in 1861, he was simply following a family tradition.

## Chapter Eighteen

# NATHANIEL MACON

Nathaniel Macon was quite possibly the most important man in the history of the Tar Heel State, North Carolina. Jefferson called him the "last of the Romans"—meaning a republican who favored limited government, frugality, and selfless service—and Macon's friend and political ally, John Randolph of Roanoke, described him as the wisest man he ever knew. Most Americans have probably never heard of Macon. Modern history texts rarely mention him, if at all. He was everything that politically correct interpretations of American history try to avoid. Macon championed states' rights, supported secession, denounced the Constitution, presided over a large tobacco plantation, served with distinction in the Revolution in defense of his state and region, and opposed every measure that tended to increase centralization and federal power. He lived a simple life, and though a genuine Southern aristocrat, was never pretentious. Macon was the personification of the Old South, and an American hero.

The first Macon, a French Huguenot named Gideon Macon, arrived in Virginia before 1680 and became a prominent tobacco planter in the tidewater region of Virginia. His grandson, Gideon Macon, moved to North Carolina in the 1730s, established a tobacco plantation, and built the family home, Macon Manor. The Macon family was well connected in both Virginia and North Carolina. For example, George Washington's wife,

## Did You Know Macon:

- Once voted against a monument to George Washington because it violated the principles of frugal government

- Believed the principles of the Revolution were best expressed in secession and nullification

- Never campaigned for office but held a position in Congress for thirty-seven years

Martha Dandridge Custis Washington, was descended from this line. Gideon Macon and his wife, Priscilla Jones, had six children. The last, Nathaniel Macon was born in 1758, and was only five when his father died. Nathaniel was bequeathed around five hundred acres, three slaves, and all of his father's blacksmith tools.

From 1766 to 1773, Macon was educated by Charles Pettigrew, grandfather of the famous Confederate general by the same name, and later attended the College of New Jersey, otherwise known as Princeton University. He left the college when the War for American Independence began in 1775 and enlisted with the New Jersey militia. He served one year, returned to North Carolina and began the study of law. He again enlisted for military duty in 1780 when his state was threatened by the British invasion of the South. Macon refused a commission, and also refused the bounty offered for enlistment. He fought at the Battle of Camden. When chosen to serve in the state Senate in 1781, he initially refused, but later accepted as a favor to General Nathanael Greene. Macon regarded his military service as service to his state—as did most Americans serving in the War for Independence—not to any union represented by the Continental Congress.

He served in the state legislature for the remainder of the 1780s. While there, he met and befriended Willie Jones, the dominant Anti-Federalist in North Carolina. The state elected Macon to serve in the Continental Congress in 1786, but he declined, and when several states called for a convention to discuss changes to the Articles of Confederation, Macon opposed North Carolina's participation. He did not attend the North Carolina ratification convention, but, along with his brother, John Macon, urged the defeat of the Constitution. North Carolina would not ratify the document until

## Books They Don't Want You to Read

*The Life of Nathaniel Macon,* by William E. Dodd (Raleigh, N.C.: Edwards & Broughton, Printers and Binders, 1903). Available for free on Google Books.

1789, and only after the Bill of Rights—especially the Ninth and Tenth Amendments—were guaranteed.

He served in the United States House of Representatives from 1791 to 1813 and in the United States Senate from 1813 to 1828. He was Speaker of the House for six years and president *pro tempore* of the Senate for one. His thirty-seven years of service occurred during the formative years of the republic, and he became a leading "negative" on federal action. Few other members cast as many "no" votes as Macon. One biographer called him a "negative radical," but this derogatory term does not do Macon justice. He voted "no" so often because he believed the federal government continually abused its authority and unconstitutionally enlarged its scope and influence. He took friend and foe alike to task for their support of unconstitutional measures.

## The Quid

Macon was identified as one of a group of thirteen "Quids" during his time in Congress. John Randolph of Roanoke bestowed the title on the group because their consistent attachment to limited government made them the other "thing" (in Latin, a *quid* is a "thing") in relation to the Federalists and the Republicans.

Macon was the recognized leader of the North Carolina delegation to the House of Representatives. He immediately characterized Alexander Hamilton as the "supreme evil-doer" and joined the opposition to his economic programs. Southerners believed that New England and New York were exercising too much influence on the general direction of the United States, especially in advancing Northern commercial interests against Southern agrarian interests. Macon shared that view.

Macon suggested a series of excise taxes in 1794 that would have extended the burden of the "whiskey tax" onto other beverages like beer, porter, and cider. His intent was to spread the pain, given that the

## Books They Don't Want You to Read

*The Old Republicans: Southern Conservatism in the Age of Jefferson*, by Norman K. Risjord (New York: Columbia University Press, 1965).

whiskey tax fell disproportionately on Western and Southern farmers. Macon and other Southern leaders felt that the whiskey tax was a political tax, imposed by Northern Federalists on Southern Republicans. In 1788, when Federalists attempted to limit free speech through the Sedition Act, Macon at once challenged the bill. He declared the provisions of the sedition law violated the spirit of 1776, and claimed that "the people suspect something is not right when free discussion is feared by government. They know that truth is not afraid of investigation." It was true, he conceded, that states had exercised the same power of the Sedition Act, but that was within their constitutional authority. He reasoned "let the States continue to punish, when necessary, licentiousness of the press"; what he denied was the federal usurpation of this right. Moreover, Macon argued the bill violated the First Amendment to the Constitution. "How can so plain language be misunderstood or interpreted into consistency with the bill before us?"

Macon consistently challenged federal designs to weaken the states and institute legislation that conflicted with republican principles of government, and he supported the Virginia and Kentucky Resolutions of 1798, where Madison and Jefferson put forward the argument that the states could nullify federal legislation. Macon went further, stating that if the states wished to end the federal government, they could do so because "the Government depends upon the State Legislatures for existence. They have only to refuse to elect Senators to Congress and all is gone." This would have worked in 1798, but after the Seventeenth Amendment (1913) and the direct election of senators, this was no longer the case. Macon would certainly have opposed that glaring reduction of state power.

But Macon did not focus singly on matters of state and federal power. He was a firm advocate of fiscal responsibility. For example, he voted against spending $7,000 (around $120,000 2007 dollars) on a monument to George Washington, not because he did not think Washington deserved the honor, but because the sum was too large and not an appropriate expenditure for the Federal government in any case. When Federalists asked for enormous sums of money to wage a war against France, Macon responded by saying, "Some people think borrowing five or six millions a trifling thing. We may leave it for our children to pay. This is unjust. If we contract a debt we ought to pay it, and not leave it to your children. What should we think of a father who would run in debt and leave it for his children to pay?" He also asked, "Ought we not to save all the expenses which are not absolutely necessary?"

Macon's independence was shown in his willingness to oppose those in his own party when they deviated from republican principles. Jefferson realized this in his second term. This is when Macon became identified as a "Quid." For a time, Macon attacked and ridiculed President Jefferson at every turn for what Macon regarded as Jefferson's inconsistent adherence to republican principles and the Constitution. Macon was not a "party man." He voted his beliefs. In fact, Macon was the model of the disinterested statesman. He did not seek election during the Revolution. When his state chose him to serve in the United States Senate, it was at the state legislature's insistence, not his. He was elected Speaker of the House three times, though he never actively campaigned for the position. When he was defeated for a fourth term in 1807, he never said a word

## Books They Don't Want You to Read

*The Missouri Controversy, 1819-1821*, by Glover Moore (New York: Peter Smith, 1967). Macon argued that Northerners wanted to exacerbate "sectional conflict" over slavery and create parties separated by the issue of slavery in order to expand their political power. The issues that led to the Civil War go all the way back to the Founding Fathers—and before.

about it. He turned down several offers of more "prestigious" positions in the federal government, from cabinet appointments to Vice President. Macon shunned the "glamour" of political office, and was a selfless public servant for his state.

## The Republican of Buck Spring

Buck Spring was a remote, sprawling tobacco plantation in Warrenton, North Carolina, that at one time covered two thousand acres. This was Macon's home and in the republican tradition of departing public life gracefully, he retired there in 1828. Macon lived twelve miles from the nearest post office and only received mail once every two weeks. His wife had died when he was thirty-two, and Macon never remarried. He lived alone but peacefully among his seventy slaves. He brought his entire group of slaves with him to church services once a month and had a separate service every Sunday at his home. His slaves were required to participate, and elder slaves would often lead a prayer. He was a genuine Southern aristocrat but a man of simple tastes. He ate what the plantation produced and preferred corn whiskey. He was fond of thoroughbreds and

## The True Statesman

The historian Clyde Wilson nicely summarized Macon's popularity this way: "Macon, like Washington and Jefferson, was not important and respected because he was elected to office. He was elected to office because he was important and respected. He never campaigned for office. He never attended a party caucus. He never promised anyone patronage to support him. Macon was elected over and over and revered because of what he was."

kept at least ten fine horses, and he enjoyed such Southern activities as fox chasing. Unless visitors called, Macon rarely had contact with the outside world. Buck Spring was his first country, North Carolina his second.

Macon did, however, stay abreast of the current political debates even in retirement. When South Carolina nullified the federal tariff in 1832, several leading Southerners pressed Macon for an opinion. He had supported nullification in 1798, but his attitude had changed. He believed nullification alone would not be enough to check Northern usurpation of power and argued secession was the only remedy. "I have never believed a State could nullify and stay in the Union, but have always believed a State might secede when she pleased, provided she would pay her proportion of the public debt, and this right I have considered the best guard to public liberty and to public justice that could be desired." He sent a strong letter to President Andrew Jackson critical of his threat to use military force to collect the tariff. Macon contended the federal government could not legally use force against a state in order to "maintain the Union."

He also opposed the re-charter of the Second Bank of the United States. Macon fought against the Bank for forty years. He voted against the Bank while Speaker of the House and once said that "Banks are the nobility of the country, they have exclusive privileges; and like all nobility, must be supported by the people and they are the worst kind, because they oppress secretly." When President Jackson vetoed a bill supporting re-charter in 1832, Macon applauded the move. Like other republicans of his day, Macon considered the bank to be a symbol of Northern corruption.

One of Macon's final forays into public life occurred in 1835 as a member of the state constitutional convention called to revise the state constitution of 1776. He pressed for religious liberty, suffrage based on "maturity" rather than property, public funding for education, and open

★★★★★★★★

## Leave No Debt Behind

According to legend, on the day he died, Macon woke and knew the end was near. He shaved, dressed, and went to bed, but not before calling his doctor and undertaker. He paid both and met his fate. Macon did not want to leave his debts, however insignificant, to his children.

government that was accountable to the people. The 1776 constitution granted the vote to free blacks who met the existing property qualifications. Macon opposed repealing that provision but was defeated. His proposal for yearly elections was also voted down. In the end, Macon opposed ratification of the new constitution, which passed anyway. Though a formidable political opponent, Macon extended Southern hospitality, even for his enemies. "While life is spared, if any of you should pass through the country in which I live, I should be glad to see you." He believed the convention was his final act, but he took an active role in the 1836 presidential contest as an elector from North Carolina. He supported the New Yorker Martin Van Buren because his election meant the triumph of "Southern Republicans" and "principle." He said after the election that it was the "best evidence in the world of the indomitable spirit of democracy."

Macon died one year later, suddenly, at Buck Spring, at the age of seventy-nine. He gave instructions to bury him next to his wife and son and to cover the grave in piles of flint rock so the plot would remain undisturbed, and it remains so today. Fifteen hundred people attended his funeral, and, as per his will, he provided all with "dinner and grog." One participant recalled that "No-one, white or black, went away hungry." Macon, Georgia, and Randolph-Macon College were named in his honor, as well as counties in Alabama, Tennessee, Illinois, and North Carolina. He called North Carolina his "beloved mother," and his son-in-law presided over North Carolina's secession convention in 1861. Macon was a republican who believed in the "principles of '76." No other man better exemplifies the devotion to states' rights that was so important a part of the Founding generation.

## Chapter Nineteen

# FRANCIS MARION

We follow where the Swamp Fox guides,
We leave the swamp and cypress tree,
Our spurs are in our coursers' sides,
And ready for the strife are we.
The Tory camp is now in sight,
And there he cowers within his den;
He hears our shouts, he dreads the fight,
He fears, and flies from Marion's men.

"The Swamp Fox," by William Gilmore Simms

### Did You Know Marion:

- Enlisted blacks to fight alongside him during the War for Independence

- Was at one time one of the most celebrated heroes of the Revolution, North and South

- Helped save the war in the South through a strategy of attrition

You won't find much information about Francis Marion in American history textbooks today. Marion did not serve in the Continental Congress or the Constitutional Convention, and he never held a position in the federal government. Yet, without him, the American War for Independence may have taken a decidedly different direction. Washington rightfully received generous accolades after the war as the great hero of the Revolution, and Franklin was the diplomatic mastermind who secured needed French assistance, but Marion, the able and determined hero of the "swamps" who fought a rear-guard guerilla war to save his state from British occupation, has disappeared from our historical consciousness. His reputation has been revived in recent years, due in part to Mel Gibson's *The Patriot*, which had a Marion-like hero, but he still presents problems for the politically correct interpretation of the Founding generation and has generally not received the attention he deserves.

Marion was born in 1732 at St. John's Parish, Berkeley County, South Carolina, to Gabriel and Esther Marion. The Marion family arrived in South Carolina in 1690 as part of a wave of French Huguenots seeking refuge in North America. Marion was a puny and sickly child, the "size of a lobster" at birth as one contemporary joked. He spent his youth at his father's plantation on the Santee Canal, and with the exception of one tragic foray into a life at sea, he remained there until his father died in 1758. Marion moved to Pond Bluff shortly thereafter and established himself as a prosperous and well respected planter.

Like many in the Founding generation, Marion received his first taste of combat on the frontier in bloody and brutal engagements against American Indian tribes. When tensions rose between the Cherokee and white settlements from Pennsylvania to Georgia in 1759, several state militias were called out to quell the distress. South Carolina mustered a considerable force, and Marion volunteered for service. The war spirit died down for a time, but after several Cherokee chiefs were butchered at a remote South Carolina outpost in 1761, the Cherokee nation called for war.

Marion again answered the call of his state and this time saw action as a lieutenant in the militia. He led his men in a desperate attack on a fortified Cherokee position and took part in the subsequent burning of Cherokee towns and crops. He lamented his role in this destruction and said he could "scarcely refrain from tears" when ordered to burn fields of mature corn. The only ones who suffered were the "little Indian children" who would know that the "white people, the Christians" made them starve.

He returned to his plantation and led a quiet and uneventful life until duty called in 1775. His community elected him to serve in the South

Carolina Provincial Congress, and Marion sat through the debates over the call for independence. After the battles of Lexington and Concord, the Congress reassembled and decided on a course of action. Marion did not participate in the debates, but he voted for war and readily accepted the will of his state in the crisis.

Even before the Congress adjourned, Marion was actively recruiting men for the cause of independence. He was elected a captain in the Second Regiment of the South Carolina militia and quickly found his quota of fifty volunteers, many of whom were Scots-Irish Protestants. Marion participated in the capture of Fort Johnson and then distinguished himself during the battle of Sul-

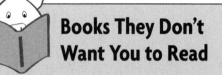

## Books They Don't Want You to Read

*The Life of Francis Marion*, by William Gilmore Simms, edited by Sean Busick (Charleston, SC: The History Press, 2007). Written in 1860 by the foremost American writer on the Revolution, this is still the best biography on Marion.

livan's Island on 28 June 1776. The British navy began a bombardment of the little American fort—Fort Sullivan, later called Fort Moultrie—in Charleston Harbor in the morning, and after an eleven-hour battle, two fifty-gun men-of-war were destroyed while the fort, made from soft palmetto logs, escaped substantial damage. Marion reportedly ordered the last shot of the engagement, a blast that killed two British officers and three seamen. In total, two hundred British sailors were killed or wounded while the South Carolina militia suffered only thirty-eight casualties. This victory kept the British out of the South for three years. For his service and leadership, Marion was rewarded with a promotion to Lieutenant-Colonel and was given command of Fort Sullivan, a prestigious honor, because the fort was the presumed focal point of any future British attack.

When the British returned to the South in 1778, however, they first attacked Savannah, Georgia. American forces attempted to retake the city in 1779. Marion moved south with the South Carolina militia but was exasperated by the French contingent who arrived first and imprudently allowed the British to fortify their positions. He reportedly flew into a fit of rage after learning of the French incompetence. "My God! Who ever heard of anything like this before? First, allow an enemy to entrench, and then fight him? See the destruction brought upon the British at Bunker's Hill—yet, our troops there were only militia; raw, half-armed clodhoppers, and not a mortar, or carronade, not even a swivel—only their ducking-guns! What, then, are we to expect from regulars, completely armed, with a choice train of artillery, and covered by a breastwork?"

Marion participated in the frontal assault on the British position at Savannah. His Second Regiment suffered heavy casualties, and in little time the British reduced the combined Franco-American forces by 1,100 men. Marion escaped, but some of the best men in his regiment did not. The British lost few men and held the city. The American forces retreated, and Marion was given the task of drilling and organizing the South Carolina militia. Everyone presumed the British would next attempt to take Charleston, and in 1780 Marion marched into the city with his men to prepare for its defense. Fate intervened. Marion was

## A Carolina Cavalier

"Of all the picturesque characters of our Revolutionary period, there is perhaps no one who, in the memory of the people, is so closely associated with romantic adventure as Francis Marion.... He was ... a man of few words and modest demeanour, small in stature and slight in frame, delicately organized, but endowed with wonderful nervous energy and sleepless intelligence. Like a woman in quickness of sympathy, he was a knight in courtesy, truthfulness, and courage. The brightness of his fame was never sullied by an act of cruelty."

—The historian John Fiske, 1891.

invited to a dinner party with friends, and when the host locked them in until all the wine was finished, the temperate and sober Marion decided to leave by jumping from a second-story window. The fall broke his ankle, and Marion was forced to retire to his home in St. John's Parish. This proved to be a stroke of luck for the American cause. Due to the incompetence of Benjamin Lincoln, the Northern general sent to defend the city, the entire American army was captured at Charleston in the ensuing assault, but Marion, home healing, escaped and ultimately became the most conspicuous officer in the Southern theater fighting for American independence.

## The Swamp Fox

While still suffering from his ankle injury, Marion organized a small group of men and moved north to meet with the Continental Army under the command of Horatio Gates. When he arrived, Gates could scarcely refrain from laughing at the disheveled band of South Carolinians. Marion hobbled on his broken ankle, and his men—both white and black— were poorly equipped and ragged. Gates ordered them to the interior of South Carolina. Officially, they were sent to scout enemy movements, but really Gates was just trying to get rid of Marion and his band. This decision proved to be vital to the American cause. Gates was routed at the Battle of Camden, leaving Marion's men to be a major obstacle against British occupation of South Carolina.

Marion's base of operations, Williamsburg, South Carolina, had a strong patriot population, and he recruited troops there. His men served without pay, and provided their own supplies and horses. They were an efficient, hard-hitting, guerilla group that could evaporate into the swamps when threatened.

Before the Battle of Camden, Marion and other South Carolinians had encouraged a "Fabian strategy" in the South, a line of attack named after the Roman General Quintus Fabius Maximus who used a war of attrition to wear down superior Carthaginian forces under Hannibal in the Punic Wars. Now that the regular American Southern army was all but destroyed, Marion, along with Generals Thomas Sumter and Andrew Pickens, adopted this approach in an effort to erode British resolve and keep them from moving north.

He would attack when the numbers favored him, and when they didn't he led the British into the swamps where he was uncatchable. He was called the "old fox" or the "swamp fox" by the British. Marion disrupted supply and communications, and acted as a nuisance to British commanders in the region. The British sent Colonel Banastre Tarleton after him in 1780, but without success. "Bloody Ban" had reportedly slaughtered Americans who had surrendered at the Battle of Waxhaws. He resorted to similar pitiless tactics in an attempt to capture Marion. Like General William Tecumseh Sherman in the War Between the States, "Bloody Ban" burned homes and other property, stole food and supplies, and left a swath of destruction in his path. Of British officers Tarleton was possibly the most despised man by the patriots. Marion sometimes resorted to similar methods—he commandeered food and supplies; he never burned homes—but whereas Tarleton left only blood and tears behind, Marion and his men left receipts, most of which were honored by the South Carolina government after the war.

Guerilla warfare took its toll on the British. Instead of methodically moving north and sacking North Carolina, they were bottled up in South

★ ★ ★ ★ ★ ★ ★ ★

## Those Resourceful Southerners

Marion's men made swords from old saws and bullets from melted down pewter. He rarely had more than thirty to forty men for an attack. Southerners during the War Between the States resorted to similar resourcefulness. Women, for example, were asked to save their urine to make "niter" for gunpowder.

Carolina chasing a "swamp fox" that often disappeared rather than fight. Marion's fame grew. South Carolina Governor John Rutledge, leading the state "from the saddle" in exile, heard of his exploits and commissioned him a brigadier-general.

Marion was ordered to take Georgetown, South Carolina, in January 1781, but failed. In the same month, however, American forces in the region won a stunning victory over the British at the Battle of Cowpens. Newly appointed commander Nathanael Greene recognized Marion's success and adopted a Fabian strategy during 1781 to keep the British out of North Carolina. He summarized it this way, "We fight, get beat, rise, and fight again." Marion's motto would have been, "We fight only the battles we should win, and we win; if not, we disappear, and fight again." Marion was able to secure Fort Watson and Fort Motte, and he rescued a small American contingent in August 1781, a deed that resulted in an official letter of appreciation from the Continental Congress. He also stopped American General Charles Lee, the man who would have lost Fort Moultrie in 1776 if not for the genius of the South Carolinians, from slaughtering Loyalist captives at the conclusion of the battle of Fort Motte. Marion despised cruelty in all its forms.

## Guerilla Warfare with Rules

"Never shall a house be burned by one of my people; to distress poor women and children is what I detest."

**— Francis Marion.**

British General Lord Charles Cornwallis determined that the American army in the South was being supplied through Virginia. In the spring of 1781, he left South Carolina for Virginia and, in the process, let Nathanael Greene slip back into the state. Marion helped Greene push the British back to the coast through a series of bloody engagements. He commanded the militia during the final battle in the Southern theater, the Battle of Eutaw Springs in September 1781, a battle immortalized in the South Carolina state song.

Marion had no more battles to fight. His heroic efforts had not only made him a household name in South Carolina, but might have provided the turning point of the war, tying up British troops that would otherwise have advanced North and possibly captured George Washington in a vise.

Marion retired to a plantation destroyed by war. The life-long bachelor, who one subordinate officer described as an "ugly, cross, knock kneed, hook-nosed son of a bitch," took his cousin, Mary Esther Videau, as his wife in 1786. She was a wealthy widow, and Marion needed the money, if nothing else. He served in the South Carolina Senate in 1781, 1782, and 1784, and as the honorary commander of Fort Johnson from 1784 to 1790. He was elected as a delegate to the state constitutional convention in 1790 and served again in the state senate the following year. Marion died at his home in St. John's in 1795 at the age of 63. His tomb-

## The Fabian Fox

"The Washington of the south, he steadily pursued the warfare most *safe* for *us* and most fatal to our enemies. He taught us to sleep in the swamps, to feed on roots, to drink the turbid waters of the ditch, to prowl nightly round the encampments of the foe, like lions round the habitations of the shepherds who had slaughtered their cubs. Sometimes he taught us to fall upon the enemy by surprise, distracting the midnight hour with the horrors of our battle: at other times, when our forces were increased, he led us on boldly to the charge, hewing the enemy to pieces, under the approving light of day."

— **Recollection of General P. Horry, one of "Marion's Men."**

stone read: "HISTORY will record his worth, and rising generations embalm his memory, as one of the most distinguished Patriots and Heroes of the American Revolution: which elevated his native Country TO HONOUR AND INDEPENDENCE, AND Secured to her the blessings of LIBERTY AND PEACE...."

## The politically incorrect soldier

Marion was a dedicated servant to South Carolina throughout his life. That is his allure. He never served in the Continental Army and considered South Carolina to be his native "country." When duty called, he served with honor, and like Washington, the more famous "citizen-soldier," returned to his plantation when the fighting was over. He owned slaves, but fought alongside blacks for much of the war. John Blake White, in an 1830s painting, portrayed Marion as a gentleman offering an "enemy" officer supper, a depiction that also included Marion's body servant, Oscar, the man who fought side-by-side with him during the darkest days of the Revolution. Washington is often chastised for his refusal to allow black soldiers to fight in the Revolution—he later changed course—but they did fight in the Southern theater. Marion proved that.

Historians have also been critical of Marion for the role he played on the frontier, fighting Indians, in 1761. Wars against the Indian tribes were typically brutal, often inhumane affairs, with barbarism exhibited on both sides. Marion showed remorse for his deeds, even during the conflict, and never appeared to be an "Indian hater."

Marion is one of the true heroes of the Founding generation, a man who played no political role, but who personified the spirit and determination of South Carolina's patriots.

## Chapter Twenty

†††

# JOHN MARSHALL

"The people made the Constitution, and the people can unmake it. It is the creature of their own will, and lives only by their will." Those are the words of Chief Justice John Marshall in his 1821 Supreme Court ruling of *Cohens v. Virginia*. It declared that the Supreme Court could review state supreme court decisions, reinforced the "supremacy clause" of the Constitution, and solidified the idea that the Constitution was a "living," "elastic" document. Marshall was wrong in 1821, at least in regard to how the ratifiers intended the Constitution to be read, but his opinions have outlasted those of his opponents. John Marshall might not be a household name to most Americans, but he is, along with Hamilton, one of the most important Federalists in American history. The federal government would not be the same (or as powerful) without him.

Marshall was born on 24 September 1755 on the Virginia frontier. His family lived a modest, comfortable life. His father, Thomas Marshall, was a second generation American of Welsh descent. His mother, Mary Randolph, came from a more prestigious lineage. She was a descendent of the Randolph and Isham families, both of which had connections to the seventeenth-century English gentry. John Marshall could count a number of important Americans among his extended family, including Thomas Jefferson, Robert E. Lee, and John Randolph of Roanoke. There is some ques-

### Did You Know Marshall:

➤ Set the stage for modern activist judges

➤ Is *the* architect of big government

➤ Used the Supreme Court as a pulpit for his personal and political battles

tion about his mother's legitimacy in the Randolph family, but she was reared by the family and was considered a "blood" member.

Marshall spent most of his youth on the frontier and had little in the way of formal education. His family was not wealthy enough to possess a library, though he was acquainted with several Roman histories and some English literature. He took an interest in the law at seventeen when his father purchased a copy of William Blackstone's *Commentaries on the Laws of England*.

His youthful passions for learning and frontier leisure were interrupted by the Revolution. At twenty, Marshall became a member of the Culpeper Minute Men and took part in the siege of Norfolk in 1775. He was commissioned a lieutenant in the 3rd Virginia Regiment of the Continental Army in 1776 and eventually reached the rank of captain. He served with distinction at the battles of Brandywine, Germantown, and Monmouth, and suffered with the rest of Washington's army at Valley Forge in 1777 and 1778. The war had an interesting effect on Marshall's political ideology. He wrote that during the war, he "was confirmed in the habit of considering America as my country and Congress as my government." This was in sharp contrast to most men in the Founding generation, particularly Southerners such as John Taylor or Nathaniel Macon, who considered their state to be their country and the "united States" as simply an expedient confederation. Marshall was fast becoming a nationalist during the war.

He returned home when his commission expired in 1779 and was mustered out of service in 1781. He attended a series of law lectures given at the College of William and Mary by noted legal scholar George Wythe in 1780 and was admitted to the bar in Fauquier County the same year. He fell in love with the state treasurer's daughter during his time in Williamsburg and the two were married in 1783. In the meantime, Marshall was elected to the Virginia legislature in 1782, moved to Richmond, and opened an office in the city. Work was slow for a man whom Jefferson called lazy and predisposed to leisure, and whom most contemporaries viewed as disheveled. And though he had little money, Marshall reportedly gambled much of his salary away, spent too much on liquor and social events, bought an occasional slave, and speculated in land. The home-spun frugality of his frontier rearing quickly evaporated in the "big city" of Richmond.

Regardless of his own financial problems, Marshall viewed Virginia politics as corrupt and was shocked by what he considered latent demagoguery by many Virginia leaders, including Patrick Henry. Democracy worried him. Many of the farmers who supported Henry and controlled the government were bankrupt, and when Shay's Rebellion took place in Massachusetts in 1786, Marshall theorized that the "common man" was incapable of self-government. Of course, Shay's Rebellion was a reaction to oppressive taxation, but to Marshall, it was a manifestation of the evils of the leveling spirit of democracy, and it needed to be checked. Constitutional reform offered that possibility.

Marshall heartily supported Madison's efforts to strengthen the central government in 1787. Both men had established reputations as opponents of Patrick Henry's firm grip on the Virginia legislature and welcomed a restraint (even at the Federal level) on his substantial power. Marshall served as a member of the state ratification convention in 1788. He supported the Constitution without amendments and spoke on a number of occasions in defense of the wide-ranging authority of the new government, particularly in relation to the new judicial branch. His statements foreshadowed his actions as Chief Justice of the Supreme Court. Marshall laid the foundation of judicial review when he remarked to the convention that the Supreme Court could declare a law "void" if the Congress violated its "enumerated" and "delegated" powers.

This statement can be read in two ways. First, Marshall considered judicial review constitutional in 1788, though the Constitution did not specifically outline such a doctrine. He was consistent on this point throughout his life. Second, Marshall implicitly argues for states' rights when he declares that any congressional law that violated the "enumerated" and "delegated" powers of the Constitution was unconstitutional. Marshall would oppose this position later in his career. He also believed that a bill of rights was "merely recommendatory" because if it were "otherwise, the consequence would be that many laws which are found convenient would be unconstitutional." The Anti-Federalists claimed that was the point. Federal power needed to be checked. Marshall believed otherwise and contended the Congress would never act beyond the scope of its "defined" powers. But Marshall came to believe that the "defined" powers of the Federal government were expansive.

Marshall voted for the Constitution, and because of his performance at the convention became a leading Federalist in Virginia. Though in sympathy with Washington, Adams, and other Federalists, he declined serving in the new government on several occasions. He refused Washington's offer of attorney general in 1795 and an appointment as minister to France in 1796. Adams persuaded him to accept the same position in 1797, though Marshall's acceptance might have been driven by financial need. His one-year salary as minister was three times his legal earnings, and Marshall used this money to save his teetering investments. Once home from France, he turned down an appointment to the Supreme Court, but was elected to Congress in 1799 as a Federalist.

He was one of the few supportive voices of the Adams administration in Congress, and within a year, Adams tapped him to be Secretary of State. He did little during his time in the executive branch, and his general laziness in the office led to a bitter court battle years later (as we'll see in *Marbury v. Madison*). When Supreme Court Chief Justice Oliver Ellsworth resigned from the bench in 1801, Adams nominated Marshall for the position. This was the most important decision of his administration. Marshall accepted, and for the next thirty-five years dominated the judicial branch of the United States and defined the powers and procedures of the court in Federalist terms.

## Chief Justice

Marshall's first official act as Chief Justice was swearing in Thomas Jefferson as president. This is ironic, because the two men would be bitter rivals all the rest of their lives. Marshall did little in his first year on the bench. His one important contribution was the reorganization of the decision system. To this point, each justice offered a separate decision on a case in question, but following 1801, the court issued one decision, typically written by Marshall, and thus appeared as a "unified court." It was not until 1805 that a "dissenting" opinion appeared alongside the "majority opinion."

The Republican-controlled Congress refused to allow the court to meet for over a year. When the court reconvened in 1803, Marshall wanted to ensure that the "prestige" of the Court would be upheld. The first case on the docket appeared under the title *Marbury v. Madison*. This case actually involved Marshall, so he should have been disqualified from presiding over it, but he didn't remove himself and ultimately issued, as the "unanimous court," one of the most important decisions in court history.

William Marbury was an Adams federal appointee to a minor position in the District of Columbia under the dubious Judiciary Act of 1801, a bill that enlarged the federal court system and allowed Adams to place several Federalist judges in the federal circuit. When Jefferson and the Republicans took power in 1801, they repealed the act. Marbury's commission was signed by Marshall, but he failed to deliver it to him, making it unofficial. Jefferson refused to allow Marbury to take his position, claiming that a sealed appointment from a previous administration did not constitute a legal, binding deed. If the appointment was not delivered, it did not exist.

### Books They Don't Want You to Read

*The Politically Incorrect Guide™ to the Constitution*, by Kevin R. C. Gutzman (Washington, D.C.: Regnery, 2007).

Marbury applied to the Supreme Court for a mandamus—a legal demand for action—for Madison to issue the appointment. Marshall sympathized with Marbury, and believed he was entitled to his position, but declared he could not rule on the case because it was outside the jurisdiction of the court. If he had stopped there, the issue would have died, but Marshall also declared part of the Judiciary Act "unconstitutional," thus creating "judicial review."

This was Marshall's personal revenge on the Virginia and Kentucky Resolutions. Jefferson and Madison pointed out in 1798 through the Virginia and Kentucky legislatures that states could interpose state sovereignty against the enforcement of laws by which the federal government exceeded its delegated authority. Marshall disagreed. Judicial review became the standard interpretation of court power following *Marbury v. Madison*, much to the dismay of Thomas Jefferson who later in life lamented, "Yet this case of Marbury and Madison is continually cited by bench and bar, as if it were settled law, without any animadversion on its being merely an *obiter* dissertation of the Chief Justice." In other words, Jefferson thought Marshall used the court as a pulpit for his personal political and legal theories and as a means to attack his enemies.

Republicans had the chance to stop Marshall in 1804. The House of Representatives impeached Supreme Court Justice Samuel Chase for partisan attacks from the bench. This was a "high crime and misdemeanor" under the traditional definition, and the Republicans hoped that by making an example of Chase they could overturn "judicial review" and any other doubtful Federalist court decisions and mute activist judges. Marshall was genuinely scared. He testified on behalf of Chase, timidly. When the Senate failed to convict Chase, Marshall went on the warpath.

The scope of his decisions over the next thirty years covered all aspects of federal power. Jefferson thought his aim was to reduce state authority and take revenge on the Republicans. He certainly had cause to believe this. Marshall once called the Republicans "speculative theorists and absolute terrorists." He ruled in 1807 that Aaron Burr was not guilty of treason, a personal affront to Jefferson who wanted Burr hanged for his suspicious activity on the frontier (where it was alleged that, among other things, Burr was conspiring to detach western territories from the United States). In the 1810 *Fletcher v. Peck* decision, Marshall declared a state law unconstitutional and determined that states could not repudiate their contracts. This strengthened federal authority and made state laws subject to federal judicial oversight, something many of the ratifiers feared. Marshall himself attempted to alleviate those fears during the Virginia Ratifying Convention in 1788. "Can they make laws affecting the mode of transferring property, or contracts, or claims, between citizens of the same state?" he asked of the federal power in 1788. He said no then, but reversed course in 1810.

★ ★ ★ ★ ★ ★ ★ ★

## Yazoo!

The *Fletcher v. Peck* decision prevented the elected Georgia legislature from revoking immense land grants (the Yazoo contracts) which had been made by an earlier bribed legislature. The decision validated corruption and led John Randolph of Roanoke to point a finger at Federalists and say, "Yazoo!"

1819 was a busy year for Marshall and a depressing and shocking year for strict constructionists. Marshall ruled in the case of *Sturges v. Crowninshield* that federal jurisdiction over contracts applied to both states and private individuals. In other words, the Supreme Court could determine if state laws in respect to *private* as well as *public* contracts were constitutional. Marshall followed a similar course in the *Dartmouth College Case.* The Court ruled that states could not void a contract, in this case the charter of Dartmouth College. This again was an affront to state power, but his most important decision of 1819 was the *McCulloch v. Maryland* case, a decision that appeared to vindicate the "loose interpretation" of the Constitution outlined by Alexander Hamilton in 1791.

The United States was in a deep depression in 1819, and many blamed the "panic" on the monetary policies of the central banking system (nothing changes). The Maryland legislature levied a tax on the Baltimore Branch of the National Bank in order to force it out of existence, but the bank president, James McCulloch, refused to pay the tax. The state sued and the case reached the Supreme Court. Marshall realized this was the perfect opportunity to crush states' rights—he wrote after the decision that he feared "the constitution [would] be converted into the old confederation." The chief issue was the constitutionality of the national bank. Marshall declared the bank constitutional under the "implied" powers of the Constitution. "Let the end be legitimate, let it be within the scope of the constitution, and all means which are appropriate, which are plainly adapted to that end, which are not prohibited, but consist with the letter and spirit of the constitution, are constitutional." So, essentially, the ends justify the means (expanding the federal government). How convenient. Under this definition, anything can be constitutional as long as it is consistent "with the letter and spirit of the constitution" as interpreted by the federal government itself.

**Wisdom of the Founders**

"The power to tax involves the power to destroy."

**—John Marshall, 1819.**

Marshall did not stop there. He unilaterally defined the "supremacy clause," and the "necessary and proper clause" of the Constitution. First, as to the "supremacy clause," "If any one proposition could command the universal assent of mankind, we might expect it would be this—that the government of the Union, though limited in its power, is supreme within its sphere of action." But the "necessary and proper clause," wrote Marshall, "purport[s] to enlarge, not to diminish the powers vested in the government. It purports to be an additional power, not a restriction on those already granted." So, the government has limited powers, but those limited powers are infinite and implied. In 1788 Marshall had said that the federal government had "enumerated" and "delegated" powers. He skirted around this apparent contradiction by stating that under a "strict interpretation" of the Constitution, even many of the enumerated powers could not be applied, so that only a "loose interpretation" of the Constitution allowed Congress to do its "job" of passing expansive legislation.

His final blows at states' rights were in the aforementioned *Cohens v. Virginia* and the 1824 decision of *Gibbons v. Ogden*. The *Cohens* decision was a follow-up to the *McCulloch* case and the *Gibbons* decision expanded federal power by declaring that the federal government, through the power to regulate commerce, had the power to "prescribe the rule by which commerce is to be governed. This power, like all others vested in Congress, is complete in itself, may be exercised to its utmost extent, and acknowledges no limitations, other than are prescribed in the constitution." Under this definition, anything that might be considered "commerce" falls under federal jurisdiction and regulation.

★ ★ ★ ★ ★ ★ ★ ★

## Marshall's Critics

Marshall's decisions were controversial and had vociferous opponents, including John Taylor of Caroline and John Randolph of Roanoke. But over time, Marshall's type of Federalism, armed with his precedent-setting decisions, simply rolled over its opponents.

## The architect of big government

Marshall distrusted the people's capacity to govern and believed that liberty was best secured by an aggressive central authority and not by local or state governments. John Randolph of Roanoke, a friend and bitter rival, agreed with Marshall on the dangers of democracy, or "King Numbers" as he called it. Marshall truly believed the Constitution was, as Madison argued in *Federalist No. 10*, the only safeguard against the "demagoguery" of Patrick Henry and other state factions. But, he unknowingly set the stage for the rapid growth of the central government in the twentieth century. His goal was a conservative one—to set up a safeguard against demagoguery—but in the end he only established the precedents for an over-mighty central government that was as subject to demagogues as any state or local faction.

Marshall died in 1835 at the age of eighty, fulfilling his lifetime appointment to the bench. His decision to stay until his death was a political one; he did not want Andrew Jackson to have the satisfaction of appointing his replacement. He died during Jackson's second term. One can argue that all of his important decisions were personally or politically motivated in some way. He felt sorry for neglecting Marbury's appointment in 1803 and indirectly ruled in his favor while giving Jefferson a lecture; he acquitted Burr in 1807 in order to humiliate Jefferson; he ruled against Georgia in 1810 because he had a vested financial stake in a similar case involving a Virginia state contract and didn't want to lose money; he believed in Hamiltonianism and thus ruled that "implied" powers were constitutional.

## Marshall: A Semi-Conservative

"These, and his other celebrated opinions, ensured that the United States would fulfill the Federalists' vision of an expanding, united, commercial nation, in which the rights of property and the division of authority were secure. These were conservative tendencies, in part; yet in another sense, they opened the way for illimitable changes of industrialization and consolidation, and they desperately wounded another sort of conservatism, that of the South and the agricultural interest."

**—Russell Kirk on John Marshall in his *The Conservative Mind*.**

He once said that "the acme of judicial distinction means the ability to look a lawyer straight in the eyes for two hours and not hear a damned word he says." Marshall had typically decided his course before arguments were made. He preferred the closing to the opening, and rarely heard what opponents had to say. His constitutional theories were "vindicated" by his protégé, Joseph Story, in an 1833 treatise on the Constitution that is still in print. For good or ill, Marshall is one of the most influential members of the Founding generation.

## Chapter Twenty-One

# GEORGE MASON

I f a list were constructed of the most important Virginians in American history, George Mason would appear near the top. His influence on public policy, the Revolution, and the Constitution was far greater than his modern, meager reputation allows. He was a giant of his time. His close friendships with Washington, Jefferson, Madison, Henry, and many others from his state allowed him to influence the direction of state and federal politics. Mason was described as a private man, fundamentally disinterested and impersonal, and the perfect definition of the gentleman statesman. He was a planter, a republican, a firm defender of states' rights and civil liberty, and one of the ablest enemies of the Constitution. He is correctly labeled the "Father of the Bill of Rights," and though a slave holder, was an early proponent of the abolition of slavery. Mason is the antidote to the "politically correct" interpretation of the Founding generation. Perhaps that is why he is so often ignored, forgotten, or misrepresented.

Mason was the fourth of a line of George Masons to live and prosper in northern Virginia. The first George Mason arrived in North America around 1651 after the Battle of Worcester, the last battle of the English Civil War, which ended in defeat for the Royalists. He was a loyal follower of King Charles II and the prototypical Virginia cavalier. He settled on his grant of 900 acres, and by the time George Mason IV was born in

## Did You Know Mason:

- Once said he would rather cut off his hand than sign the Constitution

- Is the "Father of the Bill of Rights"

- Favored compensated emancipation and opposed the international slave trade

1725, the Mason estate totaled 5,000 acres in Douge's Neck, Virginia, as well as other Virginia and Maryland plantations. George Mason III, the subject's father, died in 1735, leaving his ten-year-old son under the care of his mother and his uncle, John Mercer of Marlborough.

Mercer was one of the leading attorneys in the colony, and his 1,500-volume library served as the foundation of Mason's informal education. His mother provided private tutors for a time, but Mason was soon excelling under Mercer's care. His mind was sharp and his intellect penetrating. Learning was one of his chief sources of pleasure, and his knowledge on legal and constitutional matters was unsurpassed, even by the supposed "genius" of his more famous countryman, James Madison. Though Mason was never licensed to practice law, his contemporaries often called upon him to answer important legal questions throughout his life. Planting was his occupation; the law was his hobby.

## Books They Don't Want You to Read

*The Life of George Mason, Including His Speeches, Public Papers and Correspondence.* 2 Vols., by Kate Mason Rowland and Fitzhugh Lee (New York: G.P. Putnum's Sons, 1892). The older biographies of the Founders are almost always the best, and that's true with Mason as well. Available for free on Google Books.

As the gentleman code dictated, Mason only entered the public arena when duty required. In 1748 he became a vestryman of the Truro Parish and served as one of the overseers of the poor. The following year he became a justice of the Fairfax County Court. Mason married Anne Eilbeck in 1750, and in 1755 he commissioned the construction of Gunston Hall for his new family (Mason and his wife would have nine surviving children). Completed in 1758, the home was one of the finest in Northern Virginia. He volunteered during the French and Indian War and received the rank of colonel as a quartermaster. He also served as a trustee for the newly formed town of Alexandria from 1754 until 1779 when the town was incorporated. The freeholders of Fairfax County elected him to the Virginia House of Burgesses in 1758, and he held office until 1761.

Mason found political life mundane and petty and much preferred devoting his energies to making his plantation self-sufficient. He also suffered from severe gout, and he used his affliction to avoid public service when possible. He spent much of the 1760s interested in western land. Mason became a partner in the Ohio Company in 1752. Indian problems and the British policy of discouraging western expansion after the French and Indian War curtailed the profitability of the company, but Mason still claimed around 60,000 acres of land in western Virginia and Kentucky. In Virginia, land, not goods or factories, determined status. All of Virginia's leading men in the Founding generation owned considerable tracts of land, and most had large plantations. They were planters first, statesmen second, soldiers third. This rooted them in their community, their "country," and helped foster the traditional, conservative, agrarian society of Virginia.

## The "retired" revolutionary

Mason did not take an active public role in most of the political conflicts of the 1760s. He preferred to remain at his plantation as a "retired" member of society, but from 1765 onward, he became an influential expositor of American grievances both through the press and in private circles. Edmund Randolph claimed Mason "was behind none of the sons of Virginia in knowledge of her history and interest. At a glance he saw to the bottom of every proposition which affected her." He opposed the Stamp Act and wrote an open letter to British merchants under the name "A Virginia Planter" in 1766. His arguments were conservative and founded on legal precedent.

He reminded the British that "we are descended from the same stock... nurtured in the same principles of freedom; which we have both sucked in with our mother's milk; that in crossing the Atlantic we have only changed our climate, not our minds, our natures and dispositions remain unaltered; that we are still the same people with them in every respect...." Mason stated, "We claim nothing but the liberty and privileges of Englishmen...we cannot be deprived of them, without our consent, but by violence and injustice; we have received them from our ancestors, and, with God's leave, will transmit them, unimpaired, to our posterity." He claimed to be a man in retirement without the wild impulses of "Jacobitism," a man "who adores the wisdom and happiness of the British constitution" and who is "an Englishman in his principles." Yet, Mason warned the merchants that an infringement upon these sacred liberties would end in "revolt."

The Townshend Duties were less egregious to Mason, but he used Washington as a conduit to present bills to the House of Burgesses designed to temper their effects. When the governor dissolved the legislature in 1769, Mason authored a series of resolves that led to the Virginia Association, a formal agreement not to import British goods—including slaves—by Virginia. The resolves were later adopted by the First Continental Congress. But Mason, like his close friend Washington, shied away from talk of independence. His position was firm but temperate, particularly during the 1760s. He was loyal to the crown. It was not until 1774 that Mason publicly supported independence.

The Coercive Acts of 1774 led him to write the Fairfax Resolves. He wrote, "That it is our greatest wish and inclination...to continue our connexion with, and dependence upon, the British government; but though we are its subjects, we will use every means, which Heaven hath given us, to prevent our becoming its slaves." He viewed the rights of Englishmen as more valuable than the British Empire. Mason, then, viewed the War for Independence as a war to maintain the rights of Englishmen in America. The Fairfax Resolves were adopted at the Virginia convention and the Continental Congress and became the leading legal justification for separation from the crown.

Mason returned to public life in 1775. He served at both Virginia conventions and in 1776 framed the Virginia Declaration of Rights and most of the new Virginia constitution. Jefferson borrowed much of the language from the Declaration of Rights in drafting the Declaration of Independence, and the document also served as the foundation for the first ten amendments to the United States Constitution. Mason declared, "All men are by nature equally free and independent, and have certain inherent rights, of which, when they enter into a state of society, they cannot by any compact deprive or divest their posterity; namely, the enjoyment of life and liberty, with the means of acquiring and possessing property, and pursuing and obtaining happiness and safety." He insisted, "A well regulated militia, composed of the body of the people, trained in arms, is the proper, natural, and safe defense of a free state.... " Mason argued that "the freedom of the press is one of the great bulwarks of liberty, and can never be restrained but by despotic governments," and that religious liberty should be preserved "unless, under color of religion, any man disturb the peace, the happiness, or the safety of society. And that it is the mutual duty of all to practice Christian forbearance, love, and charity towards each other."

Notice that Mason did not claim the militia was a pseudo "National Guard." It was "composed of the body of the people," you and me. He emphasized "Christian" principles in his declaration of religious freedom and emphasized property as a pre-requisite for "happiness and safety." How politically incorrect can you get? His statements on religious liberty and gun rights are usually ignored and discounted, but in the eighteenth century, members of the Founding generation considered them the perfect expression of their rights and privileges as Englishmen. They could not be separated or reduced. They were the rights of free men, free societies, and free states. And his claim that all men were "equally free and independent" was qualified by "when they enter into a state of society."

Only freeholders were citizens "in a state of society." Citizenship, as in the ancient republics, was a privilege, not a right.

His version of the Virginia constitution "swallowed up all the rest." Mason set the intellectual foundations of the new republic. The 1776 Virginia constitution was classically republican and derived from the traditional models. It divided and limited power in an attempt to restrict the potential for corruption and abuse. He included property qualifications for members of the legislature, and the document was designed to maintain the social order of Virginia.

He served in the Virginia legislature for most of the war. Mason worked to reform the laws of Virginia, mostly through insisting on the preservation of the English common law. He helped organize the state militia and the supply and recruitment of troops for the Continental Army. Along with Patrick Henry he organized the western expedition of George Rogers Clark in 1779. Clark and Mason were "like father and son," and Clark's accounts from the western territories were first sent to Mason. In 1773, Mason defended Virginia's claim to the western territory in a document entitled *Extracts from the Virginia Charters*. This was used as the justification for the Clark expedition and boundary settlement with the British at the conclusion of the War for Independence in 1783.

## "Objections to the Federal Constitution"

Mason again retired from public life in 1780. He continued to work behind the scenes in support of various projects, including the disestablishment of the Anglican Church in Virginia. When the problems of debt, commerce, and war began to hinder the effectiveness of the Articles of Confederation, Mason supported the strengthening of the central government. He attended the Mount Vernon Conference in 1785 and was appointed to the Annapolis Convention in 1786, but did not attend.

## Thomas Jefferson on George Mason

"A man of the first order of wisdom among those who acted on the theatre of the revolution, of expansive mind, profound judgment, cogent in argument, learned in the lore of our former constitution, and earnest for the republican change on democratic principles. His elocution was neither flowing nor smooth, but his language was strong, his manner most impressive, and strengthened by a dash of biting cynicism when provocation made it seasonable."

When Virginia chose delegates for the Philadelphia Convention in 1787, Mason was regarded as a lock.

He ventured to Philadelphia in general accord with Madison and supported the initial proposals of the Virginia Plan. But when the convention dragged on for weeks and then months, he began to question the motives of the nationalists. Mason attended every session and spoke more than 140 times. He opposed the direct election of the executive, and as in Virginia, favored property qualifications for senators. But he was alarmed by proposals to abolish the states, feared that the executive was too strong, and thought that proposals for taxing exports and the creation of a standing army infringed upon the basic premises of liberty. Mason began the proceedings fully expecting to sign the new Constitution, but on 31 August 1787, he declared his intention to oppose ratification at all costs, insisting that "he would sooner chop off his right hand than put it to the Constitution as it now stands."

Mason returned to Virginia after voting against the final draft of the Constitution and quickly issued an explanation, later published in newspapers and in a handbill under the title *Objections to the Federal Constitution*, as to why he declined to sign the document. "There is no declaration of rights," he said, "and, the laws of the general government being paramount to the laws and constitutions of the several states, the declarations of rights in the separate states are no security." He feared the strength of the judicial power—"The judiciary of the United States is so constructed and extended as to absorb and destroy the judiciaries of the several states"—the powers of the executive branch, namely the power to make treaties and the "unrestrained power of granting pardon for treason," and reasoned that the five Southern states would be subjected to commercial and economic abuse by the eight states of the North and East, "whose produce and circumstances are totally different" from the South. He closed by prognosticating that "this government will commence in a moderate aristocracy: it is at present impossible to foresee whether it will, in its operation, produce a monarchy or a corrupt oppressive aristocracy," but he assumed it would "terminate in one or the other."

His old friends and allies Washington and Madison were angered and shocked by his public declaration. He would only get more aggressive. Mason and Patrick Henry formed the backbone of the opposition at the Virginia Ratifying Convention. Mason dressed in black and, like a skilled surgeon, cut the Constitution apart piece by piece. The Constitution as designed would "annihilate totally the State Governments," and he questioned, "Will powers remain to the States which are not expressly guarded and reserved?" He feared the Northern and Eastern states would destroy the institution of slavery in the South without any written protection for the institution, dreaded the judicial power which "goes to everything," and argued that the South would be subjected to "stockjobbers" and the interests of the Northern merchant class. As to the Framers, he stated,

## Mason's Wit

One delegate to the Virginia Ratifying Convention called Mason a "poor old man" who, due to age, had lost his wits. Mason replied to this insignificant delegate: "Sir, when yours fail, nobody will ever discover it."

"They have done what they ought not to have done, and have left undone what they ought to have done."

Because of the bludgeoning Mason administered to the final document, Madison agreed to present a number of amendments to the Constitution in the first Congress, and Virginia conditionally ratified the document by a close margin. Mason still voted against it. His recommendations resulted in the Bill of Rights, but other recommendations, such as a greater restriction on the power of the judiciary, were unsuccessful. He retired for the final time after the convention and rejected several offers to serve in the United States Senate. He preferred plantation life among his family to any public service, though he did write to his son shortly before his death that his public career "has been such as will administer comfort to me when I shall most want it and smooth the bed of death." Mason died in 1792 unaware that many of his dreaded prophecies of the future would come to fruition.

## Slavery

Politically correct attacks against Mason typically center on his apparent inconsistencies in regard to slavery. They emphasize that he argued for constitutional protections of the institution yet in the same breath called the slave trade "diabolical in itself and disgraceful to mankind." This was not uncommon for Virginians of his generation. There was a difference between slavery and the foreign slave trade. Only Northern merchants and Deep South rice and cotton growers (some of whom were Northern transplants) insisted on continuing the foreign slave trade. Virginians did not. They recognized the inherent evils of slavery, particularly the foreign slave trade, and regarded it as bane on society, though they did not know how to eradicate the institution without destroying their way of life. Mason, in fact, wrote several proposals for the extermination of the institution, but his ideas followed his specific belief in the rights of life, liberty, and property. Mason favored manumission, but not before slaves were educated so that the freedmen could maintain their liberty. He also wanted government to respect the rights of property and favored legal protection of the institution so that slave holders would be compensated should the institution be terminated. This would prevent a large percentage of Southern capital from evaporating. Great Britain followed the same path toward emancipation in 1833.

His statements during the Virginia Convention have also received much scrutiny. Mason desired an end to the slave trade and believed the union would be better off without it, and argued that the Constitution as written would not allow the trade to expire before 1808 regardless of amendment. His statements in regard to the protection of slavery, however, have been used against him, most skillfully by Joseph Ellis in his *Founding Brothers*.

Ellis correctly states that Mason voted against the Constitution, "in part," because of a compromise between the North and South over the slave trade and taxation, but he never explores the second part. Readers assume that slavery was the chief cause of his opposition. In fact, Mason was just as opposed to the powers given to the central government to tax and regulate commerce as he was to the slave trade. Northern merchants could tax the South out of existence—and for what benefit to the South: the continuation of the "diabolical" slave trade? To Mason the "compromise" hardly seemed fair or expedient.

Ellis accuses Mason of being disingenuous, but by reading his *complete* opposition to the document, not cherry-picking what he said in reference to slavery, one can only conclude that Mason was consistent. He feared what centralization and Northern dominance could do to the states and to his region. Slavery was simply one component of the bigger picture. As he said on 7 June 1787, "Whatever power may be necessary for the National Government a certain portion must necessarily be left in the

States. It is impossible for one power to pervade the extreme parts of the U.S. so as to carry equal justice to them." The Southern agrarian order, in his mind, would always be under assault from Northern and urban interests. Mason, like so many of his Virginia contemporaries, believed that liberty was best guarded by the states and that a man's true nation was his state.

## Chapter Twenty-Two

# ROGER SHERMAN

Thomas Jefferson once described Roger Sherman as "a man who never said a foolish thing in his life." John Adams said he was "an old Puritan, as honest as an angel and as firm in the cause of American Independence as Mount Atlas." Such lofty praise from two of the most prominent men of the Founding generation would seem to indicate that Roger Sherman would be a recognized name in American history, but he isn't. His stature has been unjustly eclipsed by other members of the generation, but the United States Constitution, for example, was as much Sherman's document as James Madison's, if not more. He was the only member of the Founding generation to affix his signature to the 1774 Articles of Association, the Declaration of Independence, the Articles of Confederation, and the United States Constitution. Sherman was the Patrick Henry of Connecticut, the most dominant political figure of his state and, aside from John Hancock, his region. He was also a "mild Federalist," a man who favored a stronger central government but recognized the importance of state power. In an era that champions federal action, big government spending, and aggressive centralized "leadership," Sherman seems archaic. But that is precisely why he should be studied.

Sherman was born in 1721 in Newton, Massachusetts. The first Sherman to settle in the British North American colonies, John Sherman, arrived in 1636, just a decade after the establishment of the Massachusetts

## Did You Know Sherman:

- Supported the Revolution, in part, because he feared the British would destroy the established Congregationalist Church in Connecticut

- Had as large a role in writing the Constitution as James Madison

- Opposed a Bill of Rights because it violated state sovereignty

Bay Colony. Roger Sherman, then, could count his family as one of the oldest in the region. His father, William Sherman, was a cobbler and farmer in Stoughton, Massachusetts. Sherman learned his father's trade and was largely self-educated, spending much of his free time in the study of theology, history, mathematics, law, and politics. After his father died, Sherman moved to New Milford, Connecticut, in 1743—according to legend he walked the entire distance with his tools on his back—and quickly became a leading man in the town.

He was appointed New Haven County surveyor in 1745, a position that led to considerable wealth and substantial land holdings. Sherman served in a variety of political and civic positions in New Milford, including juryman, town clerk, clerk of the church, deacon, school committeeman, and as town agent to the Connecticut Assembly. He owned the town's first store and published a series of almanacs between 1750 and 1761 that illustrated his depth of knowledge in mathematics and his propensity for wit and wisdom. He was admitted to the bar in 1754 and was elected to the General Assembly in 1755. Sherman was appointed justice of the peace and justice of the county court and was returned to the legislature every year except two between 1755 and 1761.

## Books They Don't Want You to Read

*The Life of Roger Sherman,* by Lewis Henry Boutell (Chicago, IL: A.C. McClurg and Company, 1896). Available for free on Google Books.

He moved to New Haven in 1761 and became involved with Yale College, first as a merchant selling supplies to the students, then as a contributor to the construction of the college chapel, and finally as the treasurer of the school. Yale awarded him an honorary Master of Arts degree in 1768. New Haven sent him to the upper house of the legislature in 1766, where he served until 1785, and he was made a judge of the superior court of Connecticut in 1766, a position he held until 1789. Sherman wrote in his almanac, "Every free-man shou'd promote the public good." The people of New Haven County deemed him an able steward of the public good for most of his life, and his service to his state was exemplary, but the Revolution would mark his career and make him a well-known public figure in all the states.

## The Atlas

Sherman was an early supporter of the Sons of Liberty, founded to resist unjust and unconstitutional Parliamentary acts such as the Stamp Act of 1765. When the organization turned to violence, however, Sherman turned against the group and charged that it tended to "weaken the authority of the government." Sherman supported boycotting British goods and chaired the New Haven Committee of Correspondence, because both were peaceful protests against unconstitutional British activity. He wanted to ensure order while still pressing the rights of Englishmen and the supremacy of Connecticut law over Parliamentary acts.

This placed him at the vanguard of public opinion in 1774. He was a conservative, but he recognized the British as a threat to the colonial order of Connecticut. The tipping point for Sherman was the Coercive Acts of 1774 and Lexington and Concord in 1775. By pushing violence on the colonies, King George III, in Sherman's mind, abdicated his authority and violated the Connecticut charter. On the eve of his election to the First Continental Congress in 1774, he informed the Massachusetts delegation to that body that he believed they should have "rescinded that part of their Circular Letter where they allow Parliament to be the supreme Legislature over the Colonies in any case." He was particularly concerned with the role of the Anglican Church in Connecticut and feared that British authority might include the further strengthening of the church in the Northern colonies, a region that had always expressed hostility to the orthodox Anglican religion. Sherman was a Congregationalist, not an Anglican, and the Congregationalist or Puritan Church

## American Laws for the American People

"The Parliament of Great Britain had authority to make laws for America in no case whatever."

—**Roger Sherman, 1774.**

was the officially established church in Massachusetts and Connecticut even after the war.

He signed the Articles of Association in 1774 and agreed with some of the more "radical" members of the Congress in regard to colonial rights, but he also signed the Olive Branch Petition of 1775 and sought to avoid war if possible. Sherman pursued the best interests of Connecticut, and was first and foremost a Connecticuter. Because of his known opposition to Parliament and his conservatism, he was appointed along with Adams, Jefferson, Franklin, and Robert Livingston to serve on the committee charged with drafting the Declaration of Independence. Sherman viewed the Declaration as the best way to preserve the traditional government and society of Connecticut, not as a formalization of abstract human rights. Secession from the empire protected the sovereignty and culture of Connecticut.

He showed his Northern partisanship during the selection of a general to lead the Continental Army. He favored a Northern candidate and did not like the thought of a Virginian leading an all New England army at the outset of the war, though he ultimately voted for Washington. He particularly reveled in the successes of Northern generals throughout the conflict. Sherman eventually considered Washington to be an able general, and Sherman's son, Isaac, rose to the rank of lieutenant-colonel under Washington's command and served with distinction in several important battles.

Sherman was an active and energetic member of the Congress and served on several important committees, including ways and means, the war and ordinance committee, and the committee on Indian affairs. He was also asked to help draft a plan of union and served on the committee that proposed the Articles of Confederation. When several delegates to the Congress argued that representation in the new union should be based on the population of the states, Sherman rose and said, "We are representatives of states, not individuals. States of Holland. The consent of everyone is necessary. Three colonies would govern the whole, but would not have a majority of strength to carry the votes into execution. The vote should be taken in two ways; Call the colonies and call the individuals, and have a majority of both." The states were sovereign, and Sherman was determined to protect their rights and integrity and not reduce the government to a "national" collection of individuals.

He dedicated much of his energy in the Congress to the public credit. Sherman opposed fiat currency—inflated paper money—argued for higher taxes, and was against unnecessary loans. He was frugal and sober, and the champion of limited spending. If the Continental Army became too expensive, Sherman suggested using more militia. If diplomatic costs piled up, he insisted on reining in their expense accounts. When commissions to supply agents spiraled out of control, he recommended placing them on salary. Sherman was the antithesis of the modern bureaucrat. He was a meticulous accountant and guardian of public money. He served in the Congress unabated from 1774 to 1781 and was returned from 1783 to 1784. By the time he left the Congress, he was considered the "Father" of the group and one of the most skilled legislators, with one contemporary describing him as "cunning as the Devil" in crafting legislation.

Retirement from Congress did not mean retirement from politics. Sherman continued to serve his state and community. He was elected mayor of New Haven in 1784, a position he held until his death, and was charged with revising Connecticut law, a task that led to the publication of *Acts and Laws of the State of Connecticut*. He held his position on the state superior court and practiced law in New Haven while attending to a large family—he had fifteen children between two wives, the first, Elizabeth Hartwell, who died in 1760, and the second, Rebecca Prescott, who survived him. He was already an old man when the Annapolis Convention of 1786 asked for a convention of all the states to meet in Philadelphia the following year. Connecticut reluctantly sent a delegation, and when the staunch Anti-Federalist Erastus Wolcott declined his selection, the legislature chose Sherman, the wise, conservative, and erstwhile defender of state power, in his place.

## The Connecticut Compromise

Sherman took his seat in the Convention on 30 May 1787, two days after Edmund Randolph presented the "Virginia Plan." He immediately showed support for a revision of the powers of the central government, but he was "not to be disposed to make too great inroads on the existing system" because he feared the states would not allow it. Sherman spoke frequently and attended most of the sessions. He was against democratic elections because the people were "constantly liable to be misled" and would not choose "fit" candidates, and he argued for an executive chosen by the legislature. This would prevent "the very essence of tyranny." He also believed the legislature should have the power to "remove the executive at pleasure" and warned against absolute executive power, for "no one man could be found so far above all the rest in wisdom." When the Convention appeared at an impasse after several weeks, Sherman seconded Benjamin Franklin's motion for prayer at daily sessions of the Convention.

Sherman represented Connecticut on the committee charged with finding a compromise between competing plans for representation in the new government. The "Connecticut" or "Great Compromise" followed the same course he advocated in the Continental Congress. The states were to have equal representation in the upper house while the lower house would have representation based on population. This is often described as a protection for the "small states," but Sherman made it clear on many occasions that equal representation protected *all* the states from arbitrary federal power. Madison reported in his journal of the proceedings that Sherman "urged the quality of the votes, not so much as a security for the small states, as for the state governments, which could not be preserved unless they were represented, and had a negative in the general government." He also successfully lobbied against a federal veto of state laws in order to protect the sovereignty of the states.

With the compromise, Sherman ensured that the Constitution would be the best document the states would approve. He did not believe that the states would willingly surrender much of their authority to a stronger central government. He was right. Ratification would be a difficult process in the most powerful states of Virginia, Massachusetts, and New York. In Connecticut, he used his considerable influence to win approval for the Constitution, which was ratified by a crushing majority. His September 1787 letter to the legislature, transmitting the Constitution for its review, specifically denied that the new government would infringe upon state sovereignty. "The equal representation of the states in the Senate, and the voice of that branch in the appointment of offices, will secure the rights of the lesser, as well as the greater states." And though "some additional powers are vested in Congress... those powers extend only to matters respecting the common interests of the Union, and are specially defined, so that the particular states retain their sovereignty in all other matters." He wanted Connecticut to support the Constitution without fear

## Books They Don't Want You to Read

*Founding Fathers: Brief Lives of the Framers of the United States Constitution*, by M. E. Bradford (Lawrence, KS: University Press of Kansas, 1994). Bradford's brief, readable work on the fifty-seven delegates to the Constitutional Convention should be required reading for anyone interested in the Founding generation.

## Sherman's Limits on Government

When pressed about the powers of the central government, Sherman stated that the only objectives of a Union of the states should be "first, defense against foreign danger; secondly, against internal disputes and a resort to force; thirdly, treaties with foreign nations; fourthly, regulating foreign commerce, and drawing revenue from it.... All other matters, civil and criminal, would be much better left in the hands of the states." Government, he thought, "ought...to be so construed as not to be dangerous to their [the people's] liberties."

because Connecticut would remain sovereign, not the central government.

Sherman's states' rights convictions led him to oppose the inclusion of a bill of rights with the Constitution. He believed that by insisting on "federal" guarantees of individual liberty, the new central government could exclude all other rights not listed and thus greatly reduce liberty. He argued that the states already had specific guarantees of rights, and because the new central government would not have the delegated authority to infringe upon those rights, the states could easily protect individual liberty from federal usurpation. His objections were sophisticated and duly noted and ultimately led to the Ninth Amendment to the Constitution.

Sherman was immediately elected as an at-large member of the United States House of Representatives in 1788, where he served one term from 1789 to 1791. He supported a Bank of the United States and the retirement of the federal debt and helped hammer out the compromise that led to the assumption of state debts in return for planting the federal capital along the Potomac, otherwise known as the "assumption scheme." He was chosen to serve in the United States Senate in 1791 and served there until his death in 1793 at the age of 72.

Sherman can be seen as an Anti-Federalist Federalist. Sherman believed the Constitution granted the federal government limited, delegated authority; he believed it maintained states' rights; and he would not have signed it and supported it otherwise. He was a Connecticuter to the end, the representative and defender of his state, and one who believed that the executive power should be limited because "no one man could be found so far above all the rest in wisdom." Sherman knew that an unchecked executive is "the very essence of tyranny," and that the best check on the power of the executive branch of the federal government was the authority of the sovereign states—an observation that seems very distant from where we are now.

## Chapter Twenty-Three

# JOHN TAYLOR OF CAROLINE

I
f anyone could be more Jeffersonian than Jefferson himself, it would probably be John Taylor of Caroline. Jefferson is the recognized champion of states' rights, individual liberty, and the agrarian tradition, but in contrast to Taylor's five published books, a handful of pamphlets, and a number of newspaper articles, Jefferson only produced one published work, his *Notes on the State of Virginia*. Modern Americans scarcely know Taylor existed, though during his life Taylor was the recognized pamphleteer of republicanism. He was an active patriot, a Southern planter, an Anti-Federalist, and he ultimately became the disinterested spokesman for the Old Republicans, a man who lived like his Roman heroes, faithful to his public duty, always defending the agrarian principles of the republic, and to the end, a resolute antagonist of aristocracy and artificial power. Taylor, in short, was the anti-John Marshall, John Adams, and Alexander Hamilton, and most of his public barbs were thrown their way. His philosophy embodied the American tradition of a limited, frugal, and state-dominated central authority, and he was as politically incorrect as a man could be.

Born in 1753 to a wealthy Virginia family, Taylor had the rearing of a gentleman. His father, James Taylor, died when he was three, and his mother, Anne Pollard, died shortly thereafter, so the task of caring for the young boy fell to his wealthy uncle, Edmund Pendleton, a member of the

### Did You Know Taylor:

- Was the "pamphleteer of Jeffersonian republicanism"

- Thought Virginia should secede from the Union in 1798

- Predicted the problems of modern state capitalism and central banking

Virginia House of Burgesses and the Justice of the Peace for Caroline County. Taylor was educated in the classical tradition at the finest schools in Virginia, including Donald Robertson's Academy, where many American statesmen received their training, and the College of William and Mary. Following his formal education, Taylor was given the opportunity to study law at his uncle's office, and, in 1774, was admitted to the Virginia Bar, but his original practice was cut short by the American Revolution. He joined the Continental Army at the outset of war, served in New York, Pennsylvania, and Virginia, and earned the rank of major before resigning his commission in 1779 when the army contracted. He returned to Virginia and served for a brief time in the Virginia House of Delegates before returning to the army at the end of the war as a lieutenant-colonel in the Virginia state militia. He served with the famous Frenchman the Marquis de Lafayette, battling Hessians in his state until the conclusion of hostilities.

After the Revolution, Taylor practiced law and accumulated a sizable fortune. In 1783, he married Lucy Penn, daughter of John Penn of North Carolina, a signer of the Declaration of Independence, and by the age thirty was well established in Virginia. His earnings from his law practice ran as high as $10,000 a year (or about $150,000 2007 dollars), but land was his true passion, and he invested most of his income in the sparsely settled West. At the height of his fortune, Taylor owned thousands of acres in Kentucky, three plantations in Virginia, and one hundred fifty slaves. He believed slavery to be an evil institution but did not favor its abolition because it was "incapable of removal and only within reach of palliation."

★★★★★★★★

## Warning: Not Beach Reading

John Randolph once said that Taylor would be very influential if his works could be translated into English. They are difficult, but not impossible, to wade through—and they're worth the effort.

His main plantation, Hazelwood, was perhaps the finest in the upper South. Taylor spent much of his time perfecting the science of planting.

He strove for self-sufficiency, and he was one of the first planters to recognize the importance of crop rotation. He served in the state legislature three times, from 1779 to 1781, 1783 to 1785, and 1796 to 1800, and in the United States Senate to complete unfinished terms from 1793 to 1794, in 1803, and again from 1822 to 1824. As an admirer of classical republics, Taylor

## Books They Don't Want You to Read

*New Views of the Constitution,* by John Taylor (Whitefish, MT: Kessinger Publishing, 2004).

refused to run for office unless called upon, and would usually return to his plantation once his term had expired or after he had resigned.

## Secessionist

Taylor served very little time in either the state or federal government, but he was productive when there. While in the Virginia legislature in 1798, he introduced the Virginia Resolves in opposition to the Sedition Act. These resolves were milder than their Kentucky counterparts, but they still emphasized that a state had the right and duty to "interpose for arresting the progress" of unconstitutional legislation. For his part, Taylor thought Virginia should just secede.

The subject had been broached before in 1794, when two Northern senators cornered Taylor and pressed the issue. It was not Taylor who insisted on secession at this point, however, but Rufus King of Massachusetts and Oliver Ellsworth of Connecticut. Taylor listened, and though in agreement that the Southern and Northern states had substantial disagreements, he believed the North desired an alliance with Great Britain for the purpose of bringing the agrarian South to its knees. He never trusted Northerners, even those who, on the surface, shared his political beliefs.

Taylor, of course, was no fan of the Constitution and favored the interests of Virginia and the South over those of Northern merchants. He did not attend the Virginia Ratifying Convention in 1788, but argued against the Constitution. He later called his philosophy the "Spirit of '76." In his view, Federalists and centralizers were working to pervert the goals of the Revolution. Taylor had not fought a war for more centralization. He, and many other Republicans, had fought for individual liberty, limited government, and the rights of Englishmen. Had Taylor lived into the 1850s, he certainly would have supported Southern secession as a remedy for sectional discord.

## The pamphleteer

From Hazelwood, Taylor wrote the most important works of Jeffersonian political economy. Taylor's essays and treatises were widely read. He intended his works to be applicable to any class of farmer, and to be read by what the historian Frank Owsley labeled the plain folk of the Old South, those free-holders with a vested interest in agricultural production and the stability of the agrarian republic. Jefferson wrote that Taylor's *An Inquiry into the Principles and Policy of the Government of the United States* should be required reading for every student of American Constitutional theory. Taylor's *Arator*, a series of essays on farming and politics, was reprinted five times before the War Between the States, and had a marked influence on Southern agriculture and society. Taylor's polemics on various subjects, from the Missouri Compromise and the *McCullough vs. Maryland* decision in his *Construction Construed and*

**Books They Don't Want You to Read**

*Arator*, by John Taylor (Indianapolis, IN: Liberty Fund, Inc., 1977).

*Constitutions Vindicated*, to the proposed federal protective tariff and the public debt in his *Tyranny Unmasked*, were the best exposition of agrarian republicanism. Agriculture and government were linked, in Taylor's opinion, and all his works displayed a solid defense of an agricultural republic.

> ## Books They Don't Want You to Read
>
> *Tyranny Unmasked*, by John Taylor (Indianapolis, IN: Liberty Fund, Inc., 1992).

In 1818, Taylor wrote, "If agriculture is good and the government bad, we may have wealth and slavery. If the government is good and the agriculture bad, liberty and poverty." Only by balancing the two would an independent society be secured, and since agriculture was the most common interest of the country, it should be protected from what he labeled as "stock-jabbers" and "a paper aristocracy." A "master capitalist" would turn "nine-tenths" of the "sound yeomanry" of the United States into "swindlers and dependents" and reduce them to the "daily bread" of the industrial age. "An aristocracy is no where agrarian. And where it has taken deep root . . . an agricultural interest has ceased [to] have any influence in the government." His two most important works, the *Inquiry* and his *Arator*, most clearly outline his ideas on American political economy and the relationship between labor and government.

Taylor designed the *Inquiry* to challenge John Adams's *Defense of the Constitutions of Government of the United States of America*. Originally written shortly after Adams published his *Defense* in 1787, the *Inquiry* was not distributed until 1814. Taylor reworked portions of the *Inquiry* during that time span in order to let his youthful passions subside, but his conclusions were unchanged. The *Arator*, published before the *Inquiry* but written after its conception, provided Southerners with a scientific handbook for increased agricultural production, but half of the sixty-four essays in the book were dedicated to the political economy of agriculture. The political themes Taylor addressed in each were consistent. Taylor attacked what he saw as the three main vices of American government: artificial aristocracy, banking, and minority rule. The government was heading, in his opinion, toward a consolidated empire ruled not by a king, as in England, but by something far worse: a president who used patronage and government hand-outs to centralize power in the name of the general welfare. Sound familiar?

Taxation was the greatest burden the laborer had to bear, and oppres-

## Wisdom of the Founders

"Thus, whilst a paper system pretends to make a nation rich and potent, it only makes a minority of that nation rich and potent, at the expense of the majority, which it makes poor and impotent."

— **John Taylor, 1814.**

sive taxation, Taylor believed, was the device used to secure artificial aristocracy. "Oppressive taxation, by law and monopoly, direct and indirect, to create or sustain the system of paper and patronage, proposes nothing retributory for reducing a people to the condition of asses, except an aristocracy to provide for them a succession of burdens." The lion, personified in the working man, would become "cowardly and stupid" if Congress implemented Alexander Hamilton's economic system of excessive taxation on agricultural products for the "common good" of society.

In Taylor's opinion, industrial capitalism (as opposed to free-market farming) could not exist without government protection in the form of tariffs, banks, internal improvements, and a permanent national debt. The protective tariff was but one device the government used to maintain finance capital at the expense of agriculture. Tariffs seized "upon the bounty taken by law from agriculture, and instead of doing any good to the actual workers in wood, metals, cotton, or other substances," they created an artificial aristocracy "at the expense of the workers in earth, to unite with government in oppressing every species of useful industry." Tariffs not only hurt agriculture, but they impoverished and enslaved workers in manufacturing. The capitalists would seize the bounty taken by the tariff, "appropriate to itself...and allow as scanty wages to its workmen, as it can." A permanent national debt facilitated this type of theft because the debt paid interest to the rich by taking it directly or indirectly from the productive wealth of agriculture. To Taylor, shuffling paper—financing debt, commercial speculation, and so on—was a dishonest trade.

Taylor believed "the excrescence of banking" constituted the major crutch for finance capital and the paper aristocracy. Inflation and interest saddled the laborer with unnecessary debt. These taxes were paid by "the public to individuals...to enrich idleness, and supply the means of luxury to a separate interest." Tariffs, federally funded "internal improvements," banking, and other government assistance to private companies or corporations transferred property to select interests. This was "the evil moral principle, in which all hereditary and hierarchical orders have been founded," and was, he argued, in sharp contrast to the founding principles of the United States.

The "logarithm of patronage" became the politicians' tool to perpetuate the usurpation of private wealth earned by honest labor. If a representative could "draw wealth from his own laws, by means of office, sinecure or monopoly," government ceased to be controlled through election. In the United States, power was given by the majority to an individual, and since a representative could not "be guided by the interest of both the minority and the majority...he will be guided by the interest to which he belongs; if he is a receiver of the tax, he will tax." Of course, the legislator would profess he was doing this in the name of the public good, but the public would be unable to check his avarice.

**Private Charity Is Better than Government Spending**

"A nation oppressed by taxes, can never be generous, benevolent or enlightened."

**— John Taylor, 1814.**

## Books They Don't Want You to Read

*An Inquiry Into the Principles and Policy of the Government of the United States,* by John Taylor (Fredericksburg, VA: Green and Cady, 1814). Available for free on Google Books.

If Congress used its power to tax to erect a "stock aristocracy," it would be "guilty of treason against the constitution, without violating its letter." Only by maintaining a balance of power between the people and the government, and the states and the federal government, could the laborer maintain his fiscal independence, cripple the "paper-jobber," and dull the sword of patronage.

Taylor spoke in majoritarian terms, but did not want the government thrown to the masses. He criticized *both* an aristocracy composed of minority interests, such as a military or stock interest, and mob rule. The business of minority interests was to "get what they can from the rest of the nation." Demagoguery would prevail, as these interests would enlist the help of government to secure their desires. Unless they could be checked or balanced, Taylor feared "paper systems"—i.e. banking and commercial speculation—because they bestowed "exorbitant wealth" at a level dangerous to society. A landed gentry would be able to hinder this process, to a degree. Though vested with a certain amount of inherited power, a landed interest was preferable to an aristocracy of paper and patronage because power radiated from the land in the former and oppressive taxation in the latter. The landed gentry were the natural ruling class, whereas a paper aristocracy was only able to maintain itself by using patronage and taxation. Taylor, for example, did not advocate the extension of the franchise to a landless proletariat because they would only help prolong the power of the demagogue. The only other safeguard in the American system was division of power, which prevented the twin dangers of excessive democracy: mob rule and minority rule.

Taylor, of course, was not some type of communist progressive who hated capitalism. What he feared was a fusion of government and finance, not markets or profit. He was wealthy, and he sold a good portion of his crops for cash, but he distrusted banks and the effect central banking could have on the yeoman farmer and the laborer. He also despised powerful central government. His ideology was grounded in the history and traditions of Virginia. Like George Mason, John Carroll, and Nathaniel Macon, and many other planters in the Founding generation, Taylor shunned political life. The historian Norman Risjord labels Taylor a conservative because he fought to preserve an agrarian society in the face of the industrial revolution, and also to sustain the interests of the landed gentry through decentralization.

Taylor died at Hazelwood in 1824 at the age of seventy-one. Jefferson wrote in 1820 that Taylor's *An Inquiry into the Principles and Policy of the Government of the United States* provided "many valuable ideas, and for the correction of some errors of early opinion, never seen in the correct light until presented to me in that work. . . . I know that Colonel Taylor and myself have rarely, if ever, differed in any political principle of importance. Every act of his life, and every word he ever wrote, satisfies me of this." Such a ringing endorsement should have provided Taylor with a more substantial reputation. But today not many historians pay attention to the wealthy planter who loathed

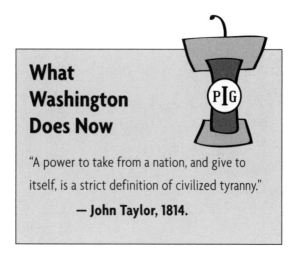

**What Washington Does Now**

"A power to take from a nation, and give to itself, is a strict definition of civilized tyranny."

— **John Taylor, 1814.**

centralized government and disparaged a future where voters would be governed by demagogues awarding government jobs and economic redistribution. Where is John Taylor when you need him?

# WHAT THE FOUNDING FATHERS WOULD DO

Barack Obama was correct when he suggested he will continue "remaking America." We no longer live in the America of the Founding generation, and in contrast to Obama's claim, we have not been "true to our Founding documents" for more than a century, at least since the War Between the States, which massively shifted power to the Federal government and forcibly denied states' rights. Politicians today who invoke the Founding Fathers and America's Founding principles often have very little idea of who the Founding Fathers were or what they stood for. If Washington, Jefferson, Henry, Mason, or Adams were to come back today and place their stamp on the federal government through a reform program short of secession, here is what they would do to reclaim the original intent of their generation.

**Follow the Constitution:** Hey, there's a novel idea. The Founding Fathers intended for the federal government to do just that, but this has been a chore rather than a mandate for those in modern government. To judge by their actions, very few members of Congress have actually read the Constitution, and most Americans can do no more than recite the Preamble, the most unimportant part of the document. This ignorance is one reason why a "Constitutional Law Professor," like Barack Obama, can ignore the Constitution's stated restraints on government power with impunity.

The Founding Fathers were cut from a different cloth than the politicians we have today, and most believed that political service was a duty rather than a career, or a way to wield power, or a tool to transform society. Public officials—statesmen—were elected in the Founding period with the understanding that they would not infringe upon individual liberty or the liberty of the states that elected them. The purpose of the Constitution was to limit government, not to grant it indefinite power.

Washington's model of executive restraint was emulated, with some exceptions, by the men of the Founding generation who succeeded him in office. The Constitution has defined roles for each branch of government. They should not be considered merely "guidelines" but rules. Executive powers should be reduced and legislative authority reasserted over key issues such as war powers and budgeting. Every spending item should be an "earmark" so that taxpayers know precisely how Congress is spending *their* money; omnibus bills and federal grants allow for too much waste and corruption. Following the Constitution seems quite simple, but the rascals in the federal government have not adhered to it since 1861. That should change.

**Cut Federal Spending and Reduce the Public Debt:** The Founding generation to a man would be shocked at the current level of spending in Washington. Even the most ardent centralizers, Hamilton and Marshall, would have railed against the bloated federal budgets of the last seventy years. Forced economic redistribution—"spreading the wealth" through government programs—was never a cornerstone of the American republic. Government spending should be reduced and applied only to essential services. Republican (with a lowercase "r") simplicity should reign. When the federal government shut down during the budget "crises" of 1995 and all "non-essential" programs went unfunded for a time, no one seemed to ask, "If the programs are not essential (or Constitutional), why do the taxpayers continue to fund them?" The Founders would ask the same question.

The Founders dedicated the principles of life, liberty, and property to their posterity. Without question, the men who have led the federal government in the last seventy years have perverted the principles of the Founding generation and in the process of piling up large federal deficits have ruined the potentially unlimited blessings of life, liberty, and property to future generations and have given them an undue burden. Jefferson made reducing the debt a priority in his first term as president, and Congress generally displayed fiscal restraint in the first thirty years of American history. Even the big spenders of the early republic would be outclassed by the current bunch in Washington, D.C. Hamilton understood that a little debt would not damage the United States, but excessive debt, such as the modern variety in the trillions of dollars, would bankrupt the country. Slashing the debt would be a priority to the Founding Fathers.

**Eliminate Taxes and Rein-in or Abolish the Federal Reserve System:** The Founders would start with a movement to repeal the Sixteenth Amendment, otherwise known as the Income Tax Amendment. An income tax would have been considered theft to the Founding generation. The Revolution would have been impossible without Charles Carroll of Carrollton and John Hancock, the two wealthiest men in the colonies at the outbreak of war in 1775. The British could have controlled them by taxing their income—but that was unfathomable to any eighteenth-century man, and the direct taxes levied by the British were light compared to modern standards and even they were resisted passionately. Even the architect of the modern state-capitalist system, Alexander Hamilton, considered direct taxes a messy Constitutional business. The Founding generation did not mind paying Constitutional and reasonable taxes, but barely anything in the modern federal tax code can be considered Constitutional or reasonable. The Founders would not only abolish the income tax, they would abolish payroll taxes and most excise taxes as well.

Just as the issue of central banking dominated the early Federal period, the abolition of the Federal Reserve would be a major sticking point for the Founding generation. There would be those, such as Hamilton and Marshall, who would defend the central banking institutions of the United States and urge their continued existence, but the republicans of the bunch—Jefferson, Taylor, Macon, Mason and others—would call for their speedy destruction. As in the Founding period, the second group might lose the argument (at least temporarily) over central banking, but they would certainly campaign against the market-distorting and inflationary policies of the Federal Reserve. Instead of blaming the "free market" for the demise of the American economy in 2008, they would insist that the Federal Reserve and Congress were culpable and blame the fusion of government and finance, otherwise known as state capitalism, for the financial meltdown. Central banking would take a needed hit.

**Reduce the Size of the Military, and End Foreign Alliances and Foreign Wars:** Since 1898, the United States has expanded its influence in ways the Founders deemed improbable and inexpedient. It has acquired colonies, sent its army and navy to every continent on the globe, has become involved in a complex alliance system with 28 countries, and has ceded its sovereignty on several occasions to a world governing body called the United Nations. Washington warned against every item on this list. Both Adams and Jefferson worked to avoid war with Great Britain and France during their administrations, and Madison was essentially drawn into a war with Great Britain (the War of 1812) because of cunning diplomacy by Napoleon Bonaparte, but not before Madison believed he had exhausted every diplomatic settlement. James Monroe, the last member of the Founding generation to occupy the executive office, declared that the United States would avoid wars in Europe and wished to see a free Latin America, but this did not mean he thought the United States would police the Western Hemisphere; the "progressive" Teddy Roosevelt added that provision to the Monroe Doctrine during his administration.

Today the Founders would seek to be good neighbors and neutral trading partners with the world, end foreign commitments to NATO and the United Nations, reduce the size of the professional military, bring the troops home, and use the Air Force, Navy, and Coast Guard to defend and safeguard our borders. After all, providing for the "common defense" is a charge of the federal government, but that does not require the current size or scope of the military-industrial complex.

**Limit Immigration:** With very few exceptions, the men who led the Founding generation were third or fourth generation Americans. Their families had immigrated to the colonies on their own hook and forged communities by their own sweat and blood. Most were British subjects from birth and considered British liberties sacred. While there were cultural differences between the sections and colonies, all understood that they must work within the British system and embrace British culture and Western Civilization. While naturalization laws of the 1790s allowed for relatively easy citizenship as long as the person was of good moral character and was "attached to the principles of the Constitution of the United States," the Founders would not have advocated "open borders" or unlimited immigration, and they would have viewed non-assimilation by immigrant groups as a threat to American liberty. We know this because the Founders expressed such fears in various contexts, including Benjamin Franklin worrying about large German communities that did not seem to be adopting the English language or English customs.

Nothing was more important to the Founders than preserving the rights of Englishmen—and they would rapidly tighten our borders and revise our immigration laws to limit immigration only to those people who share that same devotion.

**Reassert State Control over State Issues:** Since the inauguration of Barack Obama in January 2009, there has been a movement in several states to reaffirm state sovereignty. The Founders would applaud. They would demand the reassertion of state sovereignty in the language of Jefferson and Madison's Virginia and Kentucky Resolutions of 1798 as well as support an effort to repeal the Seventeenth Amendment to the Constitution (which instituted the direct election of United States Senators). The Founding generation believed in preserving and protecting cultural and sectional differences by maintaining the traditional values of society and argued that domestic issues were best addressed by the states. How the people of Massachusetts lived had no impact on Virginia or South Carolina. The Congregationalists of Connecticut would have been uneasy with the religious culture of Virginia. The states were sovereign, and federal usurpation of delegated state powers would have been unconscionable to men such as Jefferson or even Federalists like Adams. Even Hamilton insisted at one time that the federal government could not coerce a state. Moreover, the direct election of United States senators has removed a fundamental check on democracy the Founders considered important. Popular election has made Senate races little more than races of popularity, money, and promises to dole out the most pork once in office; the Founders meant senators to be disinterested defenders of the rights of their states, which is why senators were to be appointed by their state legislatures.

**Preserve the Bill of Rights:** Since the most powerful states in the Union would not have ratified the Constitution if not for the Bill of Rights, the

Founding generation would be its most ardent defenders. Gun control should never be considered; the "Fairness Doctrine" should never reach the floor of Congress for a vote; the Patriot Act, which allows the government to use unconstitutional powers, should be revised, amended, or placed in the trash-can; religious liberty, including the free expression of religious faith during government functions and prayer in public schools, should be defended; the burden of proof in a case involving "violations" of federal "regulations" should be placed on the government, not the accused; federal disregard for private property should cease. In short, federal activity should be severely curtailed.

The Founding principles of the republic have been perverted or buried precisely because they conflict with the scope and power of the modern state. The Founders were not socialists, fascists, or utopian egalitarian romantics. They understood human nature, power, and the potential for corruption better than any generation in American history, which is why they were intent on limiting the influence of government, which is the historical refuge of those with dangerous levels of avarice, ambition, and vice. They wrote the Constitution based on their understanding of history and tradition, and were true conservatives and republicans. We need them now more than ever.

# ACKNOWLEDGMENTS

This project would not have been possible without the love and encouragement from my wife, Samantha, and my family, most importantly my children, Shannon, Savannah, and Virginia, who missed time with me while I was locked up in my office pecking at a keyboard or with my nose buried in research. Words cannot express my gratitude.

I would like to thank Harry Crocker at Regnery for his support and help in this project, and Christian Tappe, Sally Brock, and all the folks behind the scenes at Regnery who have made this book possible. The Founding Fathers are *our* common heritage, and they would not have been heard without your contributions.

Clyde Wilson has been a true friend and mentor during this process. He read every word and offered advice and guidance when needed. Thank you from one of the usual suspects.

Bart Talbert at Salisbury University was my first mentor in history and my inspiration for obtaining an advanced degree. No better friend or ally can be found.

My friend Jeff Rogers and my brother Sean McClanahan offered advice and criticism in the final stages of the manuscript and helped me make the book a better product.

Five individuals who contributed to my love of history and writing and helped in my education—my grandfathers Walter R. McClanahan and Charles E. McCabe, my parents Mike and Rita McClanahan, and my middle-school English instructor Betty Manion—require thanks for putting me on the path to success.

Laurel Blackwell, Xueying Chen, Corey Williams, Angela Harris, and Dakota Goode at Chattahoochee Valley Community College provided support and research assistance; I have the longest list of overdue books in the history of the college. Thanks again for wiping my fines.

# BIBLIOGRAPHY

L isted below are a number of works either consulted for the project or provided for general interest. I did not include American history textbooks. If I used them, I cited each individually in the notes section. This is by no means a comprehensive bibliography on the literature of the Founding generation. Such a project is outside the space and scope of this work, but for those who have a passion for the group as a whole, the following works are a good start. Not all are written from a conservative viewpoint—in fact many aren't—but they allow the reader to "sharpen his pencil," so to speak. Knowing the opposition is in many ways more important than knowing yourself. The Internet has also become an invaluable source for many of the "primary" works used in this book. Most of the government records and Revolutionary War pamphlets are a "click" away on a good search engine, and some of the older books with expired copyrights can be accessed online as well.

Adams, Charles F. ed. *The Works of John Adams.* 10 vols. Boston: Little, Brown, 1850–1856.

Adams, Henry. *History of the United States of America During the Administrations of Thomas Jefferson.* New York: Library of America, 1986.

*Annals of Congress.*

Austin, James T. *The Life of Elbridge Gerry, with Contemporary Letters.* 2 vols. New York: Da Capo Press, 1970.

Bailyn, Bernard. *The Ideological Origins of the American Revolution.* Cambridge, MA: Harvard University Press, 1967.

Baker, Leonard. *John Marshall: A Life in Law.* New York: Macmillan Publishing Co., 1974.

Banning, Lance. *The Jeffersonian Persuasion: Evolution of a Party Ideology.* Ithaca, NY: Cornell University Press, 1978.

Bauer, Elizabeth Kelley. *Commentaries on the Constitution, 1790-1860.* New York: Russell and Russell, 1965.

Beard, Charles A. *An Economic Interpretation of the Constitution of the United States.* New York: The Free Press, 1986.

Bennett, Walter Harwell, ed. *Letters from the Federal Farmer to the Republican.* Tuscaloosa, AL: University Press of Alabama, 1978.

Billias, George A. *Elbridge Gerry: Founding Father and Republican Statesman.* New York: McGraw Hill, 1976.

Boardman, Roger Sherman. *Roger Sherman: Signer and Statesman.* New York: Da Capo Press, 1971.

Boutell, Lewis Henry. *The Life of Roger Sherman.* Chicago: A.C. McClurg, 1896.

Boyd, Julian P. et al, eds. *The Papers of Thomas Jefferson.* Princeton: Princeton University Press, 1950–.

Bradford, M. E. *A Better Guide Than Reason: Federalists and Anti-Federalists.* New Brunswick, NJ: Transaction Publishers, 1994.

_____. *Founding Fathers: Brief Lives of the Framers of the United States Constitution.* Lawrence, KS: University Press of Kansas, 1994.

_____. *Original Intentions: On the Making and Ratification of the United States Constitution.* Athens, GA: University of Georgia Press, 1993.

_____. *Remembering Who We Are: Observations of a Southern Conservative.* Athens, GA: University of Georgia Press, 1985.

_____., ed. *Arator: Being a Series of Agricultural Essays, Practical and Political: In Sixty-Four Numbers by John Taylor.* Indianapolis, IN: Liberty Fund, 1977.

Brandt, Irving. *James Madison.* 6 vols. Indianapolis: Bobbs-Merrill, 1941–1961.

Brookhiser, Richard. *What Would the Founders Do? Our Questions, Their Answers.* New York: Basic Books, 2006.

Burnett, Edmund C., ed. *Letters of Members of the Continental Congress.* 8 vols. Washington, D.C.: Carnegie Institute of Washington, 1921.

_____. *The Continental Congress.* Westport, CT: Greenwood Press, 1975.

Busick, Sean, ed. *The Life of Francis Marion by William Gilmore Simms.* Charleston, SC: The History Press, 2007.

Carey, George W., ed. *The Political Writings of John Adams.* Washington, D.C.: Regnery, 2000.

Collier, Christopher. *Roger Sherman's Connecticut: Yankee Politics and the American Revolution.* Middletown, CT: Wesleyan University Press, 1971.

Dickinson, John. *The Political Writings of John Dickinson, Esquire.* 2 vols. Wilmington, DE: Bonsal and Niles, 1801.

*Dictionary of American Biography.* 17 vols. New York: Charles Scribner's Sons, 1964–1981.

DiLorenzo, Thomas J. *Hamilton's Curse: How Jefferson's Arch Enemy Betrayed the American Revolution—and What It Means for Americans Today.* New York: Crown Forum, 2008.

Dodd, William E. *The Life of Nathaniel Macon.* Raleigh, N.C.: Edwards & Broughton, Printers and Binders, 1903.

Elliot, Jonathan, ed. *The Debates in the Several State Conventions on the Adoption of the Federal Constitution as Recommended by the General Convention at Philadelphia in 1787.* 5 vols. New York: Burt Franklin Reprints, 1974.

Ellis, Joseph J. *American Creation: Triumphs and Tragedies at the Founding of the Republic.* New York: Vintage Books, 2007.

_____. *Founding Brothers: The Revolutionary Generation.* New York: Vintage Books, 2002.

Evans, M. Stanton. *The Theme Is Freedom: Religion, Politics, and The American Tradition.* Washington, D.C.: Regnery, 1994.

Farrow, Anne, Jenifer Frank, Joel Lang. *Complicity: How the North Promoted, Prolonged, and Profited from Slavery*. New York: Ballantine Books, 2005.

Ferling, John. *Almost a Miracle: The American Victory in the War of Independence*. New York: Oxford University Press, 2007.

Fischer, David Hackett. *Albion's Seed: Four British Folkways in America*. New York: Oxford University Press, 1989.

_____. *Paul Revere's Ride*. New York: Oxford University Press, 1995.

Fiske, John. *The American Revolution*. 2 vols. Boston: Houghton, Mifflin and Co., 1891.

Fitzpatrick, John C., ed. *The Writings of George Washington*. 39 vols. Washington, D.C.: U.S. Government, 1931–1944.

Flower, Milton E. *John Dickinson: Conservative Revolutionary*. Charlottesville, VA: University of Virginia Press, 1983.

Ford, Paul L., ed. *The Writings of Thomas Jefferson*. 10 vols. New York: G.P. Putnam's Sons, 1892–1899.

Fowler, William M., Jr. *The Baron of Beacon Hill. A Biography of John Hancock*. Boston: Houghton Mifflin Company, 1980.

Fox-Genovese, Elizabeth and Eugene Genovese. *The Mind of the Master Class: History and Faith in the Southern Slaveholders' Worldview*. Cambridge, MA: Cambridge University Press, 2005.

Freeman, Douglas Southall. *George Washington: A Biography*. 7 vols. New York, Charles Scribner's Sons, 1951. Vol. 7 by John A. Carroll and Mary W. Ashworth.

Freeman, Joanne B., ed. *Alexander Hamilton: Writings*. New York: Library of America, 2001.

Frisch, Morton J., ed. *The Pacificus-Helvidius Debates of 1793-1794: Toward the Completion of the American Founding*. Indianapolis, IN: Liberty Fund, 2007.

Frohnen, Bruce, Ed. *The Anti-Federalists: Selected Writings and Speeches*. Washington, D.C.: Regnery, 1999.

Graham, John Remington. *A Constitutional History of Secession*. Gretna, LA: Pelican, 2002.

Greene, Jack. *Peripheries and Center: Constitutional Development in the Extended Polities of the British Empire and the United States, 1607-1788*. New York: W.W. Norton, 1990.

Gutzman, Kevin R. C. *Virginia's American Revolution: From Dominion to Republic, 1776-1840*. Lanham, MD: Lexington Books, 2007.

_____. *The Politically Incorrect Guide to the Constitution*. Washington, D.C.: Regnery, 2007.

Halbrook, Stephen P. *The Founders' Second Amendment: Origins of the Right to Bear Arms*. Chicago: Ivan R. Dee, 2008.

Hamilton, John C., ed., *The Federalist*. Washington, D.C.: Regnery, 1998.

Hawke, David F. *Franklin*. New York: Harper and Row, 1976.

Henry, William Wirt. *Patrick Henry. Life, Correspondence, and Speeches*. 2 vols. New York: Charles Scribner's Sons, 1891.

Jensen, Merrill. *The Founding of a Nation: A History of the American Revolution, 1763-1776*. New York: Knopf, 1968.

_____. *The New Nation: A History of the United States During the Confederation 1781-1789*. New York: Alfred A. Knopf, 1967.

*Journals of the Continental Congress, 1774-1789.*

Kaminski, John. *George Clinton: Yeoman Politician of the New Republic*. Lanham, MD: Madison House Publishing, Inc., 1993.

Kennedy, James R. and Walter D. Kennedy, eds. *A View of the Constitution by William Rawle, LL.D 1825: Secession as Taught at West Point*. Baton Rouge, LA: Land and Land Publishing, 1993.

Kesler, Charles R., ed. *The Federalist Papers*. New York: Signet Classics, 2003.

Ketcham, Ralph. *James Madison: A Biography*. New York: Macmillan, 1971.

Kirk, Russell. *The Conservative Mind: From Burke to Elliot*. Washington, D.C.: Regnery, 1995.

Labaree, Leonard et al., eds. *The Autobiography of Benjamin Franklin*. New Haven: Yale University Press, 1964.

Lee, Richard Henry. *Memoir of the Life Of Richard Henry Lee and His Correspondence with the Most Distinguished Men in America and Europe: Illustrative of Their Characters and of the Events of the American Revolution.* Whitefish, MT: Kessinger Publishing, 2007.

Lemay, J. A. Leo, ed. *Benjamin Franklin: Writings.* New York: Library of America, 1987.

Lipscomb, A. A. and Albert Ellery Bergh, eds. *The Writings of Thomas Jefferson.* 20 vols. Washington, D.C.: Jefferson Memorial Association, 1903.

Litwack, Leon F. *North of Slavery: The Negro in the Free States 1790-1860.* Chicago: University of Chicago Press, 1961.

Loewen, James W. *Lies My Teacher Told Me: Everything Your American History Textbook Got Wrong.* New York: Touchstone, 2007.

Lucier, James P., Ed. *The Political Writings of James Monroe.* Washington, D.C.: Regnery, 2001.

Malone, Dumas. *Jefferson and His Time.* 6 vols. Boston: Little, Brown, 1948–1981.

Mayer, Henry. *A Son of Thunder: Patrick Henry and the American Republic.* New York: Franklin Watts, 1986.

McCullough, David. *1776.* New York: Simon and Schuster, 2006.

_____. *John Adams.* New York: Simon and Schuster, 2008.

McDermott, Scott. *Charles Carroll of Carrollton: Faithful Revolutionary.* New York: Scepter, 2002.

McDonald, Forrest. *Alexander Hamilton: A Biography.* New York: W.W. Norton and Company, 1979.

_____. *E Pluribus Unum: The Formation of the American Republic, 1776-1790.* Indianapolis, IN: Liberty Fund, 1979.

_____. *Novus Ordo Seclorum: The Intellectual Origins of the Constitution.* Lawrence, KS: University Press of Kansas, 1985.

_____. *The Presidency of George Washington.* Lawrence, KS: University Press of Kansas, 1974.

_____. *The Presidency of Thomas Jefferson.* Lawrence, KS: University Press of Kansas, 1976.

Bibliography

_____. *We the People: The Economic Origins of the Constitution*. Chicago: University of Chicago Press, 1958.

McManus, Edgar J. *Black Bondage in the North*. Syracuse, NY: Syracuse University Press, 1973.

McMurry, Rebecca L., and James F. McMurry Jr., *Anatomy of a Scandal: Thomas Jefferson and the Sally Story*. Shippensburg, PA: White Mane Books, 2002.

Miller, F. Thornton, ed. *Tyranny Unmasked by John Taylor*. Indianapolis, IN: Liberty Fund, 1992,

Miller, Helen Hill. *George Mason: Gentleman Revolutionary*. Chapel Hill, NC: University of North Carolina Press, 1975.

Miller, John C. *Sam Adams: Pioneer in Propaganda*. Stanford: Stanford University Press, 1936.

Moore, Glover Moore. *The Missouri Controversy, 1819-1821*. New York: Peter Smith, 1967.

Nevins, Allan. *The American States During and After the Revolution 1775-1789*. New York: Augustus M. Kelley, 1969.

Palmer, Dave R. *George Washington and Benedict Arnold: A Tale of Two Patriots*. Washington, D.C.: Regnery, 2006.

Paul, Ron. *A Foreign Policy of Freedom: Peace, Commerce, and Honest Friendship*. Lake Jackson, TX: Foundation for Rational Economics and Education, 2007.

_____. *Pillars of Prosperity*. Auburn, AL: Mises Institute, 2008.

Peterson, Merrill D., ed. *Thomas Jefferson: Writings*. New York: Library of America, 1984.

Pocock, J. G. A. *The Machiavellian Moment: Florentine Political Thought and the Atlantic Republican Tradition*. Princeton: Princeton University Press, 1975.

Rakove, Jack N., ed. *James Madison: Writings*. New York: Library of America, 1999.

Rhodhamel, John, ed. *George Washington: Writings.* New York: Library of America, 1997.

Richard, Carl J. *The Founders and the Classics: Greece, Rome, and the American Enlightenment.* Cambridge, MA: Harvard University Press, 1995.

Richardson, James D. *A Compilation of the Messages and Papers of the Presidents 1789-1897.* 10 vols. Washington, D.C.: Bureau of National Literature and Art, 1901.

Risjord, Norman K. *The Old Republicans: Southern Conservatism in the Age of Jefferson.* New York: Columbia University Press, 1965.

Rowland, Kate Mason, and Fitzhugh Lee. *The Life of George Mason, Including His Speeches, Public Papers and Correspondence.* 2 Vols. New York: G.P. Putnum's Sons, 1892.

_____. *The Life of Charles Carroll of Carrollton 1737-1832 with his Correspondence and Public Papers.* 2 vols. New York: G. P. Putnam's Sons, 1898.

Rutland, Robert. *George Mason, Reluctant Statesman.* Charlottesville, VA: University of Virginia Press, 1963.

Sanders, Jennings B. *The Presidency of the Continental Congress 1774-89: A Study In American Institutional History.* New York: Peter Smith, 1971.

Sears, Lorenzo. *John Hancock: The Picturesque Patriot.* Boston: Little, Brown, and Company, 1913.

Skousen, Mark, ed. *The Compleated Autobiography* by Benjamin Franklin. Washington, D.C.: Regnery, 2006.

Stille, Charles J. *The Life and Times of John Dickinson 1732-1808.* New York: Burt Franklin, 1969.

Stoll, Ira. *Sam Adams: A Life.* New York: Free Press, 2008.

Storing, Herbert J. *The Anti-Federalist: An Abridgement, by Murray Dry, of the Complete Anti-Federalist.* Chicago: University of Chicago Press, 1985.

Syrett, Harold C. et al, eds. *The Papers of Alexander Hamilton.* 27 vols. New York: Columbia University Press, 1962–.

Taylor, John. *An Inquiry into the Principles and Policy of the Government of the United States*. Fredericksburg, VA: Green and Cady, 1814.

_____. *New Views of the Constitution.*, James McClellan, ed. Washington, D.C.: Regnery, 2001.

Taylor, Robert J., et al eds. *The Papers of John Adams*. Cambridge, MA: Harvard University Press, 1977-.

Van Doren, Carl. *Benjamin Franklin*. Westport, CT: Greenwood Press, 1973.

Wilson, Clyde N. ed. *View of the Constitution of the United States with Selected Writings by St. George Tucker*. Indianapolis, IN: Liberty Fund, 1999.

Wood, Gordon. *Creation of the American Republic, 1776-1787*. Chapel Hill, NC: University of North Carolina Press, 1969.

Wood, Kirk. *Nullification, A Constitutional History, 1776-1833: Volume One: James Madison, Not the Father of the Constitution*. Lanham, MD: University Press of America, 2008.

Woods, Thomas E. *Meltdown: A Free-Market Look at Why the Stock Market Collapsed, the Economy Tanked, and Government Bailouts Will Make Things Worse*. Washington, D.C.: Regnery, 2009.

_____. *The Politically Incorrect Guide to American History*. Washington, D.C.: Regnery, 2004.

Wright, Louis B. *The First Gentlemen of Virginia. Intellectual Qualities of the Early Colonial Ruling Class*. Charlottesville, VA: Dominion Books, 1964.

Zinn, Howard. *A People's History of the United States: 1492-Present (P.S.)*. New York: Harper Perennial Modern Classics, 2005.

# INDEX

Index